Silverlight™ 1.0

Foreword xix
Introduction xxi
Chapter 1: Introduction to Silverlight 1
Chapter 2: Building Silverlight Applications Using XAML 29
Chapter 3: Designing Silverlight Applications Using Expression Blend 2 59
Chapter 4: Coding Silverlight Applications with JavaScript and XAML 91
Chapter 5: Using Silverlight with ASP.NET 139
Chapter 6: Silverlight 1.1 and the CLR 189
Chapter 7: Video Player: Silverlight 1.0 Case Example 201
Appendix A: Silverlight Object Reference 221
Appendix B: XAML Reference. 251
Appendix C: Silverlight Online Resources 273
Index 275

Silverlight™ 1.0

Silverlight™ 1.0

Devin Rader
Jason Beres
J. Ambrose Little
Grant Hinkson

BICENTENNIAL 1807 WILEY 2007 BICENTENNIAL

Wiley Publishing, Inc.

Silverlight™ 1.0

Published by
Wiley Publishing, Inc.
10475 Crosspoint Boulevard
Indianapolis, IN 46256
www.wiley.com

Published simultaneously in Canada

ISBN: 978-0-470-22840-1

Manufactured in the United States of America

10 9 8 7 6 5 4 3 2 1

Library of Congress Cataloging-in-Publication Data

Silverlight 1.0 / Devin Rader... [et al.].
p. cm.
Includes index.

ISBN 978-0-470-22840-1 (paper/website)
1. Silverlight (Electronic resource) 2. Multimedia systems. 3. Web sites—Design. 4. Application software—Development. I. Rader, Devin, 1976-
QA76.575.S5674 2007
006.7--dc22
2007035569

For general information on our other products and services please contact our Customer Care Department within the United States at (800) 762-2974, outside the United States at (317) 572-3993 or fax (317) 572-4002.

Wiley also publishes its books in a variety of electronic formats. Some content that appears in print may not be available in electronic books.

To my wife, Kathleen

— Devin Rader

I would like to dedicate this book to my beautiful wife, Sheri, and amazing daughter, Siena, who put up with my crazy schedule and who forgive me every time I need to do things like write a book chapter or two when I should really be having fun with them.

— Jason Beres

Non nobis Domine non nobis sed nomini Tuo da gloriam.

— J. Ambrose Little

To Ania, my best friend, for your constant support and encouragement. To Mom and Dad, who encouraged me to create from the very beginning.

— Grant Hinkson

About the Authors

Devin Rader is a Product Manager on the Infragistics Web Client team, responsible for leading the creation of Infragistics ASP.NET and Silverlight products. Devin is also an active proponent and member of the .NET developer community, being a co-founder of the St. Louis .NET User Group, an active member of the New Jersey .NET User Group, a former board member of the International .NET Association (INETA), and a regular speaker at user groups. He is also a contributing author on the Wrox title *Professional ASP.NET 2.0* and a technical editor for several other Wrox publications and has written columns for *ASP.NET Pro* magazine, as well as .NET technology articles for MSDN Online. You can find more of Devin's musings at `www.geekswithblogs.com/devin`.

Jason Beres is the Director of Product Management for Infragistics, the world's leading publisher of presentation layer tools. Jason is also one of the founders of Florida .NET User Groups, he is founder of the New Jersey .NET User Group, he is a Visual Basic .NET MVP, he is on the INETA Speakers Bureau, and he is on the INETA Board of Directors. Jason is the author of several books on .NET development, an international speaker, and a frequent columnist for several .NET publications. He also keeps very active in the .NET community.

J. Ambrose Little is the User Experience and Guidance group lead at Infragistics. He is a Microsoft Solutions Architect MVP, an ASPInsider, author of numerous articles, co-author of *Professional ADO.NET 2* and *ASP.NET 2.0 MVP Hacks and Tips* from Wrox, and he has spoken at various user groups, events, and conferences. He's been designing and developing web sites and applications professionally for more than 8 years.

Grant Hinkson is Director of Visual Design at Infragistics, a software company specializing in reusable interface components and application design. He is passionate about design, usability, and technology and is rewarded by working with a team of people who share similar passions. He loves both design and development and thrives in the worlds of Silverlight and WPF, where he gets to exercise both sides of his brain. Grant has been involved with both WPF and Silverlight since their pre-Beta days, working with Expression Blend when it was affectionately known by its codename Sparkle. Grant is author of the Fireworks to XAML Exporter, is a frequent contributor to Adobe's Developer Center site, and has spoken at major industry design events.

Credits

Executive Editor
Bob Elliott

Senior Development Editor
Kevin Kent

Technical Editors
Derek Harmon
Tom Puglisi
Ed Blankenship

Production Editor
Debra Banninger

Copy Editor
Kim Cofer

Editorial Manager
Mary Beth Wakefield

Production Manager
Tim Tate

Vice President and Executive Group Publisher
Richard Swadley

Vice President and Executive Publisher
Joseph B. Wikert

Acquisitions Director
Jim Minatel

Project Coordinator, Cover
Adrienne Martinez

Compositor
Happenstance Type-O-Rama

Proofreader
Nancy Carrasco

Indexer
Jack Lewis

Anniversary Logo Design
Richard Pacifico

Acknowledgments

Writing a book like this is a team effort like no other. It takes effort and support from the authors, the editors, the publishers, and the families of all involved to make it possible. For myself, I thank my wife Kathleen for putting up with the late nights and working weekends. I know I always say this is the last time, but you know it's probably not. Thanks also to my parents for all of your support and advice.

Thanks to my co-authors who put so much time and effort into the book, some not really knowing what they were getting into. Thanks to all of those at Wiley, especially Kevin Kent, Bob Elliot, and Jim Minatel, for giving us the opportunity to do this book and for keeping us moving in the right direction through its creation. Thanks to Tim Sneath at Microsoft for taking the time to contribute the foreword to the book.

Finally, thanks to Bill Evjen, who offered me my first step into writing and is the reason I am fortunate enough to be working with Wrox. — Devin Rader

I would like to take this opportunity to thank the Wrox team, especially Kevin Kent, who kept this book on track and made sure we all did what we needed to do to keep our tight schedule. I would also like to shout out a very special thanks to the great author team in Devin, Ambrose, and Grant for making this book happen. It was awesome doing this book and even more awesome working with you guys at Infragistics every day. — Jason Beres

Thanks to my wonderful wife and kids who patiently let me abscond to work on this book, to my co-authors for bearing a lot of the burden in making this book a reality, and to the editors for helping us stay on track and ensuring quality. — J. Ambrose Little

I'd like to thank my co-authors and editors — what a great team of people to work with, not only on this book but every day. To the Visual Design Group at Infragistics — what a fun, creative, and passionate group of artists. I've enjoyed growing with all of you. — Grant Hinkson

Contents

Acknowledgments x
Foreword xix
Introduction xxi

Chapter 1: Introduction to Silverlight 1

What Is Silverlight? 1
- What Does DOM Really Mean? 4

Silverlight Versions Explained 5
Getting the Silverlight Plug-In 6
Getting the Silverlight SDK 9
Building Silverlight Applications 13
- Creating the Silverlight Object in HTML 17
- Silverlight Object Attributes 18
- Adding Multiple Silverlight Objects to a Page 20
- Resizing a Silverlight Control 21
- Displaying in Full Screen Mode 23

Understanding XAML 25
Summary 27

Chapter 2: Building Silverlight Applications Using XAML 29

Rendering Silverlight Content 29
- Working with XAML in This Chapter 30

Layout of Silverlight Content 31
- Positioning Objects Using ZIndex 34
- Positioning Objects Using Transforms 38

Drawing with Text and Brushes 41
- Using the TextBlock Object 41
- Creating Hyperlinks 43

Silverlight Video 45
- Adding Video to Web Pages 46
- Supported Audio and Video Formats 46
- Interacting with the MediaElement Object 47
- Using Markers and Timelines in Video 49
- Painting Video onto Objects 52
- Creating Video Reflections 53

Animating Silverlight Elements 56
Summary 58

Chapter 3: Designing Silverlight Applications Using Expression Blend 2 59

Getting the Latest Blend 2 Preview **60**
Creating a New Silverlight Project **60**
The Silverlight Project Starter Template 61
Blend Workspace Overview 62
Layout and Design in Blend 74
Creating and Understanding Timelines **79**
Understanding Storyboards in Silverlight 80
Creating a Timeline 80
Working with Artwork Created Outside of Blend **84**
Designing with Blend/Silverlight in Mind 84
Exporting to XAML in Other Tools 86
Summary **89**

Chapter 4: Coding Silverlight Applications with JavaScript and XAML 91

The JavaScript Programming Model **92**
Creating the Player Using JavaScript **92**
Refactoring the Silverlight Player Creation 95
Dissecting the Silverlight.js Helper Library **96**
createObject and createObjectEx 96
isInstalled 103
Accessing the Silverlight Player Object 104
Accessing XAML Content **105**
Locating XAML Content Elements 105
Getting and Setting XAML Properties 106
Instantiating and Inserting XAML Elements 108
Examining Events in Silverlight **113**
Player Events 113
XAML Element Events 115
Accessing Storyboards Programmatically **125**
Using the Downloader Object **128**
Downloading Packages 131
Downloading Fonts 133
Using JavaScript and the MediaElement **134**
Using DownloadProgressChanged and BufferingProgressChanged Events 136
Working with Markers 137
Summary **138**

Chapter 5: Using Silverlight with ASP.NET **139**

Creating Custom Controls **142**
Setting Up the Project 142
Adding the Silverlight JavaScript Library 146
Adding Xaml Control Properties 150
Rendering the Xaml Control 154
Using ASP.NET AJAX with Silverlight **158**
Refactor into a ScriptControl 158
Adding Client-Oriented Properties 160
Creating the Client-Side (JavaScript) Default Type 161
Embedding and Registering the New Client-Side Type 164
Implementing AJAX Extension Methods 164
Creating Dynamic Silverlight User Interfaces with ASP.NET **166**
Creating the Button Template 166
Creating the ButtonBar Server-Side Code 170
Creating the ButtonBar Client-Side Code 178
Using the ButtonBar Control 184
Final Thoughts/Recommendations 187
Summary **187**

Chapter 6: Silverlight 1.1 and the CLR **189**

The CLR **191**
The Framework **192**
Base APIs 193
Data APIs 194
Communications APIs 195
Presentation APIs 196
Debugging **199**
Dynamic Language Support **199**
A Quick Silverlight 1.1 Example **199**
Summary **200**

Chapter 7: Video Player: Silverlight 1.0 Case Example **201**

Getting Started **202**
Designing the Application Architecture **202**
Designing the User Interface **202**
Managing the Developer/Designer Workflow 204
Preparing the Media for the Application **205**
Creating the Data Layer **206**

Creating the Host Web Page 207
Coding Lumos 208
Scene Class 209
Button Class 216
VideoArea Class 217
Summary 220

Appendix A: Silverlight Object Reference 221

ArcSegment 221
BeginStoryboard 221
BezierSegment 222
Canvas 222
ColorAnimation 222
ColorAnimationUsingKeyFrames 223
ColorKeyFrame 223
ColorKeyFrameCollection 223
DiscreteColorKeyFrame 224
DiscreteDoubleKeyFrame 224
DiscretePointKeyFrame 224
DoubleAnimation 224
DoubleAnimationUsingKeyFrames 225
DoubleCollection 225
DoubleKeyFrame 225
DoubleKeyFrameCollection 225
Downloader 226
DrawingAttributes 226
Duration 226
Ellipse 227
EllipseGeometry 227
FontFamily 227
GeometryCollection 228
GeometryGroup 228
Glyphs 228
GradientStop 229
GradientStopCollection 229
Image 229
ImageBrush 230
InkPresenter 230
KeyboardEventArgs 230
KeySpline 231
KeyTime 231

Line	231
LinearColorKeyFrame	232
LinearDoubleKeyFrame	232
LinearGradientBrush	232
LinearPointKeyFrame	232
LineBreak	233
LineGeometry	233
LineSegment	233
MatrixTransform	233
MediaAttributeCollection	234
MediaElement	234
MouseEventArgs	234
ParserErrorEventArgs	235
Path	235
PathFigure	235
PathFigureCollection	236
PathSegmentCollection	236
PointAnimation	236
PointAnimationUsingKeyFrames	236
PointCollection	237
PointKeyFrame	237
PointKeyFrameCollection	237
PolyBezierSegment	238
Polygon	238
Polyline	238
PolyLineSegment	239
PolyQuadraticBezierSegment	239
QuadraticBezierSegment	239
RadialGradientBrush	239
Rectangle	240
RectangleGeometry	240
RepeatBehavior	240
ResourceCollection	241
RotateTransform	241
Run	241
RuntimeErrorEventArgs	241
ScaleTransform	242
Silverlight Control	242
SkewTransform	242
SolidColorBrush	242
SplineColorKeyFrame	243
SplineDoubleKeyFrame	243

SplinePointKeyFrame **243**
Storyboard **243**
Stroke **244**
StylusInfo **244**
StylusPoint **244**
StylusPointCollection **244**
TextBlock **245**
Timeline **245**
TimelineCollection **245**
TimelineGroup **246**
TimelineMarker **246**
TimelineMarkerCollection **246**
TimelineMarkerEventArgs **246**
TimeSpan **247**
TransformCollection **247**
TransformGroup **247**
TranslateTransform **247**
TriggerAction **248**
TriggerActionCollection **248**
TriggerCollection **248**
UIElementCollection **248**
VideoBrush **249**

Appendix B: XAML Reference **251**

Introducing XAML **251**
Silverlight XAML Basics **253**
Declaring Objects in XAML **255**
Object or Content Element Syntax 255
Attribute Element Syntax 255
Property Element Syntax 256
Setting a Property Using Implicit Collection Syntax 256
Deciding When to Use Attribute or Property Element Syntax to Set a Property 258
XAML Hierarchy **258**
Adding XAML Objects to the Silverlight Object Hierarchy 260
Events and the Silverlight Control **261**
Code Behind and x:Name 262
Silverlight Player Events 264
Defining Event Handlers 266
Defining Events in JavaScript 268
Referencing the Silverlight Control 269
Summary **272**

Appendix C: Silverlight Online Resources **273**

Author Blogs 273
Silverlight Influential Blogs 273
Resource Web Sites 274

Index 275

Foreword

When we set out to create Silverlight, we knew that we wanted to bring many of the strengths of Windows Presentation Foundation, our flagship Windows-based client platform, to the web, while retaining the openness and transparency of HTML and JavaScript. Silverlight is a cross-platform, cross-browser runtime that enables developers and designers to add animation, vector graphics, and HD-quality media to any web page. In its first release, it's a natural complement to HTML, offering a powerful graphics rendering subsystem that lets you build all kinds of interactive applications from media players to casual games and embed them in any web page.

One of the great attractions of Internet development is the ability to use open technologies like XHTML and JavaScript; nothing is hidden or obfuscated, and you can edit code with any text editor and treat each individual file as an independent asset. Silverlight was built from the ground up to support that same ethos of openness and transparency and is designed to seamlessly integrate with the web technologies you use today.

For example, XAML (the markup language that Silverlight uses) is an open, XML-based format that can be embedded directly within an HTML page or served as a separate text file. Every XAML element can be accessed or manipulated from the same client-side JavaScript that would be used to interact with any HTML element. There are no artificial boundaries or barriers, and you can even overlay HTML elements directly on top of Silverlight content. If you later want to build a desktop application, you can use many of the same skills and assets in WPF, providing a continuum that supports both online and offline uses.

Powerful though it is, the 1.0 release of Silverlight is just a start. As I write this, the development team is already making great progress on the next release of Silverlight, which adds the ability to use .NET languages such as C# and Visual Basic and dynamic languages like Python and Ruby. With strongly typed compiled languages that support the latest .NET innovations such as LINQ, as well as an extensible, template-based control model, Silverlight will develop over time to be the ultimate Rich Internet Application (RIA) framework for building web-based applications.

I'm excited to see this book — it makes a great companion for anyone who wants to learn the fundamentals of Silverlight without wading through the reference material in the SDK. The authors have an extensive track record with WPF as well as Silverlight and have the real-world experience of having built some of the first third-party controls for Silverlight; if you're looking for a trustworthy guide to show you how Silverlight can light up your web applications, you'll find this book a great starting point.

Silverlight opens up a new wave of opportunities for developers and designers to push the boundaries of the web still further. I knew we really had something on our hands when one of our designers showed me a jaw-dropping demo midway through the development cycle: a jigsaw puzzle composed of seventy pieces, each of which was a different fragment of an HD movie. I'm proud of our new baby and eager to see what others accomplish with it. I think we've provided a valuable tool for the web developer's arsenal and hope you agree after having read this book.

—Tim Sneath
Group Manager, Client Platform Evangelism
Microsoft Corp.

Introduction

In the age of Web 2.0, AJAX, and RIA, web developers continue to push the boundaries of the browser platform, yet remain locked in a world limited by HTML. Silverlight 1.0 aims to change this by bringing a new paradigm of web development to the table, giving you more powerful tools in your web development arsenal, while simultaneously allowing you to leveraging your existing development skills.

This book introduces you to the Silverlight 1.0 platform through example and explanation. Reading it will give you a thorough understanding of the capabilities of Silverlight 1.0, will allow you to begin to integrate it into your applications, and will even show you a real-world example of building a Silverlight 1.0 web application.

Who This Book Is For

This book is written for the professional developer looking to create web-based applications that include a rich, interactive user interface, which can include high-resolution graphics, animation, or integrated high-definition audio or video media. Silverlight 1.0 is the perfect platform for developers looking to create these applications while leveraging their existing development skills and not having to suffer a long and steep learning curve.

The book is designed to educate both traditional web application developers who are familiar with existing web technologies, but need to understand new XAML-based development technologies, as well as rich client developers who are familiar with XAML but want to create web-based applications.

Because Silverlight is primarily a web development platform, it is recommended that you have a basic familiarity with HTML and JavaScript before reading this book. Additionally, prior familiarity with ASP.NET will help you better understand how you can leverage the power of ASP.NET's server-side development model with Silverlight.

What This Book Covers

The Internet has changed dramatically from its early days of vanilla, static HTML pages, and Silverlight represents a revolutionary step forward. In this book, you will find everything you need to make the transition to the newest development platform for the Internet.

This book covers the initial release version of Microsoft's Silverlight 1.0 platform, a new browser-based development platform created by Microsoft to enable the creation of Rich Internet Applications. The platform leverages existing familiar technologies such as JavaScript, XAML, ASP.NET, and AJAX, and delivers a powerful new browser plug-in "player" to give developers the power to create highly immersive, interactive web-based applications. Additionally, enhancements to existing development tools like Visual Studio and Expression Blend, combined with new tools like Expression Encoder, make it easy for developers to create applications that can far exceed the traditional HTML-based web user experience, allowing easy integration of rich media and animation into Internet applications.

This book demonstrates the use of this platform with its supporting technologies (XAML, JavaScript, and ASP.NET) as well as discusses the tools available for developing Silverlight applications, including Microsoft Expression Blend, Microsoft Expression Encoder, ASP.NET 2.0, ASP.NET 2.0 AJAX Extensions 1.0, and Visual Studio 2005.

This book shows developers exactly how to build everything from basic, static Silverlight-enabled HTML pages, to advanced, Silverlight-enhanced ASP.NET applications. Along with these various applications, this book addresses security, data access using AJAX, and the latest tools for building Silverlight applications, including Visual Studio 2008, Expression Blend 2.0, and Expression Encoder.

How This Book Is Structured

This book is structured in a way that will allow you to quickly and easily understand the fundamentals of Silverlight 1.0, in both designing powerful user interfaces and creating engaging interactive applications.

- The initial two chapters introduce you to the Silverlight 1.0 platform and give you an overall look at its capabilities.
- The next three chapters offer in-depth looks at the three primary components of Silverlight: designing user interfaces using Expression Blend and XAML, leveraging the Silverlight 1.0 JavaScript APIs to add logic to your application, and finally, leveraging the existing server-side power of ASP.NET to create integrated client-server style applications with Silverlight.
- Chapter 6 gives you a look into the future, discussing the Silverlight 1.1 platform and the additional capabilities it will provide.
- Finally, Chapter 7 shows you how you can tie all of the technologies together into a real-world application by dissecting the Lumos video player reference application written using Silverlight 1.0.

Although all the chapters can generally be read independently, it is recommended that if you are just beginning to explore Silverlight, you start with the first two overview chapters. The book also includes three appendixes, which give you a quick reference to the player object model, Silverlight 1.0 XAML, and available online references.

In addition to all this, you can find a bonus chapter available for download with the rest of the code from the book at `www.wrox.com`. This chapter continues the Silverlight 1.1 conversation from Chapter 6 and has an actual sample Silverlight 1.1 application that you can download, play with, and learn from. We'll be doing our best to keep it up to date as Silverlight 1.1 develops and matures.

What You Need to Use This Book

Though most basic Silverlight applications consist primarily of XAML, HTML, and JavaScript, the only tool that is truly required is a text editor. In fact, most of the samples in this book can actually be duplicated using a simple text editor such as Notepad.

However, in order to help you be as productive as possible, Microsoft has created a variety of design and development tools specifically for the creation of Silverlight applications. The following is a list of the tools we recommend you have installed prior to beginning your Silverlight application development:

- Microsoft Silverlight 1.0 SDK
- Microsoft Expression Blend 2 August 2007 Preview
- Microsoft Expression Encoder
- Microsoft ASP.NET 2.0 AJAX Extensions 1.0
- Microsoft Visual Studio 2005

Conventions

To help you get the most from the text and keep track of what's happening, we've used a number of conventions throughout the book.

Tips, hints, tricks, and asides to the current discussion are offset and placed in italics like this.

Also, Visual Studio's code editor provides a rich color scheme to indicate various parts of code syntax. That's a great tool to help you learn language features in the editor and to help prevent mistakes as you code. To reinforce Visual Studio's colors, the code listings in this book are colorized using colors similar to what you would see on screen in Visual Studio working with the book's code. In order to optimize print clarity, some colors have a slightly different hue in print than what you see on screen. But all of the colors for the code in this book should be close enough to the default Visual Studio colors to give you an accurate representation of the colors.

As for styles in the text:

- We *highlight* new terms and important words when we introduce them.
- We show keyboard strokes like this: Ctrl+A.
- We show file names, URLs, and code within the text like so: `persistence.properties`.

Source Code and Web Sites Supporting This Book

As you work through the examples in this book, you may choose either to type in all the code manually or to use the source code files that accompany the book. All of the source code used in this book is available for download at `http://www.wrox.com`. Once at the site, simply locate the book's title (either by using the Search box or by using one of the title lists) and click the Download Code link on the book's detail page to obtain all the source code for the book.

Because many books have similar titles, you may find it easiest to search by ISBN; this book's ISBN is 978-0-470-22840-1.

The Silverlight 1.0 application featured in Chapter 7, a video player named Lumos, can be viewed online at `http://labs.infragistics.com/wrox/silverlight1_0/chapter7`. However, the source code for this application is included along with the other code from the book and is available for download from `www.wrox.com`. Please note that to keep the file size of the download manageable, the code for the Lumos application available for download includes only a couple of the video clips from the full application.

Once you download the code, just decompress it with your favorite compression tool. Alternately, you can go to the main Wrox code download page at `http://www.wrox.com/dynamic/books/download.aspx` to see the code available for this book and all other Wrox books.

Don't forget — in addition to the source code you will also find online and ready for download a bonus chapter for the book detailing an actual sample Silverlight 1.1 application.

Errata

We make every effort to ensure that there are no errors in the text or in the code. However, no one is perfect, and mistakes do occur. If you find an error in one of our books, like a spelling mistake or faulty piece of code, we would be very grateful for your feedback. By sending in errata you may save another reader hours of frustration, and at the same time you will be helping us provide even higher quality information.

To find the errata page for this book, go to `http://www.wrox.com` and locate the title using the Search box or one of the title lists. Then, on the book details page, click the Book Errata link. On this page you can view all errata that has been submitted for this book and posted by Wrox editors. A complete book list including links to each book's errata is also available at `www.wrox.com/misc-pages/booklist.shtml`.

If you don't spot "your" error on the Book Errata page, go to `www.wrox.com/contact/techsupport.shtml` and complete the form there to send us the error you have found. We'll check the information and, if appropriate, post a message to the book's errata page and fix the problem in subsequent editions of the book.

p2p.wrox.com

For author and peer discussion, join the P2P forums at `p2p.wrox.com`. The forums are a Web-based system for you to post messages relating to Wrox books and related technologies and interact with other readers and technology users. The forums offer a subscription feature to e-mail you topics of interest of your choosing when new posts are made to the forums. Wrox authors, editors, other industry experts, and your fellow readers are present on these forums.

At `http://p2p.wrox.com` you will find a number of different forums that will help you not only as you read this book, but also as you develop your own applications. To join the forums, just follow these steps:

1. Go to `p2p.wrox.com` and click the Register link.
2. Read the terms of use and click Agree.

3. Complete the required information to join as well as any optional information you wish to provide and click Submit.
4. You will receive an e-mail with information describing how to verify your account and complete the joining process.

You can read messages in the forums without joining P2P but in order to post your own messages, you must join.

Once you join, you can post new messages and respond to messages other users post. You can read messages at any time on the Web. If you would like to have new messages from a particular forum e-mailed to you, click the Subscribe to this Forum icon by the forum name in the forum listing.

For more information about how to use the Wrox P2P, be sure to read the P2P FAQs for answers to questions about how the forum software works as well as many common questions specific to P2P and Wrox books. To read the FAQs, click the FAQ link on any P2P page.

Silverlight™ 1.0

1

Introduction to Silverlight

Announced at the Mix '07 conference in May of 2007, Silverlight took the world by storm with a vision of Adobe Flash–like Rich Internet Applications (RIAs) built using a standards-based, open approach with HTML and XAML using tools like Visual Studio .NET and the new Microsoft Expression Blend. The idea for Silverlight is nothing new; Microsoft had been talking about a technology called WPF/e for the previous 8 or 10 months. Interestingly enough, there was so much confusion around what WPF/e meant, the name needed to change to something completely different, a name that did not associate WPF/e with the smart client, next-generation UI platform Windows Presentation Foundation (WPF). The idea was to tack the letter "e" on the end of WPF to convey Windows Presentation Foundation Everywhere. But this was simply not the case. This WPF is a core part of .NET 3.0 and has a 30MB runtime that requires a Windows-based desktop to run. WPF/e was a 2MB download, ran in the browser, and ran on multiple platforms. And multiple platforms here does not mean Windows XP and Windows Vista; it means Windows and Apple Macintosh. It means the Safari web browser on an Apple Macintosh being served up from an Apache web server running on Linux. Yes, you read that correctly, Linux, Mac, Safari, and Windows, too. There are other significant differences as well, which you'll learn about throughout the next few chapters. Needless to say, the name WPF/e was not going to adequately represent this amazing new technology, so Silverlight was announced as the new name at Mix '07. This chapter does two basic things:

- It gives you an introduction to Silverlight.
- It sets the groundwork with the essentials on creating Silverlight applications that will help you move on to the next chapter and the rest of the book.

What Is Silverlight?

Silverlight is simply a web-based platform for building and running RIAs. The web-based platform part of that equation is essentially the plug-in that runs inside the web browser. Silverlight applications execute within a browser plug-in that installs onto the local machine via the web browser in the exact same manner you install Adobe Flash to run Flash-based animations on web pages. The Silverlight plug-in supports all of the wow factor that you'd expect from an RIA, such as vector-based graphics and animations, full video integration, and even high-definition video. You can boil down the coolness of Silverlight to the following bullets:

- It's a cross-platform, cross-browser platform for delivering RIAs.
- It supports playback of Windows Media video and audio files on PC and Mac with no dependency on Windows Media Player.
- Using XAML, HTML, and JavaScript, it delivers rich multimedia, vector graphics, animations, and interactivity beyond what AJAX can deliver.
- The installation package is less than 2MB.
- The same XAML created for Silverlight can be used in WPF applications with no changes.

The Silverlight player (or plug-in, or control — those terms are used interchangeably in the book and you will see those variances when others talk about Silverlight as well) itself is a completely standalone environment; there is no dependency on the .NET Framework on the client, on the .NET Framework on the server, or even on a specific version of the .NET Framework. The initial association to the .NET Framework comes from the fact that you are using eXtensible Application Markup Language (XAML) to build the user interface for Silverlight applications, which is of course the foundation of the rich WPF applications built on .NET 3.0. The XAML is downloaded to the browser and executes within the Silverlight runtime on the client. When the XAML is running in the Silverlight player in the web browser, you can access all of the Silverlight objects via JavaScript code that lives in your HTML page. Figure 1-1 demonstrates this interaction between the web browser, the Silverlight player, the XAML, and the HTML page.

You might be asking why Microsoft is pushing out another web-based, client-side technology. There is already ASP.NET, and the ASP.NET AJAX Extensions have been released as well. The simple answer is that users are demanding an even richer experience on the web. Even though AJAX does a lot for improved user experience — the postback nightmare of Web 1.0 is finally going away — it does not do enough. There is demand for a richer, more immersive experience on the web. This has been accomplished with WPF on the rich client side. WPF gives a unified approach to media, documents, and graphics in a single runtime. The problem with WPF, as stated earlier, is that it is a 30MB runtime that runs only on the Windows OS. Microsoft needed to give the same type of experience that WPF offers, only in a cross-platform, browser-delivery mechanism. So what Microsoft did was take the concept of a plug-in model like Adobe Flash, mixed it with the WPF declarative language in XAML, and came up with a way to develop highly rich, immersive, Web 2.0 applications.

Was the Name Silverlight a Surprise?

For the true It-Getters out there (It-Getters are the "ones who get it"), the new name Silverlight was not such a huge surprise. For the previous months of Community Technology Previews (CTPs) of WPF/e, the JavaScript file that contained the core logic to create the browser object that actually runs the WPF/e code was named `agHost.js`. For the savvy web surfers out there, you might recognize "ag" as the Internet domain suffix for Antigua and Barbuda. But in terms of `agHost.js` in a WPF/e project, the "ag" represented the atomic symbol for silver. If you are a developer and a chemist, you might have recognized this. I am not so sure anyone ever actually did, but it does show how clever these names really are.

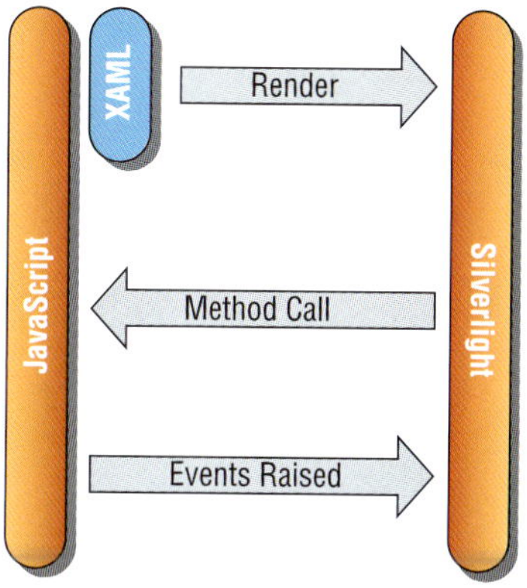

Figure 1-1

The big picture of Silverlight from an architectural perspective is in Figure 1-2. Each area is covered in more detail as you read along in the book, but the important thing to note now is that in using JavaScript you have access to the entire document object model (DOM) of the HTML page that Silverlight is running, which includes Silverlight objects themselves.

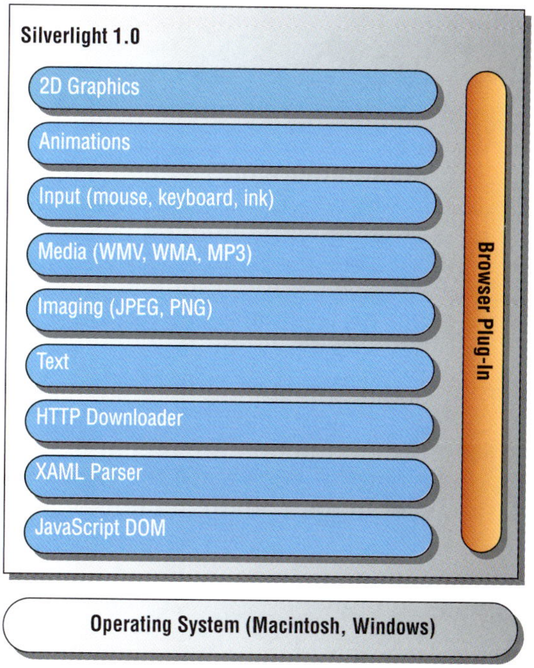

Figure 1-2

As mentioned earlier, Silverlight is fully supported across multiple browsers and operating systems. The current status for browser and OS support is identified in Table 1-1.

Table 1-1: Browser and Operating System Support for Silverlight

Browsers Note that when the Silverlight runtime is installed, a browser plug-in that exposes the Silverlight control is installed. Based on the platform, the control is packaged differently. On Windows, Internet Explorer uses an ActiveX, COM-based model to host Silverlight controls In all other combinations of browsers and platforms the Netscape plug-in technology is used to host Silverlight controls.	Internet Explorer 6 and 7 (Windows) Firefox 1.5.0.8, 2.0+ (Windows and Mac, with Linux support announced) Safari 2.0.4+ (Mac) Konqueror, WebKit, and Opera are being looked at by the Mono team and Novell.
Operating Systems	Windows XP SP2 Windows Vista Mac OS X (10.4.8+) Moonlight, a Linux-based version of Silverlight, is being created by the Mono team at Novell. BSD and Solaris are being discussed for future support, but are not currently available..

What Does DOM Really Mean?

Those new to the web world and programming web pages might not understand what the DOM actually is. In order to effectively work with elements in HTML or XML (the document), the information in the web page needs to be represented in a way that allows programmatic access the document's contents. This document object is the root node and object structure that represents the HTML in the page, and each node or object can have its own properties, methods, and events. Using languages like JavaScript (or even VBScript if you are using Internet Explorer), you can access these nodes and objects via code to manipulate them. This is what is commonly known as *client-side scripting*.

For example, the following code shows how to use the `getElementById` method to return an HTML element that has an ID property set, and then some JavaScript updates the content of the `div` element. When accessing elements via the DOM programmatically, an element must have an ID assigned.

```
<html xmlns="http://www.w3.org/1999/xhtml">
<head>
 <title>Page 1</title>
</head>

<body>
 <div id="message"></div>
 <script type="text/javascript">
   document.getElementById("message").innerHTML = "This is DOM access";
 </script>
</body>
```

In Chapter 4, you learn more about the DOM and interacting with page elements using JavaScript.

Silverlight Versions Explained

If you have been following Silverlight, you might be a little confused over the versions that are available:

- Currently, **Silverlight 1.0** is the first version of Silverlight and supports the JavaScript programming model that is described in the previous section. This means that your language choice is simple — JavaScript. You use JavaScript to interact with Silverlight objects that are executing within the Silverlight player in the browser.
- **Silverlight 1.1** supports the .NET Framework. This means that you can use any Common Language Runtime (CLR) language to code Silverlight applications, and you have the full power of the .NET Framework to interact with Silverlight objects.

In this book we concentrate on Silverlight 1.0, because it is in full release. Figure 1-3 compares Silverlight 1.0 and 1.1.

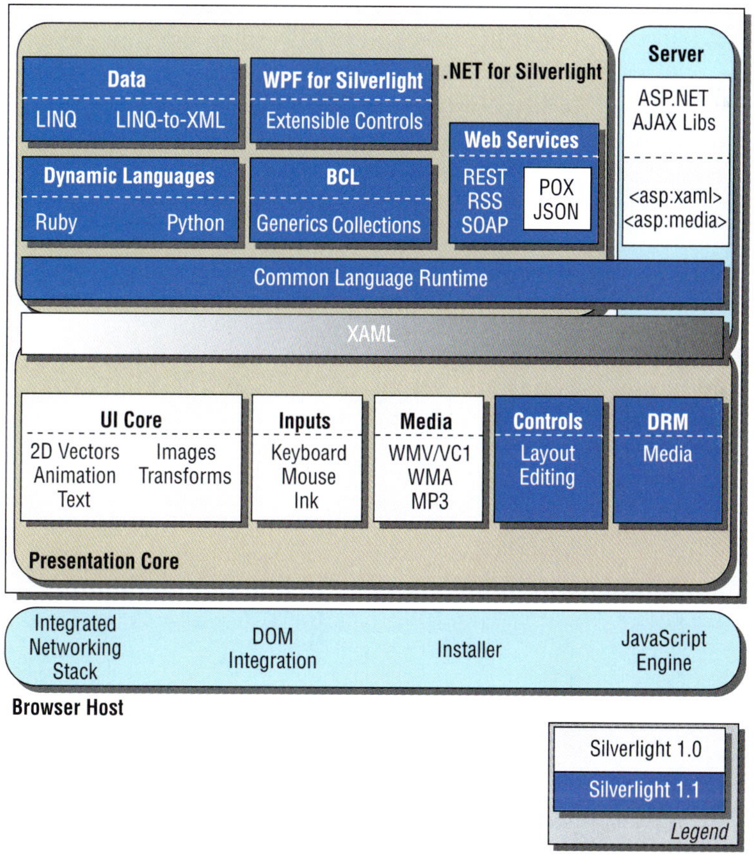

Figure 1-3

In Chapter 6 you get more insight into the next release of Silverlight and how having access to the CLR will impact your Silverlight development.

Getting the Silverlight Plug-In

The first time you navigate to a web page that contains a Silverlight application, the Silverlight player is not installed automatically; the installation is similar to the Adobe Flash experience. There is a nonintrusive image on the page where the Silverlight content is placed to run that gives a link to download the player. Silverlight has two different prompts for install — the standard install and the in-place install:

- In a standard install, the Get Microsoft Silverlight image tells you that you need to install Silverlight to complete the experience on the web page you have arrived at. Figure 1-4 demonstrates a page with the standard install images.

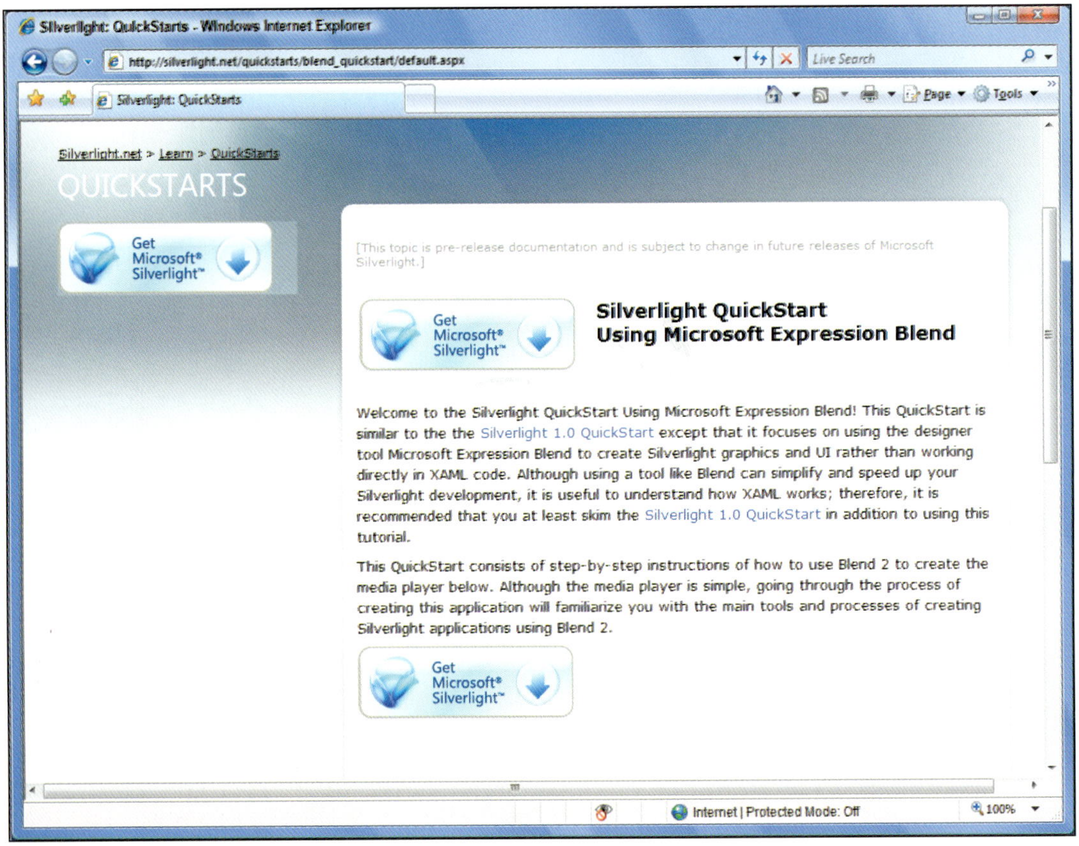

Figure 1-4

- Once you click the Get Microsoft Silverlight install image, you are taken to the Silverlight install page on the Microsoft site, as Figure 1-5 demonstrates.

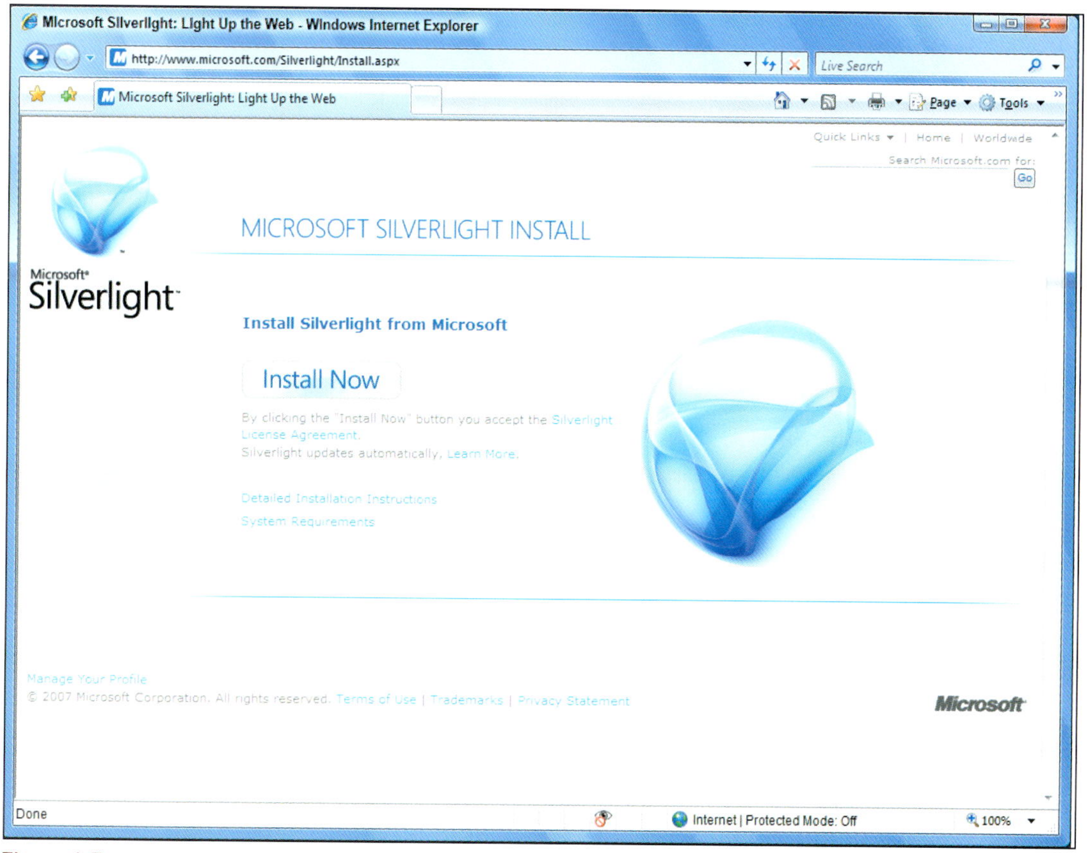

Figure 1-5

- Once you click the Install Now button, you are prompted to either download or install the Silverlight player in the same manner you would get any download from the web. Once you have successfully installed the Silverlight player, you are shown the Welcome to Silverlight page (Figure 1-6), which has a nice animation that shows off the capabilities of Silverlight. There is also a convenient link back to the page that had the Get Silverlight prompts, so the flow of your experience is fairly seamless.
- If a page is using the in-place install, the image is slightly different, and the experience is different as well. During an in-place install, the download begins without having to navigate to a special download page. Figure 1-7 shows the in-place install image. Notice the difference from the standard install image in Figure 1-4.

Figure 1-6

Figure 1-7

After the Silverlight player is installed, you never have to install it again. Silverlight also has built into it the knowledge of updates, so once a new version of Silverlight is available, you are asked if you would like to install the update to get the latest version of the player.

Getting the Silverlight SDK

To actually build Silverlight applications, you need more than the Silverlight player itself. If you have not arrived at a page where you are prompted to install the Silverlight runtime, you can easily get it on the Silverlight SDK page. There are also supporting files, help files, samples, and quick starts in the Silverlight Software Development Kit (SDK) that will give you the files you need to start building Silverlight applications. To get the SDK, go to `http://www.silverlight.net/getstarted/default.aspx`, shown in Figure 1-8.

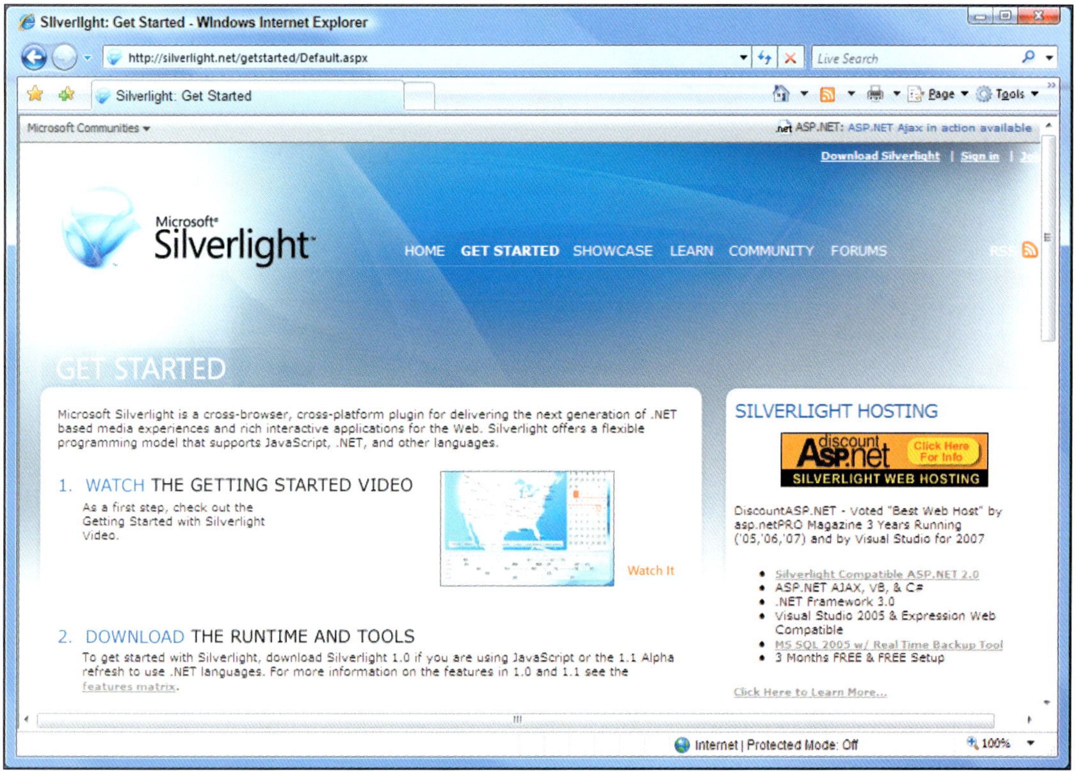

Figure 1-8

On the Silverlight SDK page, you can download all of the tools that you use to create Silverlight 1.0 or 1.1 applications:

- ❑ Runtimes:
  - ❑ Silverlight 1.0 for Mac and Windows
  - ❑ Silverlight 1.1 Alpha for Mac and Windows

- Developer Tools:
    - Microsoft Visual Studio Beta 2
    - Microsoft Silverlight Tools Alpha for Visual Studio
- Designer Tools:
    - Expression Blend
    - Expression Encoder
    - Expression Design
- SDKs:
    - Microsoft Silverlight 1.0 Software Development Kit (SDK)
    - Microsoft Silverlight 1.1 Alpha Software Development Kit (SDK)

If you need to install the 1.0 runtime, you should do that from this page. You should also download the Microsoft Silverlight 1.0 SDK. You need this to get the files and examples required to learn Silverlight. The SDK download is a standard MSI package. It installs the files necessary to create Silverlight applications, including the project templates for Visual Studio. Figure 1-9 is what the folder structure for the installed SDK looks like.

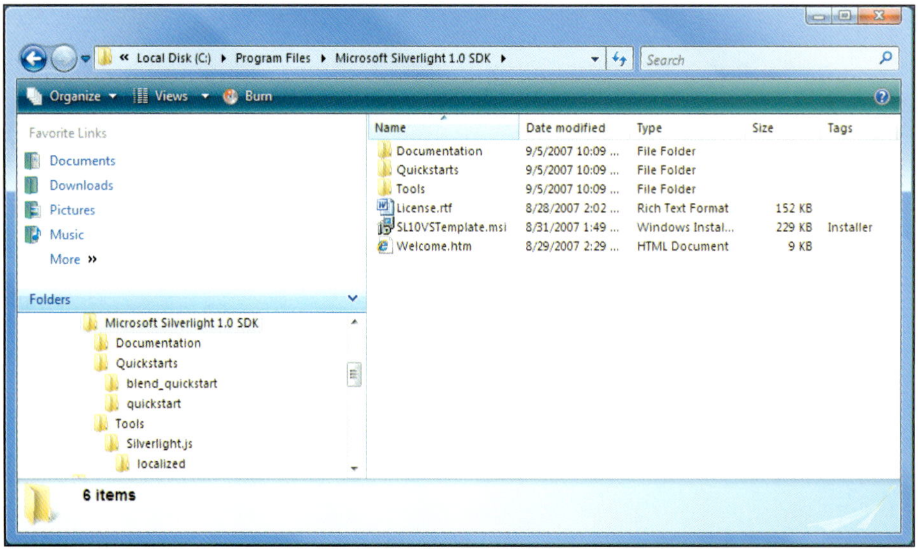

Figure 1-9

To view the samples that ship with Silverlight, you can browse to the community gallery at `http://silverlight.net/community/communitygallery.aspx`. Here you can view and download all of the samples built on Silverlight. Most of the samples are built by Microsoft, but there are also community contributions as well. Because Silverlight 1.0 is based on HTML, JavaScript, and XAML, you do not need to execute the samples within the context of a web server like IIS. So when you download a sample and run it locally, in each of the project folders there is a Default.html file that you can simply double-click to run the sample. (Note that the Internet Explorer security warning will appear because you are running pages with ActiveX on them locally.)

In Figures 1-10, 1-11, and 1-12, I have highlighted some of the more impressive examples of what you can do with Silverlight. The Page Turner example in Figure 1-10 demonstrates the ability to flip and skew images to mimic the real-life behavior of turning pages in a book.

Figure 1-10

The Grand Piano Player example shown in Figure 1-11 mimics the playing of a keyboard by mapping keys of the piano to their corresponding keyboard values.

Shown in Figure 1-12, SilverPad, an interactive application, lets you view the results of XAML that you add dynamically to the editor area of the application.

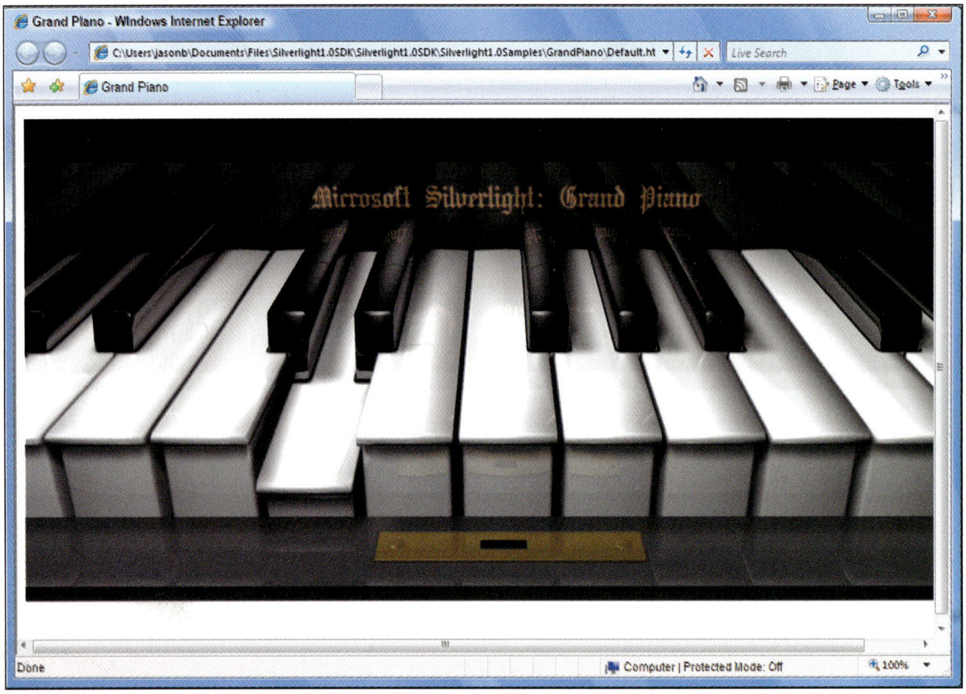

Figure 1-11

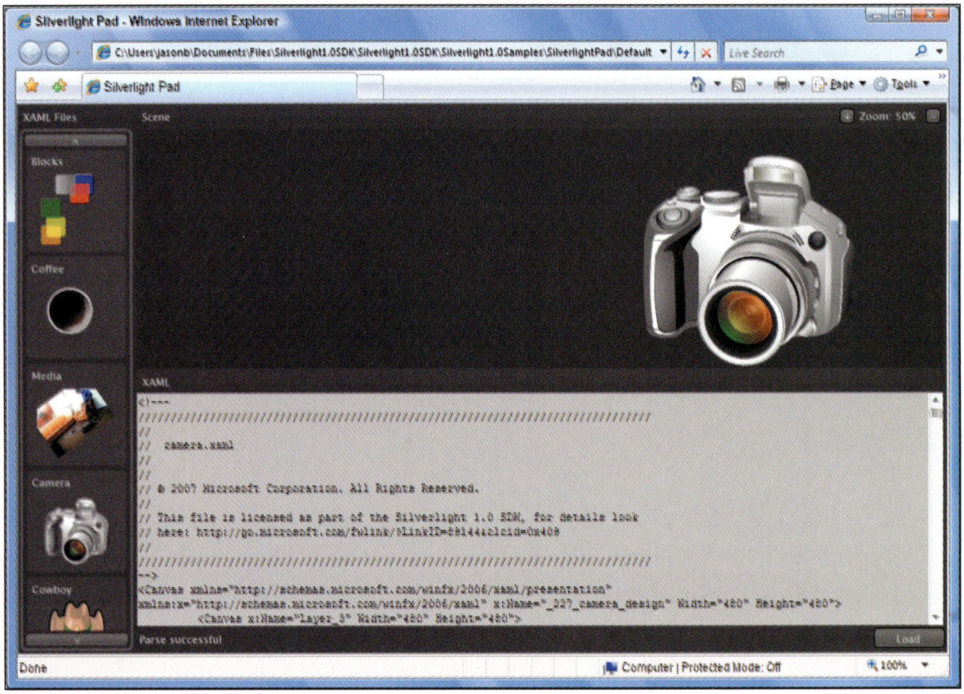

Figure 1-12

Now that you have seen some real-life examples of how powerful Silverlight is, you can start to learn more about building Silverlight applications in the next sections and, subsequently, the next chapters.

Building Silverlight Applications

Now that you have the Silverlight player installed and you have the SDK, you can start building Silverlight applications. There are several ways to create Silverlight applications:

- Visual Studio 2008 Silverlight project template. (These templates target Silverlight 1.1 only.)
- Visual Studio 2005 with the Silverlight 1.0 project templates installed from the Silverlight 1.0 SDK
- Expression Blend 2.0 using the Silverlight 1.0 and Silverlight 1.1 project templates
- Using any text editor to create the HTML, XAML, and JavaScript needed to run a Silverlight 1.0 application

Because this book is focused on Silverlight 1.0, we are going to look at building Silverlight applications using Visual Studio 2005 with the project templates from the SDK. The project template is installed when you run the initial SDK install. If you chose not to install the project template during the install, there is a package you can run from the Microsoft Silverlight 1.0 SDK from the Start Menu that will install it for you.

To start, open Visual Studio 2005 and hit Ctrl+Shift+N to open the New Project dialog. Select Visual C# Projects, because there is no template for Visual Basic in the SDK. Even if you are a hard-core VB developer, it does not really matter what language the template is under because you are only using HTML, JavaScript, and XAML to build Silverlight 1.0 applications. The New Project dialog should look something like Figure 1-13, with the Silverlight Javascript Application template under My Templates. This is the template extracted from the zip file you copied to the templates' folder previously.

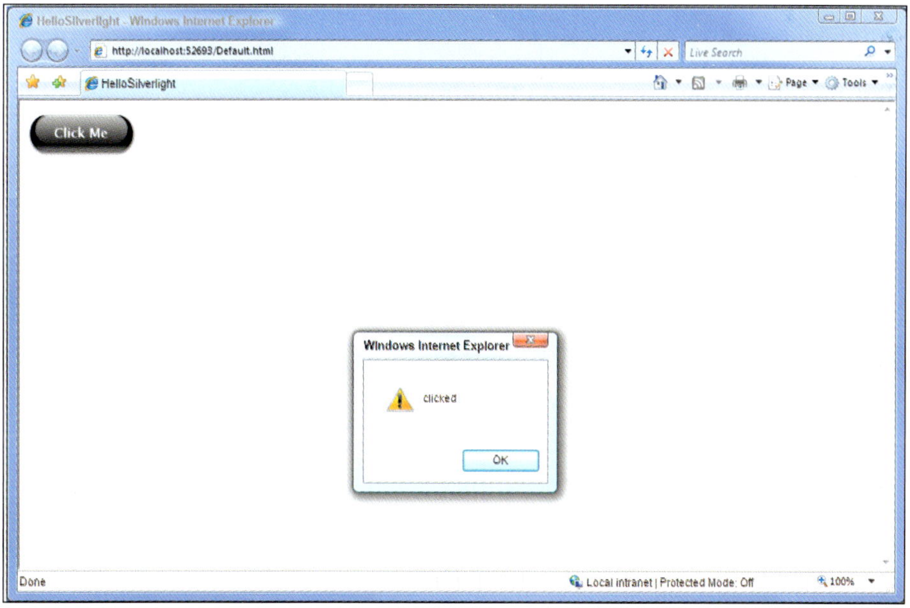

Figure 1-13

Change the Name of the project to HelloSilverlight, as Figure 1-13 shows, and click the OK button to create the solution. You should be looking at Visual Studio now, with a Solution Explorer that looks similar to Figure 1-14.

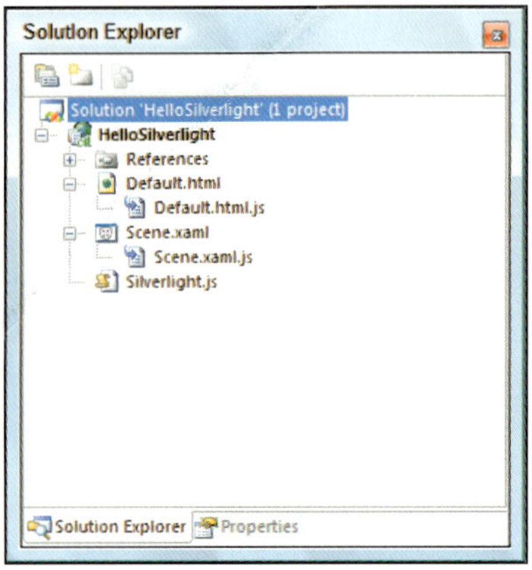

Figure 1-14

Table 1-2 outlines the files in the solution, along with their definitions.

Table 1-2: Default Files in a Silverlight Project and Their Descriptions

File	Description
`Default.html`	Default HTML file that hosts the Silverlight player and contains references to the JavaScript files required by the Silverlight player.
`Default.html.js`	The JavaScript file associated with the `Default.html` file.
`Scene.xaml`	The default XAML file that contains the objects and elements that make up the user interface that plays in the Silverlight player that is embedded in `Default.html`.
`Scene.xaml.js`	The JavaScript file for the control events specified in the XAML file. This can be likened to the code behind file of a `.cs` file.
`Silverlight.js`	The core JavaScript library that ensures the Silverlight player is on the client machine and then creates the Silverlight object that runs in the page.

Now that you have a little bit of an understanding of the files in the solution, go ahead and run the project to see how the default Silverlight template works. You should see a web page with a button on it. If you click the button, you should see something similar to Figure 1-15.

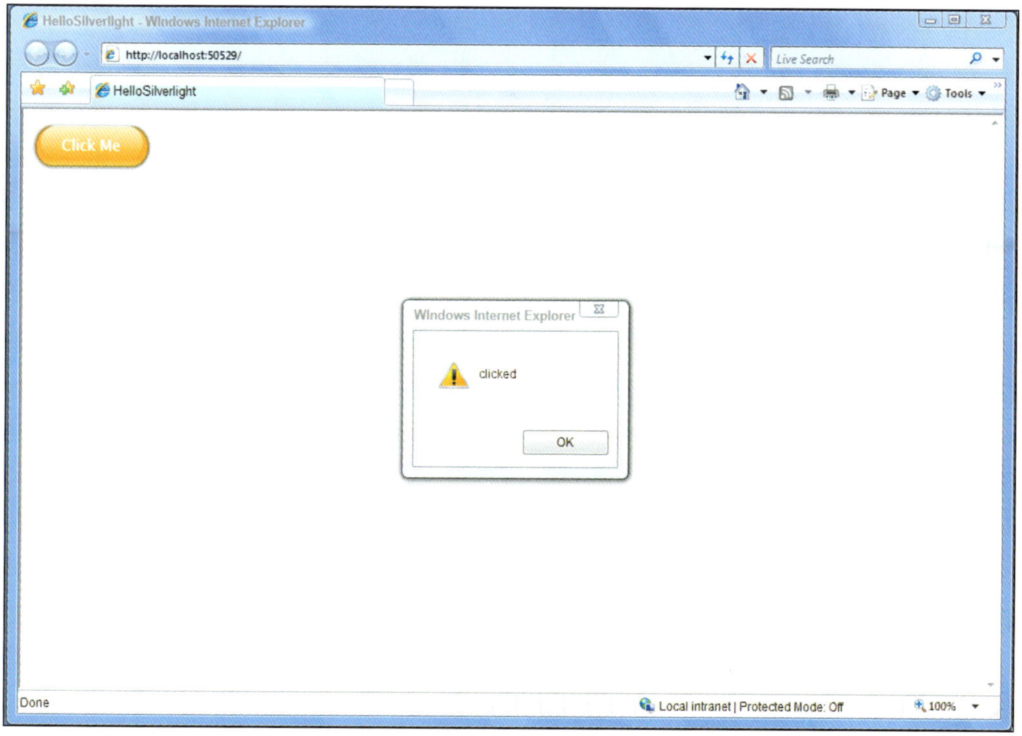

Figure 1-15

If you look at the HTML (Listing 1-1) in the `Default.htm` file, you will notice that there is no ActiveX control on the page. There are, however, several references to JavaScript files that contain the code that is needed to create the instance of the Silverlight player in the HTML page.

Listing 1-1: HTML from the Default.htm File That Hosts the Silverlight Control

```
<!DOCTYPE HTML PUBLIC "-//W3C//DTD HTML 4.01
    Transitional//EN" "http://www.w3c.org/TR/1999/REC-html401-19991224/loose.dtd">
<html xmlns="http://www.w3.org/1999/xhtml">
<head>
    <title>HelloSilverlight</title>

    <script type="text/javascript" src="Silverlight.js"></script>
    <script type="text/javascript" src="Default.html.js"></script>
    <script type="text/javascript" src="Scene.xaml.js"></script>
```

Listing 1-1: *(continued)*

```
</head>

<body>
    <div id="SilverlightControlHost">
        <script type="text/javascript">
            createSilverlight();
        </script>
    </div>
</body>
</html>
```

The embedded script in the <body> tag contains a call to the JavaScript function `createSilverlight()`, which is located in the `default.html.js` file, is listed in Listing 1-2, and is responsible for creating the Silverlight object in the HTML page.

Listing 1-2: The createSilverlight Function

```
function createSilverlight()
{
    var scene = new HelloSilverlight.Scene();
    Sys.Silverlight.createObjectEx({
       source: "Scene.xaml",
        parentElement:
        document.getElementById("SilverlightControlHost"),
        id: "SilverlightControl",
        properties: {
            width: "400",
            height: "400",
            version: "0.9"
        },
        events: {
            onLoad:
            Sys.Silverlight.createDelegate
            (scene, scene.handleLoad)
        }
    });
}
```

The core code in the JavaScript file is the call to `Sys.Silverlight.createObjectEx`. This function, shown in Figure 1-16, is responsible for creating the actual Silverlight object and returning it to the page. It also makes sure that the Silverlight control is installed on the client computer, so when it creates the object and accepts the parameters passed in, there are no errors.

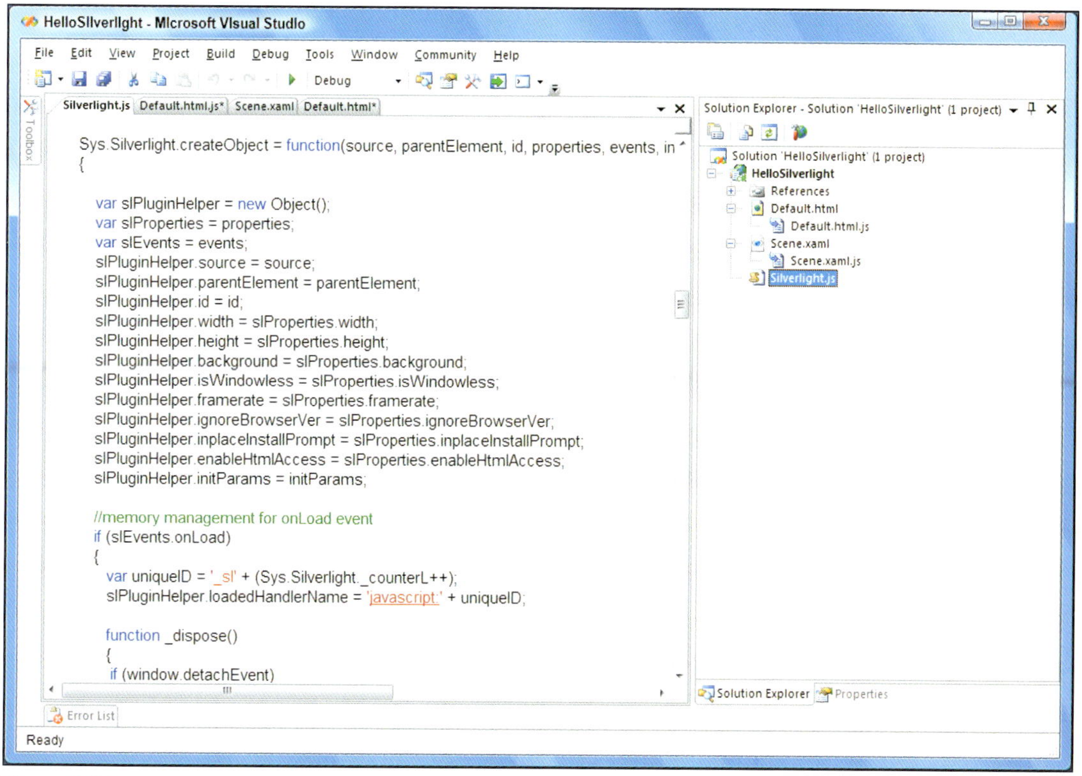

Figure 1-16

The `Sivlerlight.js` file is the core JavaScript needed to instantiate and run the Silverlight player in the browser. It is required in any Silverlight applications you create.

Creating the Silverlight Object in HTML

There are other ways to create the Silverlight player; you do not have to use the method that the default template uses. You can simply use the `object` or `embed` tag in your HTML page to get a Silverlight player. The HTML in Listing 1-3 demonstrates using the `object` tag to create an instance of a Silverlight player named `silverlight1`.

Listing 1-3: Creating a Silverlight Control Using the object Tag in HTML

```
<object
  type="application/ag-plugin"
  id="silverlight1"
  width="350"
  height="350">
  <param name="background" value="#ffebcd" />
  <param name="enableFramerateCounter" value="true" />
```

Listing 1-3: *(continued)*

```
    <param name="enableHtmlAccess" value="true" />
    <param name="initParams" value="paramValue1, paramValue2" />
    <param name="maxFrameRate" value="30" />
    <param name="onError" value="myErrorHandler" />
    <param name="onLoad" value="onLoad" />
    <param name="source" value="HelloSilverlight.xaml" />
    <param name="windowless" value="true" />
  </object>
```

The `object` tag works only in Internet Explorer browsers, whereas the `embed` tag is used for Firefox and Macintosh browsers. The HTML listed in Listing 1-4 is an example of creating a Silverlight player instance using the `embed` tag.

Listing 1-4: Creating a Silverlight Control Using the embed Tag in HTML

```
<embed
  type="application/ag-plugin"
  id="silverlight1"
  width="350"
  height="350"
  background="#ffebcd"
  enableFramerateCounter="true"
  enableHtmlAccess="true"
  initParams="paramValue1, paramValue2"
  maxFrameRate="30"
  OnError="myErrorHandler"
  OnLoad="onLoad"
  source="HelloWorld.xaml"
  windowless="false"
 />
```

The obvious observation is that you would probably not want to do this yourself, because you are limiting yourself to a specific browser type by using `embed` or `object` tags. Your best bet is to use the technique in the default Silverlight project template, which uses generic JavaScript to call the `createObjectEx` function in the `Silverlight.js` file. This ensures you are not making any mistakes in how the Silverlight player is created in the client browser.

Silverlight Object Attributes

In the various examples you have just read about that create the Silverlight player in the browser, you've seen that you can also pass parameters to the object during its creation to set various properties on the control. Table 1-3 (which paraphrases a table that can be found online at `http://msdn2.microsoft.com/library/en-us/bb412394.aspx`) lists the attributes you can use on the Silverlight control when you are creating it.

Table 1-3: Object Attributes for the Silverlight Control

Tag	Type	Description
`Type`	String	The MIME type for the installed plug-in.
`Id`	String	Gives the Silverlight control a unique identifier, because there can be multiple controls on a page.
`width`	String	The rectangular width that displays the Silverlight content in pixels. You can also specify the width as a percentage of the displayable area of the tag containing the Silverlight control — for example, `"40%"`.
`Height`	String	The rectangular region that displays the Silverlight content in pixels. You can also specify the height as a percentage of the displayable area of the tag containing the Silverlight control — for example, `"50%"`.

In addition to the object tag parameters in Table 1-3, the `object` tag also supports a set of optional parameter attributes for the control. Table 1-4 (which paraphrases a table that can be found online at `http://msdn2.microsoft.com/library/en-us/bb412394.aspx`) lists the optional parameter tags that map to properties on the Silverlight control.

Table 1-4: Optional Parameter Tags for the Silverlight Control

Parameter Tag	Type	Description
`background`	String or hexadecimal	The background color of the rectangular region that displays XAML content. The default value is `null`, which is equivalent to the color white.
`enableFramerateCounter`	Boolean	Indicates whether to display the current frame rate in the hosting browser's status bar. The default value is `false`.
`enableHtmlAccess`	Boolean	Determines whether the hosted content in the Silverlight control has access to the browser DOM. The default value is `true`.
`initParams`	String	Specifies an optional set of user-defined initialization parameters.
`maxFramerate`	Integer	Specifies the maximum number of frames to render per second, which defaults to `24`.

Table 1-4: *(continued)*

Parameter Tag	Type	Description
`onError`	String	Specifies the JavaScript error handling function for the `OnError` event. The default value is `default_error_handler`.
`onLoad`	String	Specifies the JavaScript event handling function for the `OnLoad` event. `null` is the default.
`source`	String	Specifies the XAML content that is rendered.
`windowless`	Boolean	Determines whether the Silverlight control displays as a windows-less control. The default value is `false`.

Adding Multiple Silverlight Objects to a Page

Just like any other element or object on an HTML page, you can run multiple Silverlight players on a page as well. To enable multiple Silverlight players on a page, make sure there is a unique `<div>` tag with a unique ID representing the player you are creating.

```
<div id="SilverlightControlHost">
    <script type="text/javascript">
        createSilverlight();
    </script>
</div>
```

In the default `createSilverlight` function, the name of the `<div>` element is hard coded, as demonstrated in Listing 1-5.

Listing 1-5: createSilverlight Function Showing the createObjectEx Method Call

```
function createSilverlight()
{
    var scene = new HelloSilverlight.Scene();
    Sys.Silverlight.createObjectEx({
        source: "Scene.xaml",
        parentElement:
        document.getElementById("SilverlightControlHost"),
        id: "SilverlightControl",
        properties: {
            width: "400",
            height: "400",
            version: "0.9"
        },
        events: {
            onLoad:
```

Notice the XAML file is also hard coded, as is the control host you are attempting to pass the Silverlight player back to. To ensure there are no errors, you may want to consider creating a generic `createSilverlight` function that accepts parameters for the information that you need to make unique, as the code in Listing 1-6 demonstrates.

Listing 1-6: Sample of Parameterized createSilverlight Function

```
function createSilverlight(xamlFile, hostId, controlId, height, width)
{
    var scene = new HelloSilverlight.Scene();
    Sys.Silverlight.createObjectEx({
        source: xamlFile,
        parentElement:
        document.getElementById(hostId),
        id: controlId,
        properties: {
            width: height,
            height: width,
            version: "0.9"
        },
        events: {
            onLoad:
```

As you can see, adding multiple Silverlight players to a page is pretty simple, and in many cases, will be the default scenario.

Resizing a Silverlight Control

The Silverlight control provides both resize capabilities and full screen mode. When the control is displayed in embedded mode, it is playing in the default height and width specified when it was created. In embedded mode, the `OnResize` event fires, which allows you to write code that resizes the player and the elements in the player.

The JavaScript in Listing 1-7 shows how to define an `OnResize` event for a Silverlight control.

Listing 1-7: Resizing a Control Using the OnResize Event

```
// function call from the OnResize event
function ResizeControl(width, height)
{
    // Reference the control in the DOM
    var control = document.getElementById("silverlight1");

    // Set the size
    control.width = width;
    control.height = height;
}
```

Whenever the `actualHeight` or `actualWidth` property of the Silverlight control changes, the `OnResize` event occurs. An effective way to assign a function to this event is during the control's creation. For example, you can assign the `ResizeControl` function in the `createSilverlight` function described earlier in this section:

```
silverlightObject.content.onResize = "ResizeControl"
```

When resizing a Silverlight control or when switching to full screen mode, the performance of any running video or animations should not be affected.

In full screen mode, the player is displayed in the full height and width of the screen's resolution on top of all other running applications. When the player goes from embedded mode to full screen mode, the `OnResize` event does not fire, but the `ActualHeight` and `ActualWidth` properties do change. They will reflect the height and width of your screen's resolution.

Figure 1-17 demonstrates a Silverlight player embedded in the browser, and Figure 1-18 shows the same Silverlight player in full screen mode.

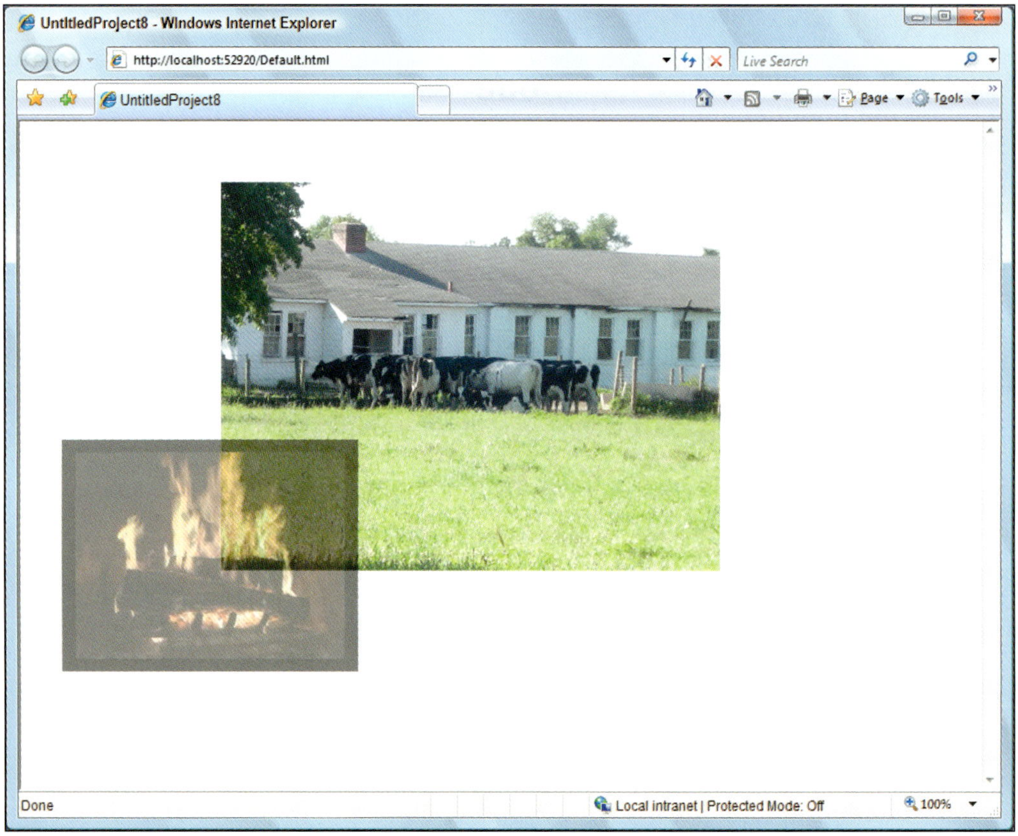

Figure 1-17

Figure 1-18

Displaying in Full Screen Mode

To display a Silverlight player in full screen mode, the `fullScreen` property must be set to `true`. If the `fullScreen` property is not set to `true`, the Silverlight control assumes its normal height and width and displays in embedded mode. Note that only one Silverlight player can be in full screen mode at a time; if a control is displayed in full screen mode, it must be returned to embedded mode before another control can go to full screen. Listing 1-8 shows how to use JavaScript to get the Silverlight player into full screen mode.

Listing 1-8: Using JavaScript to Get the Silverlight Player into Full Screen Mode

```
function GoFullScreen(sender, eventArgs)
{
        host = sender.getHost();
        host.content.fullscreen = true;
}
```

To use the function, you would need to specify an event on an XAML element. For example, because the user needs to trigger the action to go into full screen, you might have a `TextBlock` or a `Rectangle` element that indicates to users that if they click on the element, the browser goes into full screen mode. Notice in the following XAML the call to the `GoFullScreen` function on the `MouseLeftButtonUp` event.

```
<Rectangle Height="100" Width="100"
           Canvas.Top="100" Canvas.Left="100"
           Fill="Red"
           MouseLeftButtonUp="GoFullScreen" />
```

Note that you cannot set the mode to full screen in the `Loaded` event of the control. It must be set in response to user actions, such as the `MouseLeftButtonDown`, `MouseLeftButtonUp`, `KeyDown`, and `KeyUp` events. The following code toggles the screen mode based on the `MouseLeftButtonUp` event:

```
function GoFullScreen(sender, eventArgs)
{
        host = sender.getHost();
        host.content.fullscreen = !host.content.fullscreen;
}
```

When a Silverlight player switches to full screen, the message demonstrated in Figure 1-19 is displayed for several seconds, giving the user instructions on how to return to embedded mode.

Figure 1-19

Once a Silverlight player is in full screen mode, keyboard events are prevented from being passed on to keyboard event handlers in the application. The only valid keyboard input that is acted upon is the set of keystrokes that return the Silverlight control to embedded mode. This limitation of keyboard input during full screen mode is a security feature and is intended to minimize the possibility of unintended information being entered by a user. The other way to return from full screen mode to embedded mode is to simply use the following keystroke combinations:

- **Windows** — Esc, Ctrl+W, or Alt+F4
- **Macintosh** — Esc

Understanding XAML

The one file we have not touched on yet is the `Scene.xaml` file from the HelloSilverlight sample. The XAML file is the most important part of the Silverlight application. It is the markup that defines what should actually get displayed in the Silverlight player itself. The XAML in the `Scene.xaml` file is fairly complex for your first Silverlight application, so we are not going to delve into the details of what the XAML is actually doing. Over the next several chapters, you will get a better understanding of what XAML can do for you in Silverlight, the various ways you can get XAML into the Silverlight player, and how you can create very interactive user interfaces with not so complex XAML. For now, you'll just get an understanding of XAML and look at a couple of examples of how it can be used in Silverlight.

If you are not familiar with WPF, you are probably not familiar with XAML. Since the dawn of Visual Studio, way back around 1997 or so when when we used its precursor Visual InterDev, there was always the promise of code and user interface design separation. This means that a developer can write code, while a designer just works on the design and layout aspects of an application. This has never been realized, mostly because a developer and a designer are always using different tools and different languages. With the introduction of XAML, there was finally a unified markup that could not only describe what a control is and how it fits into a page, but also how layout, and more importantly, the overall look and feel of the controls on a page are defined. A designer can use XAML to create a mock-up of a page or an application, and a developer can take that XAML markup and use it directly in his project files. Because partial classes and code behind files in Visual Studio .NET allow you to separate the code logic from the layout and control definitions, using XAML gives the opportunity to have this separation of the design from the code. To give you an idea of how XAML works, look at the code in Listing 1-9. This is an XAML snippet from a Silverlight application that shows Hello World in a `TextBlock`.

Listing 1-9: Basic XAML to Display Hello World in a Silverlight Player

```
<Canvas x:Name="parentCanvas"
        xmlns="http://schemas.microsoft.com/client/2007"
        xmlns:x="http://schemas.microsoft.com/winfx/2006/xaml"
        Width="640"
        Height="480"
        Background="White"
        >
    <TextBlock>Hello World</TextBlock>
</Canvas>
```

Listing 1-10 shows how the XAML can get more complex, demonstrating adding various animations to the text block control. In this example, four different transforms are occurring:

- `ScaleTransform` — Stretches or shrinks an object horizontally or vertically.
- `SkewTransform` — Creates the illusion of three-dimensional depth in a two-dimensional object.
- `RotateTransform` — Rotates an object by a specified angle around the CenterX and CenterY of an object.
- `TranslateTransform` — Translates, or moves, an object in the two-dimensional x-y coordinate system.

Listing 1-10: XAML Showing a Custom Transform on a TextBlock Element

```
<Canvas
    xmlns="http://schemas.microsoft.com/client/2007"
    xmlns:x="http://schemas.microsoft.com/winfx/2006/xaml"
    Width="640" Height="480"
    Background="White"
    >
    <Canvas.Triggers>
        <EventTrigger RoutedEvent="Canvas.Loaded">
            <BeginStoryboard>
                <Storyboard x:Name="Timeline1"/>
            </BeginStoryboard>
        </EventTrigger>
    </Canvas.Triggers>
    <TextBlock Width="349" Height="67"
        Canvas.Left="150"
        Canvas.Top="140" Text="Hello World"
        TextWrapping="Wrap"
        RenderTransformOrigin="0.5,0.5"
        x:Name="textBlock">
        <TextBlock.RenderTransform>
            <TransformGroup>
                <ScaleTransform ScaleX="1" ScaleY="1"/>
                <SkewTransform AngleX="0" AngleY="0"/>
                <RotateTransform Angle="0"/>
                <TranslateTransform X="0" Y="0"/>
            </TransformGroup>
        </TextBlock.RenderTransform>
    </TextBlock>
</Canvas>
```

Appendix B gives a more in-depth explanation of XAML and how you can use it to define and create your Silverlight applications. You will also be getting your fair share of XAML throughout the book, because it is how you will create most of the examples that we have defined. Tools like Microsoft Expression Blend 2.0, Visual Studio 2005 with the Silverlight project support, and Visual Studio 2008 are all Rapid Application Development (RAD) tools that you can use to create your Silverlight applications. The problem right now is that Microsoft Expression Blend 2.0 is really the only tool that gives you a nice design-time experience, where you can drag and drop controls onto the design surface and switch between the designer view and the XAML view. We know these problems will work themselves out. As Silverlight matures and goes into a release stage, and as Visual Studio 2008 nears release, the appropriate tools will be released that will let you design applications in a RAD fashion. The good thing about not having the perfect tool right now to create Silverlight applications is that you are forced to type XAML, which will give you the understanding you need to know what is happening behind the scenes of the runtime player.

Summary

This chapter gave you the groundwork you need to move forward in the book. You learned that Silverlight is a rich platform for delivering next-generation RIAs based on XAML, HTML, and JavaScript. Using tools like the Silverlight project template in the Silverlight 1.0 SDK, it is easy to get started writing Silverlight applications. In the next chapter, you continue where you left off here with more information on creating the user interface using XAML. If you ever need a reference on XAML, refer to Appendix B to find out additional information on XAML.

2

Building Silverlight Applications Using XAML

In Chapter 1, you learned about the basics of Silverlight and how it helps build Rich Internet Applications (RIAs). In this chapter, you dig deeper into XAML and how XAML builds out the user interface that the Silverlight control renders. You learn the following:

- How positioning works in Silverlight
- The types of objects you can render in Silverlight
- How video works in Silverlight
- How animation works

Rendering Silverlight Content

As you might have noticed in Chapter 1, you are typing all of the XAML into the `.xaml` files to render the output of the user interface. There is no design-time experience in Visual Studio 2005, with drag-and-drop onto a convenient design surface. This also means there is no toolbox of controls that you can use in Visual Studio 2005 to create the UI. You'll learn in Chapter 3 that Expression Blend does have better support for this type of development. Because we are using Visual Studio 2005, it is important to understand what controls (or objects) there are for you to render output.

In Silverlight, there is a base class named `UIElement` that all objects that render output are based on. This means that you can create an instance of these objects using XAML, and the output will render when hosted in the Silverlight control. The objects in Silverlight 1.0 are `Canvas`, `Ellipse`, `Glyphs`, `Image`, `InkPresenter`, `Line`, `LineBreak`, `MediaElement`, `Path`, `Polygon`, `Polyline`, `Rectangle`, `Run`, `Shape`, and `TextBlock`.

Each of these objects has methods and properties that are consistent across each object, listed in Table 2-1.

Table 2-1: Properties, Methods, and Events of Base Silverlight UIElement Class Objects

Properties	`Canvas.Left`, `Canvas.Top`, `Canvas.ZIndex`, `Clip`, `Cursor`, `Height`, `IsHitTestVisible`, `Name`, `Opacity`, `OpacityMask`, `RenderTransform`, `RenderTransformOrigin`, `Resources`, `Triggers`, `Visibility`, `Width`
Methods	`AddEventListener`, `CaptureMouse`, `FindName`, `GetHost`, `GetParent`, `GetValue`, `ReleaseMouseCapture`, `RemoveEventListener`, `SetValue`
Events	`GotFocus`, `KeyDown`, `KeyUp`, `Loaded`, `LostFocus`, `MouseEnter`, `MouseLeave`, `MouseLeftButtonDown`, `MouseLeftButtonUp`, `MouseMove`

As you go through this chapter and the rest of the book, you will undoubtedly be wondering "Where is the `TextBox` control; where is the `DataGrid` control?" You are used to these types of controls using ASP.NET and Windows Forms, but in Silverlight 1.0, they are not available. You do have access to the keyboard events, so you can detect when a keystroke occurs and what the keystroke is, but if you want to accomplish data entry, you'll be using the ASP.NET server controls positioned in a `div` element on top of the Silverlight control. If you remember, the goal of Silverlight 1.0 was RIAs, with an emphasis on multimedia web sites and enhanced interaction compared to traditional HTML- or AJAX-based web sites. The size of the runtime is important, so removing all unnecessary elements was critical to an optimal download experience.

Working with XAML in This Chapter

To work with the XAML in this chapter, you should create a new Visual Studio 2005 Silverlight project. Follow the next few steps to create an application that will run, but is such that you can type in the XAML or JavaScript in this chapter to test the code that you are learning about.

1. In Visual Studio, create a new Silverlight project named `SilverlightWrox1`.
2. Delete all of the XAML in the `Scene.xaml` file except the root `Canvas` declaration and the namespace references. It should look like the following code:

```
<Canvas xmlns="http://schemas.microsoft.com/client/2007"
        xmlns:x="http://schemas.microsoft.com/winfx/2006/xaml">

</Canvas>
```

3. Delete all of the JavaScript in the `Scene.xaml.js` file except the following JavaScript:

```
if (!window.SilverlightWrox1)
    window.SilverlightWrox1 = {};

SilverlightWrox1.Scene = function()
{
}

SilverlightWrox1.Scene.prototype =
```

```
{
    handleLoad: function(plugIn, userContext, rootElement)
    {

    }
}
```

You now have a basic template that you can add XAML and JavaScript code to so you can test the concepts in this chapter. Most of the XAML listed in this chapter can simply be typed in the `Scene.xaml` file inside of the root `Canvas` object. If there is anything special that needs to be done to get code to work, we will point it out.

Layout of Silverlight Content

The layout mechanism that we briefly touched on in Chapter 1 for most elements on a Silverlight surface is the `Canvas` object. Each Silverlight XAML file has a root `<Canvas>` element. Within the root, there can be any number of child elements, including additional `canvas` elements, with any number of child `canvas` elements. In WPF, the layout of a page can be more complex, including `DockPanel` objects, `FlowLayout` objects, and `Grid` objects. In order to keep the Silverlight 1.0 runtime to a minimum, the only layout option is `Canvas`. The canvas essentially becomes the container for other child elements, and all objects are positioned using their x and y coordinates relative to their location in the parent canvas. In Silverlight, this is done with the `Canvas.Top` and `Canvas.Left` attached properties, which provide the resolution-independent pixel value of a control's x and y coordinates. Attached properties allow different child elements to set property values for properties that are actually defined in their parent element.

Using these attached properties is not the only way to position elements. Certain objects, such as geometric shapes (`Line` objects, `Polygon` objects), have other ways to position where they draw themselves on the Silverlight control. You learn more about those objects in Chapter 4. For now, we'll focus on the `Canvas.Top` and `Canvas.Left` attached properties. Listing 2-1 demonstrates the root `Canvas` object, with controls positioned within the canvas.

Listing 2-1: Positioning Elements within a Canvas Object

```
<Canvas
    xmlns="http://schemas.microsoft.com/client/2007"
    xmlns:x="http://schemas.microsoft.com/winfx/2006/xaml"
    Width="640" Height="480"
    Background="White"
    >

    <Rectangle
            Canvas.Top ="30"
            Canvas.Left="30"
            Fill="Blue"
            Height="100" Width="100"/>

    <Rectangle
            Canvas.Top ="75"
            Canvas.Left="130"
```

(Continued)

Listing 2-1: *(continued)*

```
                Fill="Red"
                Height="100" Width="100"/>

        <Ellipse
                Canvas.Top ="100"
                Canvas.Left="30"
                Fill="Green"
                Height="100" Width="100"/>

    </Canvas >
```

The same XAML from Listing 2-1 is explained in more detail in Figure 2-1, which shows the location of the objects in the canvas.

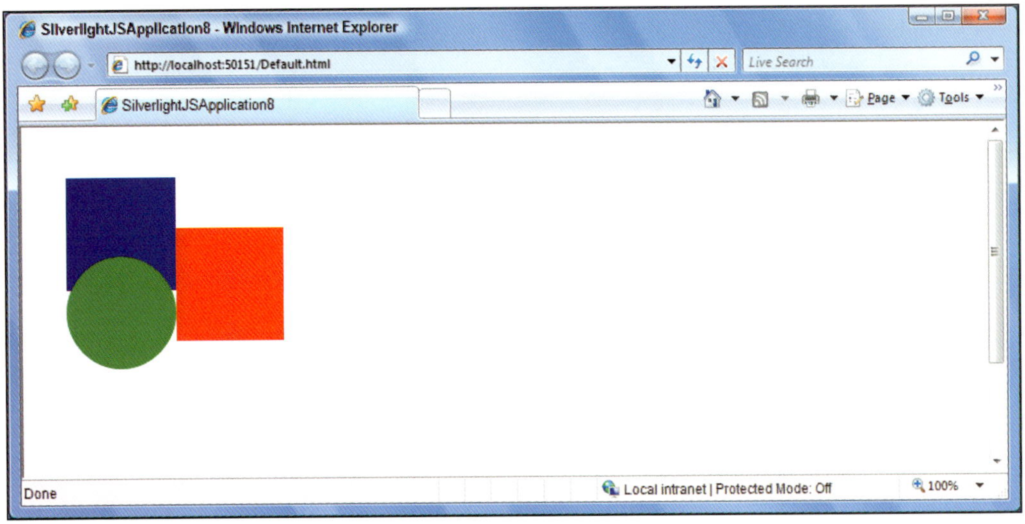

Figure 2-1

If you nest canvas objects within canvas objects, remember that the child elements in a canvas are positioned relative to their parent canvas, not the root canvas. Listing 2-2 gives an example of this, which is further explained in Figure 2-2.

Listing 2-2: Canvas Objects with Nested Canvas Objects That Have Child Elements

```
<Canvas
    xmlns="http://schemas.microsoft.com/client/2007"
    xmlns:x="http://schemas.microsoft.com/winfx/2006/xaml"
    Width="640" Height="480"
    Background="White"
    >

    <Canvas
```

Listing 2-2: *(continued)*

```
            Canvas.Top ="30"
            Canvas.Left="30">
                <Rectangle Fill="Blue" Height="100" Width="100"/>
    </Canvas>

    <Canvas
            Canvas.Top ="75"
            Canvas.Left="130">
                <Rectangle Fill="Red" Height="100" Width="100"/>
    </Canvas>

    <Canvas>
        <Ellipse
            Canvas.Top ="100"
            Canvas.Left="30"
            Fill="Green" Height="30" Width="30"/>
    </Canvas>

    <Canvas
            Canvas.Top ="75"
            Canvas.Left="130">
         <Ellipse Canvas.Top ="100" Canvas.Left="30"
            Fill="Green" Height="100" Width="100"/>
    </Canvas>
</Canvas >
```

Figure 2-2 shows the results of the XAML in Listing 2-2. Notice the position of the elements is different than Figure 2-1.The positioning of the `Canvas` objects is different, as is the position of the elements within the `Canvas` objects.

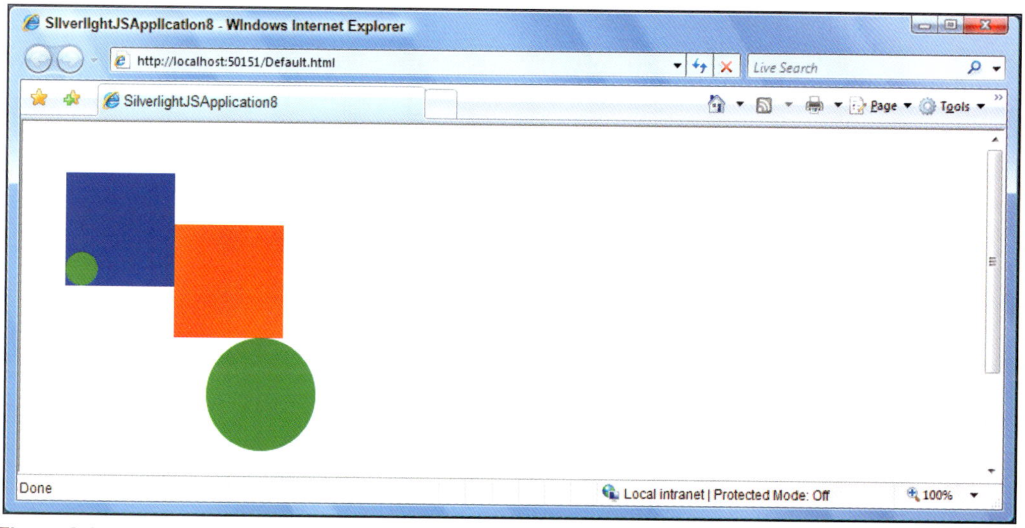

Figure 2-2

A lesson you need to learn early on is to make sure that you do not specify a `Canvas.Top` or `Canvas.Left` position beyond the size of the actual Silverlight control. When you add a Silverlight control to an HTML page, you give it a `height` and `width`, as Listing 2-3 demonstrates.

Listing 2-3: Silverlight Control Placed on an HTML Page

```
Silverlight.createObjectEx({
    source: "Scene2.xaml",
    parentElement: document.getElementById
    ("SilverlightControlHost"),
    id: "SilverlightControl",
    properties: {
        width: "300",
        height: "300",
        version: "0.9",
        background: "black"
},
```

Or you could even set the `height` and `width` properties the Silverlight control using CSS, as Listing 2-4 shows.

Listing 2-4: Positioning the Silverlight Control Using CSS

```
<style type="text/css">
    .silverlightHost {
        height: 480px;
        width: 640px;
    }
</style>

...

<div id="SilverlightControlHost" class="silverlightHost">
    <script type="text/javascript">
        createSilverlight();
    </script>
</div>
```

If your control height is 480 pixels, and you set a `Canvas.Top` property to a value of 500, the object will be outside of the viewable area of the Silverlight control. The nice thing is that the elements are still on the control, so you can animate them into view based on some other interaction if you need to.

Positioning Objects Using ZIndex

As you begin building Silverlight applications, you will be working with multiple elements on multiple canvas objects. In many cases, many of the elements will be overlapping each other, and there will be positioning issues. In these cases, you can use the `ZIndex` property to change the order in which controls are rendered on a canvas. This is the same concept as "send to back" or "bring to front" when working with elements in applications like PowerPoint and Visual Studio. `ZIndex` values that are higher are rendered on top of elements with a lower `ZIndex` property value. If no `ZIndex` is specified, the order in which elements are listed in the XAML file is how they will render.

Listing 2-5 demonstrates the use of the `ZIndex` property to position one rectangle in front of another rectangle. Figure 2-3 shows the output from Listing 2-5. Notice the two sets of rectangles, how they are positioned with the `Canvas.Top` and `Canvas.Left` properties, as well as the `ZIndex` property to specify the layering of the objects.

Listing 2-5: Using ZIndex for Positioning Elements

```
<Canvas
   xmlns="http://schemas.microsoft.com/client/2007"
   xmlns:x="http://schemas.microsoft.com/winfx/2006/xaml"
   Width="640" Height="480"
   Background="White">

    <Rectangle
        Canvas.ZIndex="3"
        Canvas.Left="5" Canvas.Top="5"
        Height="200" Width="200" Fill="Blue" />

    <Rectangle
        Canvas.ZIndex="2"
        Canvas.Left="50" Canvas.Top="50"
        Height="200" Width="200" Fill="Green" />

    <Rectangle
        Canvas.ZIndex="1"
        Canvas.Left="95" Canvas.Top="95"
        Height="200" Width="200" Fill="Red" />

    <!-- Reverse the ZIndex Property by removing the ZIndex property
         and letting the object render in the order they are listed -->
    <Rectangle
        Canvas.Left="500" Canvas.Top="5"
        Height="200" Width="200" Fill="Blue" />

    <Rectangle
        Canvas.Left="545" Canvas.Top="50"
        Height="200" Width="200" Fill="Green" />

    <Rectangle
        Canvas.Left="590" Canvas.Top="95"
        Height="200" Width="200" Fill="Red" />

</Canvas>
```

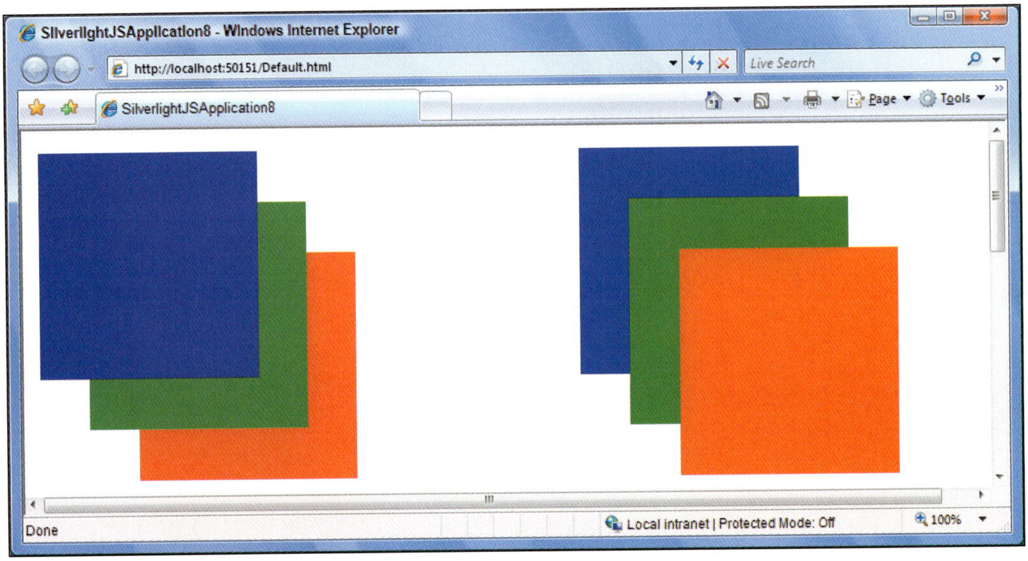

Figure 2-3

Looking at ZIndex with a bunch of rectangles may not give you a real-world example of why ZIndex matters. So, consider Listing 2-6 and Figure 2-4, which demonstrate an example of using different elements on a canvas using ZIndex. The Opacity property is also used; notice that the logo area in the upper-left of the browser has a semi-transparent background. You can see details of the image that is behind the logos. When using the Opacity property, the lower the percentage, the more the transparency. For example, the default opacity of 100 percent on all objects means they are solid. A value of zero would mean the object is invisible.

Listing 2-6: Using ZIndex and Opacity with Image and MediaElement Objects

```
<Image Width="1253.874" Height="768" Canvas.ZIndex="1"
       Source="Resources/compositeBG.png" Stretch="Fill"/>

<MediaElement Opacity="2"
              Width="342" Height="202"
              Canvas.Left="30" Canvas.Top="283" Canvas.ZIndex="4"
              Source="Resources/Grass_loop.wmv" Stretch="Fill"/>

<Image Opacity="0.5" Width="298" Height="241"
       Canvas.Left="30" Canvas.Top="19.018" Canvas.ZIndex="3"
       Source="Resources/IG_Silverlight.png" Stretch="Fill"/>

<Image Width="25" Height="24"
       Canvas.Left="976" Canvas.Top="20"
       Canvas.ZIndex="4"
       Source="Resources/xCloseButton.png" Stretch="Fill"/>

<Image Width="261" Height="167"
```

Listing 2-6: *(continued)*

```
            Canvas.Left="739" Canvas.Top="93"
            Canvas.ZIndex="5"
            Source="Resources/thumbDataVisualization.png"
            Stretch="Fill"/>

    <Image Width="261" Height="167"
            Canvas.Left="739" Canvas.Top="283"
            Canvas.ZIndex="6"
            Source="Resources/thumbOrcas.png"
            Stretch="Fill"/>
```

Figure 2-4

The `Image` elements in Listing 2-6 use the `Stretch` property to specify how the image is rendered. The `Stretch` property also applies to `VideoBrush`, `Image`, `ImageBrush`, `MediaElement`, and `Shape` objects. The `Stretch` property contains the `Stretch` enumeration, which includes:

- `None` — The content does not stretch to fill the output dimensions.
- `Uniform` — The content is scaled to fit the output dimensions and the aspect ratio of the content is preserved.

- `UniformToFill` — The content is scaled so that it completely fills the output area and preserves its original aspect ratio.
- `Fill` — The content is scaled to fit the output dimensions, which means the original aspect ratio of the content might not be preserved because the height and width are scaled independently.

Positioning Objects Using Transforms

You can also use transforms to manipulate and position objects. Using *transforms*, you can move, rotate, skew, and scale objects. Transforms are very important for real-world RIAs. In an interactive and highly styled application, not all objects are positioned in a straight, flat, two-dimensional space. To achieve higher fidelity and to allow for interactions, objects can be skewed and rotated, and based on mouse input, they can be translated and scaled. The following types of transforms are allowed in Silverlight:

- `RotateTransform` — Rotates an element by the specified angle.
- `ScaleTransform` — Scales an element by the specified `ScaleX` and `ScaleY` amounts.
- `SkewTransform` — Skews an element by the specified `AngleX` and `AngleY` amounts.
- `TranslateTransform` — Moves (translates) an element by the specified `X` and `Y` amounts.

To apply a transform, you use the `RenderTransform` property. Using a special `TransformGroup` object, you can apply multiple transforms to a single element, or you can use a `MatrixTransform` to apply special transforms to objects.

One purpose of MatrixTransforms is to allow intensely mathematical operations based on linear algebra to be performed on graphics' objects. Further discussion of such operations can be found in books on computer graphics, but are beyond the scope of this book.

Listing 2-7 shows how to apply various transforms, as well as how to use a `TransformGroup` object. The results of Listing 2-7 are shown in Figure 2-5.

Listing 2-7: Applying a Rotate, Scale, and Skew Transform to an Image Object

```
<TextBlock Canvas.Left="860" Foreground="Black"
           Text="This is Rotated Text" FontSize="48">
    <TextBlock.RenderTransform>
        <RotateTransform Angle="90" />
    </TextBlock.RenderTransform>
</TextBlock>

<!-- Original Image -->
<TextBlock Width="236" Height="29"
           Canvas.Left="28" Text="Original Image"
           TextWrapping="Wrap" Canvas.Top="10"
           FontWeight="Bold"/>

<Image Width="261" Height="167"
       Canvas.Left="21" Canvas.Top="27"
       Source="Resources/thumbSilverlight.png"
       Stretch="Fill"/>
```

Listing 2-7: *(continued)*

```
<!-- Applying a RotateTransform
     at a 23 degree angle -->
<TextBlock Width="236"
           Height="29" Canvas.Left="310"
           Canvas.Top="40" Text="RotateTransform"
           TextWrapping="Wrap" FontWeight="Bold"/>

<Image Width="261.867" Height="167.379"
       Canvas.Left="350" Canvas.Top="48"
       Source="Resources/thumbSilverlight.png"
       Stretch="Fill"
       RenderTransformOrigin="0.5,0.5">
    <Image.RenderTransform>
        <RotateTransform Angle="-23"/>
    </Image.RenderTransform>
</Image>

<!-- Applying a ScaleTransform for 2 times the width (X)
     and 1.5 times the height (Y) -->
<TextBlock Width="236" Height="29"
           Canvas.Left="238" Canvas.Top="289"
           Text="ScaleTransform"
           TextWrapping="Wrap" FontWeight="Bold"/>

<Image Width="261.867" Height="167.379"
       Canvas.Left="354" Canvas.Top="341"
       Source="Resources/thumbSilverlight.png"
       Stretch="Fill"
       RenderTransformOrigin="0.5,0.5">
    <Image.RenderTransform>
        <ScaleTransform ScaleX="2" ScaleY="1.5"/>
    </Image.RenderTransform>
</Image>

<!-- Applying a SkewTransform at a 25 degree angle inside
     of a TransformGroup element -->
<TextBlock Width="236" Height="29"
           Canvas.Left="36" Canvas.Top="557"
           Text="SkewTransform"
           TextWrapping="Wrap" FontWeight="Bold"/>

<Image Width="261.867" Height="167.379"
       Canvas.Left="62" Canvas.Top="572"
       Source="Resources/thumbSilverlight.png"
       Stretch="Fill"
       RenderTransformOrigin="0.5,0.5">
    <Image.RenderTransform>
        <TransformGroup>
            <SkewTransform AngleX="25" AngleY="0"/>
            <RotateTransform Angle="0"/>
            <TranslateTransform X="0" Y="0"/>
        </TransformGroup>
    </Image.RenderTransform>
</Image>
```

Figure 2-5

If you examine the XAML for the `TransformGroup` object for the last image rendered:

```
<TransformGroup>
        <SkewTransform AngleX="25" AngleY="0"/>
        <RotateTransform Angle="0"/>
        <TranslateTransform X="0" Y="0"/>
</TransformGroup>
```

you will notice that the `RotateTransform` and `TranslateTransform` do not have any values. This was intentional because we wanted to demonstrate the syntax for a `TransformGroup`. The goal of using a `TransformGroup` is that when using a transform on an object, you can affect the object differently by applying a translate, then a rotate, then a scale transform. The order is significant because based on the type of transform you are applying, the origin of the coordinate system changes. When an object is scaled on a center origin, the result will differ if the object was translated, or moved, from its center origin before being scaled.

Drawing with Text and Brushes

Now that you have the basics of layout and positioning, there are two more key elements that can be considered the basics of a Silverlight application: drawing text and painting with brushes. Though we have touched on some aspects of this already, the next two sections get into more detail in each area.

Using the TextBlock Object

The `TextBlock` object is used to display formatted, single line, and multiline text. You can use the `TextBlock` in a similar fashion to a label control in ASP.NET or Windows Forms, where you have a read-only element that can display text in a single line or multiple lines. The difference between a standard label-like control and the `TextBlock` is the support for brushes in the `TextBlock`, which give you additional options when painting the text content of the `TextBlock`. The following brushes are supported for `TextBlock` objects:

- `SolidColorBrush` — Paints an area with a solid color.
- `LinearGradientBrush` — Paints an area with a linear gradient.
- `RadialGradientBrush` — Paints an area with a radial gradient.
- `ImageBrush` — Paints an area with an image.

The `TextBlock` object in Silverlight also has the advantage of two additional characteristics that make it a more interesting control: `Run` and `LineBreak`.

- The `Run` object represents a string of text within a `TextBlock`.
- The `LineBreak` does what its name indicates; it adds a line break to text to make it render on multiple lines.

`Run` is interesting because it allows you to create formatted text within a text string. For example, the following text uses the `Foreground` property to display text in the color red:

```
<TextBlock Foreground="Red">
        This text is Red
</TextBlock>
```

If you just want the word *Red* to be in the color red, you can use a `Run` object and apply the `Foreground` property to it, as the following code demonstrates:

```
<TextBlock>
        This text is <Run Foreground="Red">Red</Run>
</TextBlock>
```

With the `Run` object, you can apply the same properties that you normally would against the `TextBlock` object, which include `FontFamily`, `FontSize`, `FontStretch`, `FontStyle`, `FontWeight`, `Foreground`, `Name`, `Text`, and `TextDecorations`.

If you want your text to simply wrap based on the width of the `TextBlock` object, you can set the `TextWrapping` property to `Wrap` or `NoWrap`, as Listing 2-8 demonstrates.

Listing 2-8: Using the TextWrapping Property

```
<!-- TextBlock with no text wrapping -->
<TextBlock
  Canvas.Top="20"
  Text="The TextBlock object supports wrapping of text."
  Width="200"
  TextWrapping="NoWrap" />

<!-- TextBlock with text wrapping -->
<TextBlock
  Canvas.Top="90"
  Text="The TextBlock object supports wrapping of text."
  Width="200"
  TextWrapping="Wrap" />
```

The Silverlight player natively supports the following font families: Arial, Arial Black, Comic Sans MS, Courier New, Georgia, Lucida Grande, Lucida Sans Unicode, Times New Roman, Trebuchet MS, and Verdana.

As with any font family, you have additional styles for each font, including italic and font weight, such as bold. The default font for all Silverlight rendered text is Lucida Sans Unicode, Lucida Grande, with a default `FontSize` of 14.66 pixels, or 11 points. If you want to use an additional font that is not part of the default player, you can use the `setFontSource` method to download and add additional fonts to a `TextBlock`.

Figure 2-6, which is the result of code in Listing 2-9, demonstrates the output of using various properties and brushes on a `TextBlock` object.

Listing 2-9: Using TextBlock with Various Properties

```
<!-- Simple TextBlock with single brush -->
<TextBlock
  FontFamily="Trebuchet MS"
  FontSize="36"
  FontWeight="Bold"
  Foreground="OrangeRed">
    OrangeRed Text in TextBlock
</TextBlock>

<!-- TextBlock with multiple brushes -->
<TextBlock
  Canvas.Top="60"
  FontFamily="Comic Sans MS"
  FontSize="36"
  FontWeight="Bold"
```

Listing 2-9: *(continued)*

```
      Foreground="Navy">
        Navy
        <Run Text="Spring Green" Foreground="SpringGreen"/>
        <Run Text="Dim Gray" Foreground="DimGray"/>
    </TextBlock>

    <!-- TextBlock with a linear gradient brush -->
    <TextBlock
      Canvas.Top="100"
      FontFamily="Verdana"
      FontSize="32"
      FontWeight="Bold">
        Linear Gradient Brush
        <TextBlock.RenderTransform>
            <ScaleTransform ScaleY="4.0" />
        </TextBlock.RenderTransform>
        <TextBlock.Foreground>
            <LinearGradientBrush StartPoint="0,0" EndPoint="1,1">
                <GradientStop Color="Red" Offset="0.0" />
                <GradientStop Color="Blue" Offset="0.2" />
                <GradientStop Color="Green" Offset="0.4" />
                <GradientStop Color="Olive" Offset="0.6" />
                <GradientStop Color="DodgerBlue" Offset="0.8" />
                <GradientStop Color="OrangeRed" Offset="1.0" />
            </LinearGradientBrush>
        </TextBlock.Foreground>
    </TextBlock>

    <!-- TextBlock with an image brush applied to the text. -->
    <TextBlock
      Canvas.Top="250"
      FontSize="72"
      FontFamily="Verdana"
      FontStyle="Italic"
      FontWeight="Bold">
        Wheat Image
        <TextBlock.Foreground>
            <ImageBrush ImageSource="thumbWheat.png"
                        Stretch="Fill"/>
        </TextBlock.Foreground>
    </TextBlock>

    <!-- Oringal Image used for ImageBrush -->
    <Image Canvas.Top="350" Canvas.Left="250"
           Source="thumbWheat.png"></Image>
```

Creating Hyperlinks

Like any web page, the Silverlight player needs to support navigation. There is no built-in way to navigate from page to page in a Silverlight control, so you need to do some additional work to create a hyperlink that can serve as a navigation tool.

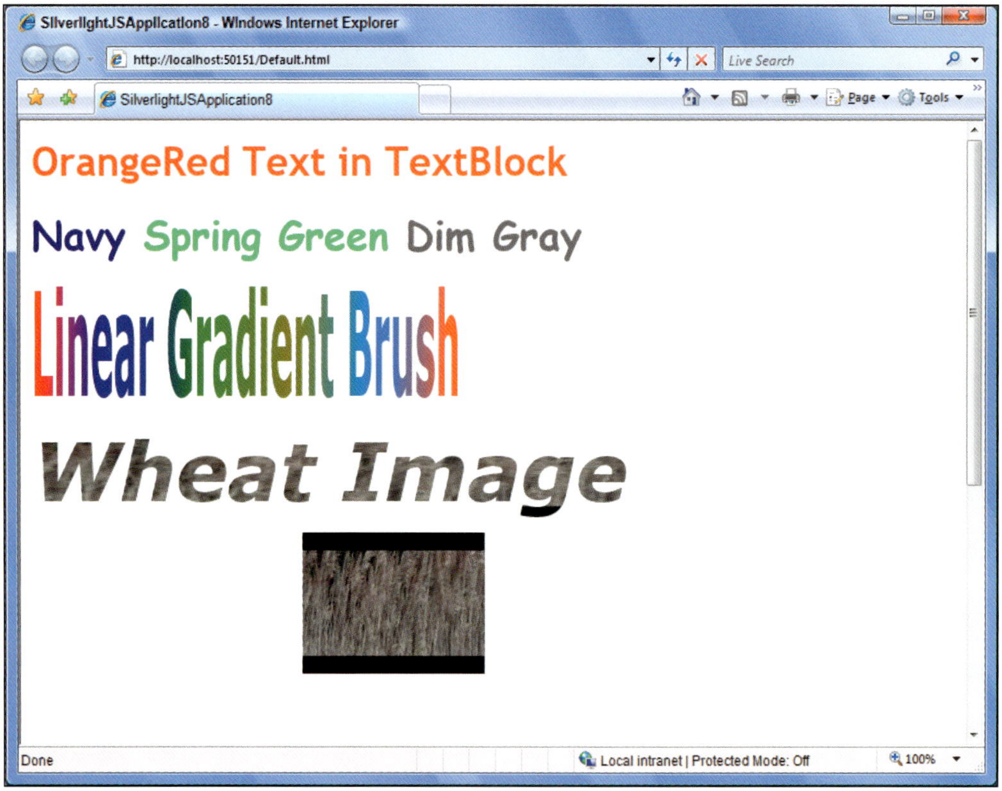

Figure 2-6

Using the `TextDecoration` and `Cursor` properties, along with some JavaScript events, you can mimic a hyperlink. The XAML in Listing 2-10 is an example of how you would define your `TextBlock`.

Listing 2-10: TextBlock for Creating a Hyperlink

```
<TextBlock
  Text="Product Details"
  TextDecorations="None"
  Cursor="Hand"
  FontSize="14" FontWeight="Bold"
  MouseEnter="onMouseEnter"
  MouseLeave="onMouseLeave"
  MouseLeftButtonUp="onMouseLeftButtonUp" />
```

The `TextDecorations` enumeration supports the `None` or `Underline` value, which is how a hyperlink would be represented when the mouse hovers over the `TextBlock`. The JavaScript in Listing 2-11 sets the `textDecorations` and `foreGround` properties programmatically to represent the natural behavior of a hyperlink. You can see the output of the JavaScript code executing on the mouse events in Figure 2-7.

Listing 2-11: Setting Hyperlink Properties in JavaScript

```
function onMouseEnter(sender, mouseEventArgs)
{
    sender.textDecorations = "Underline";
    sender.foreground="Maroon";
}

function onMouseLeave(sender, mouseEventArgs)
{
    sender.textDecorations = "None";
    sender.foreground="Black";
}

function onMouseLeftButtonUp(sender, mouseEventArgs)
{
    alert("You are Navigating on MouseLeftButtonUp");
}
```

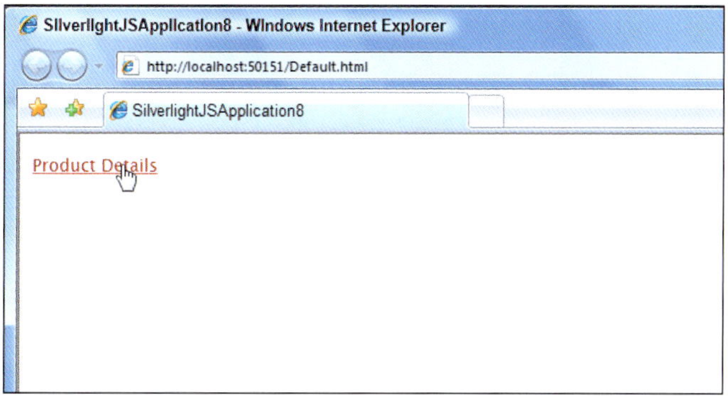

Figure 2-7

Silverlight Video

In pretty much every demo of the new Silverlight technology, the product demos show off a video integrated into a web page. As mentioned earlier, this was intentional. The goal of the initial release of Silverlight was to provide rich, multimedia experiences on web pages, which in the case of Silverlight 1.0, means audio and video on web pages. If you take a look at the top 100 trafficked web sites on the Internet, almost all of them have video playing on the home page or have video prevalent throughout. If Microsoft was to take the next step of having a complete stack of capabilities for web pages, having multimedia integration was essential. Adobe Flash is pretty much the dominant cross-platform vehicle for any media playing.

Adding Video to Web Pages

To add video or audio to a web page, you set the `Source` property on the `MediaElement` object. The following code demonstrates playing the video file `water.wmv` automatically when the canvas is loaded:

```
<Canvas
    xmlns="http://schemas.microsoft.com/client/2007"
    xmlns:x="http://schemas.microsoft.com/winfx/2006/xaml"
    Width="640" Height="480">

    <MediaElement Source="water.wmv"></MediaElement>

</Canvas>
```

The `Source` property is the URI of a valid video or audio file. In the preceding code example, the source file is located in the directory where the XAML file and the HTML page that loaded the XAML file is located. Your media files can be located in various locations, including the web site folder structure you are running the page from, or from a remote site. In either case, in order to maintain cross-platform support, you must use the "`/`" in place of the "`\`" in your URIs. For example:

```
<MediaElement Source="..\..\media\water.wmv"></MediaElement>
```

should read:

```
<MediaElement Source="../../media/water.wmv"></MediaElement>
```

If the `Source` property is pointing to a file on a Windows Media Server using the MMS protocol, the player will automatically attempt to stream the video down to the client. The default behavior is a progressive download, which means the audio or video will begin playing immediately and background load as you are playing the media. The drawback to progressive downloads is that even if you pause the video, it still downloads the media file, even if you never intend to continue playing it. With streaming media, the only data that is downloaded is the data that you actually play, which is a more efficient use of network resources.

At Mix '07, Microsoft announced a free media streaming service for Silverlight applications, named Silverlight Streaming Services. Using Silverlight Streaming Services, anyone can upload up to 4 gigabytes of Silverlight content to stream to your pages. There is an SDK and other tools that make it easy to work with the streaming service, but the end goal is to provide an easy-to-use service that eliminates barriers for adopting and using the Silverlight platform. To get a free account for this service, visit `https://silverlight.live.com`.

Supported Audio and Video Formats

The `MediaElement` supports the Advanced Stream Redirector (ASX) playlist file format, as well as the audio and video formats listed in the following table.

Audio Format	Description
WMA 7	Windows Media Audio 7
WMA 8	Windows Media Audio 8
WMA 9	Windows Media Audio 9
MP3	ISO/MPEG Layer-3 in the following configurations:
	ISO/MPEG Layer-3 compliant data stream input
	Mono or Stereo channel configurations
	8. 11.025, 12, 16, 22.05, 24. 32. 44.1 and 44.8 kHz sampling frequencies
	8-320 kbps and variable bit rates
	Free format mode (ISO/IEC 11172-3, sub clause 2.4.2.3) is not supported.
Video Format	**Description**
WMV 1	Windows Media Video 7
WMV 2	Windows Media Video 8
WMV 3	Windows Media Video 9
WMVA	Windows Media Video Advanced Profile, non-VC1
WMVC1	Windows Media Video Advanced Profile, VC1a

It is important to note that the actual file extension of a media file is irrelevant; the player will determine the encoding and play the media file with the appropriate codec. To encode audio and video to the various formats described, you can use the new Expression Encoder, another tool in the Expression Suite of products. Using Expression Encoder, you can set the encoding to the aforementioned formats, as well as add markers, overlays, and even perform cropping on your media files. In my experience, I have attempted to play files with the WMV extension, but they did not play. This is most likely because the tool that was used to stream the video was using some other custom codec, not one of the supported encodings for Silverlight. The `water.wmv` video used in Listing 2-12 was originally an MPEG video that I recorded using my digital camera. To get the WMV format that is optimized for Silverlight 1.0 Mbps broadband, I used the Expression Encoder.

Interacting with the MediaElement Object

When you add a `MediaElement` to a page, you can get or set a number of properties that will change the state of the media in the `MediaElement`. Table 2-2 lists some of the properties that the `MediaElement` exposes.

Table 2-2: Properties Exposed on the MediaElement

Property	Description
`AutoPlay`	Gets or sets a value indicating if media will begin playback automatically when the `Source` property is set.
`Balance`	Gets or sets the ratio of volume across stereo speakers.
`BufferingProgress`	Gets a value that indicates the current percentage of buffering progress.
`BufferingTime`	Gets or sets the time at which this timeline should begin.
`CurrentState`	The current state of the `MediaElement`: `Buffering`, `Closed`, `Error`, `Opening`, `Paused`, `Playing`, or `Stopped`.
`DownloadProgress`	A value indicating the percentage of download completed for content located on a remote server. The value ranges from 0 to 1.
`IsMuted`	Gets or sets a value indicating whether the audio is muted.
`Markers`	The collection of timeline markers (represented as `TimelineMarker` objects) associated with the currently loaded media file.
`NaturalDuration`	Gets the natural duration of the media.
`Position`	Gets or sets the current progress through the media's playback time. If the media does not support seek operations, setting this property will have no effect on media playback.
`Source`	Gets or sets a media source on the `MediaElement`.
`Volume`	Gets or sets the media's volume represented on a linear scale between 0 and 1.

The `MediaElement` also exposes a number of properties that let you interact with the `MediaElement` in a similar fashion that you would with any video or audio player, such as Play, Pause, and Stop. To create a more interactive media player, you need to add `Image`, `TextBlock`, or `Rectangle` objects to a `Canvas` and write the JavaScript to interact with the elements to play, pause, and stop the media. Listing 2-12 is the XAML needed to create a simple, interactive media player.

Listing 2-12: Adding Play, Pause, and Stop Capabilities to a MediaElement Object

```
<MediaElement x:Name="media"
     Source="water.wmv"
     Width="480" Height="360"/>

<!-- Plays media-->
<Canvas MouseLeftButtonDown="mediaPlay"
  Canvas.Left="10" Canvas.Top="365">
```

Listing 2-12: *(continued)*

```
        <TextBlock Canvas.Left="5"
                   Canvas.Top="5">Play</TextBlock>
    </Canvas>

    <!-- Pauses media playback-->
    <Canvas MouseLeftButtonDown="mediaPause"
      Canvas.Left="70" Canvas.Top="365">
        <TextBlock Canvas.Left="5"
                   Canvas.Top="5">Pause</TextBlock>
    </Canvas>

    <!-- Stops media playback-->
    <Canvas MouseLeftButtonDown="mediaStop"
      Canvas.Left="130" Canvas.Top="365">
        <TextBlock Canvas.Left="5"
                   Canvas.Top="5">Stop</TextBlock>
    </Canvas>
```

Listing 2-13 is the JavaScript needed to set the actual state of the media. Notice the use of `findName` on the sender object passed into the function call. Remember that `findName` will search the object tree of the entire XAML DOM to locate the elements you are attempting to find.

Listing 2-13: Using JavaScript to Interact with the MediaElement State

```
function mediaStop(sender, args) {

    sender.findName("media").stop();
}

function mediaPause(sender, args) {

    sender.findName("media").pause();
}

function mediaPlay(sender, args) {

    sender.findName("media").play();
}
```

Figure 2-8 is what the output of the video player will look like.

Using Markers and Timelines in Video

Using tools like the Expression Encoder, you can add markers to video files. *Markers* are metadata that is stored in the video file when it is encoded. Using markers, you can create timelines that allow seek operations, and you can use the metadata associated with the marker to display additional information during playback. Markers and timelines are especially useful for doing video overlay and closed captioning. Based on a marker timeline metadata, you can display custom text or images over the playing video.

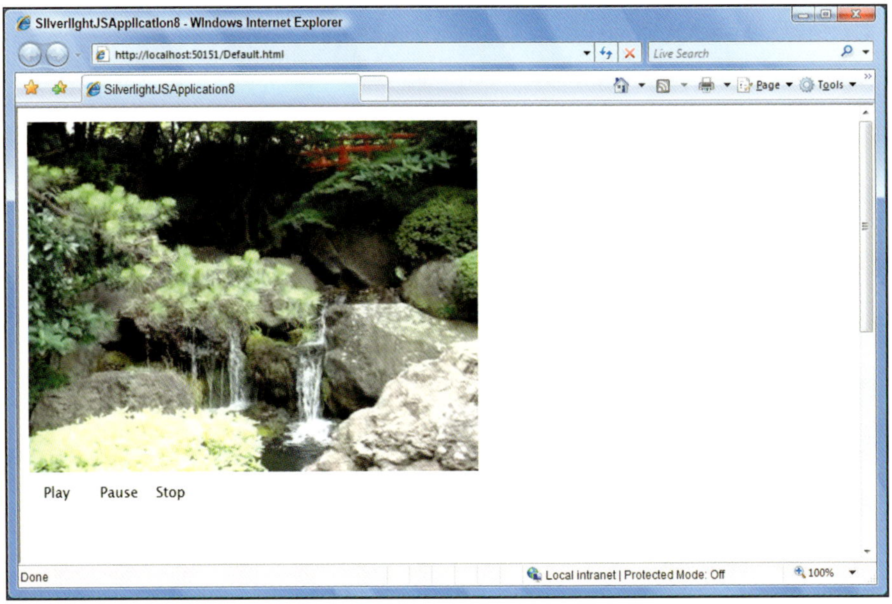

Figure 2-8

When the MediaElement object reaches a marker during playback, the MarkerReached event is raised. You can handle this event in JavaScript, which allows you to perform operations based on the marker metadata. The following properties associated with the marker metadata can be accessed via JavaScript:

- Time — A TimeSpan object that specifies the time when the marker is reached.
- Type — A string that specifies the marker's type. This value can be any user-defined string.
- Text — A string that specifies the marker's value. This value can be any user-defined string.

The XAML in Listing 2-14 demonstrates the syntax for specifying the MarkerReached event in the MediaElement. Listing 2-15 demonstrates the JavaScript that updates the TextBlock elements to display the metadata associated with the markers in the video file.

Listing 2-14: Registering the MarkerReached Event on a MediaElement Object

```
<MediaElement x:Name="media"
     Source="watermarkers.wmv"
     MarkerReached="onMarkerReached"
     Width="480" Height="360"/>

<Canvas Canvas.Left="525" Canvas.Top="5">

    <TextBlock>Time:</TextBlock>
    <TextBlock x:Name="timeTextBlock"
      Canvas.Left="60"/>

    <TextBlock Canvas.Top="30">Type:</TextBlock>
```

Listing 2-14: *(continued)*

```
        <TextBlock x:Name="typeTextBlock"
          Canvas.Left="60" Canvas.Top="30"/>

        <TextBlock Canvas.Top="60">Value:</TextBlock>
        <TextBlock x:Name="valueTextBlock"
          Canvas.Left="60" Canvas.Top="60"/>
    </Canvas>
```

Listing 2-15 is the JavaScript that handles the `MarkerReached` event and retrieves the `Time`, `Type`, and `Text` values of the marker that triggered the event and updated the `TextBlock` objects with the correct information. The results are shown in Figure 2-9.

Listing 2-15: The onMarkerReached Function

```
function onMarkerReached(sender, markerEventArgs)
{

  sender.findName("timeTextBlock").Text =
 markerEventArgs.marker.time.seconds.toString();

  sender.findName("typeTextBlock").Text =
       markerEventArgs.marker.type;

  sender.findName("valueTextBlock").Text =
       markerEventArgs.marker.text;

}
```

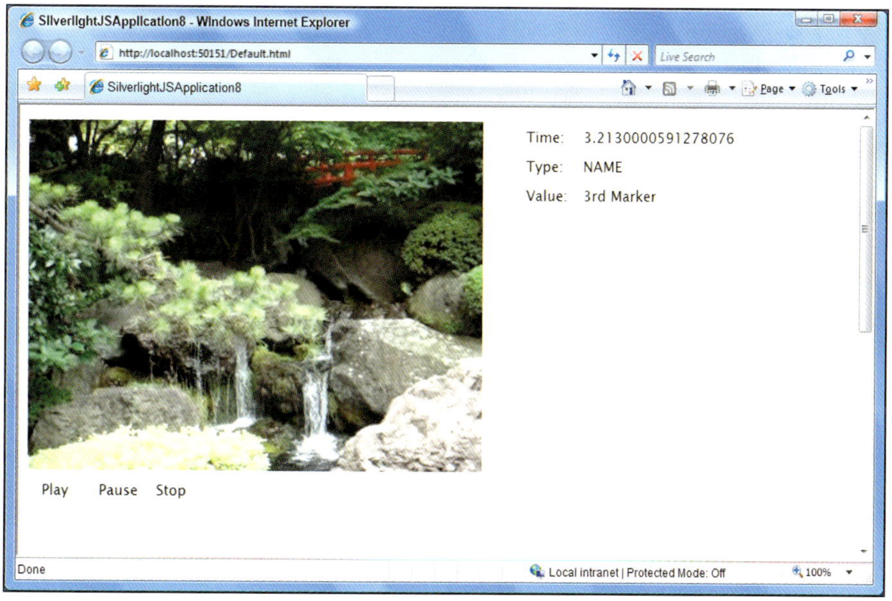

Figure 2-9

Figure 2-10 is the Expression Encoder that I used to add the markers to the video. Notice the Markers window that lists the timeline of the various markers that were added.

Figure 2-10

Painting Video onto Objects

Earlier in this chapter you were introduced to the various brushes that you can apply to objects such as the `TextBlock` element and `Rectangle` element. The `VideoBrush` is a type of brush object that lets you paint video onto other elements using the `MediaElement` control. You can paint video onto the `ForeGround` of a `TextBlock`, the `Fill` of `Rectangle`, or the `BackGround` of a `Canvas` object.

Listing 2-16 demonstrates applying a `VideoBrush` to a `TextBlock` object, which is reflected in Figure 2-11.

Listing 2-16: Adding a VideoBrush to a TextBlock

```
<MediaElement x:Name="media"
              Source="water.wmv"
              Opacity="0"/>

<TextBlock Canvas.Left="5" Canvas.Top="30"
```

Listing 2-16: *(continued)*

```
            FontFamily="Verdana" FontSize="90"
            FontWeight="Bold" TextWrapping="Wrap"
            Text="Video Brush">

         <!-- Add the VideoBrush object  -->
         <TextBlock.Foreground>
             <VideoBrush SourceName="media"
                     Stretch="UniformToFill" />
         </TextBlock.Foreground>

     </TextBlock>
```

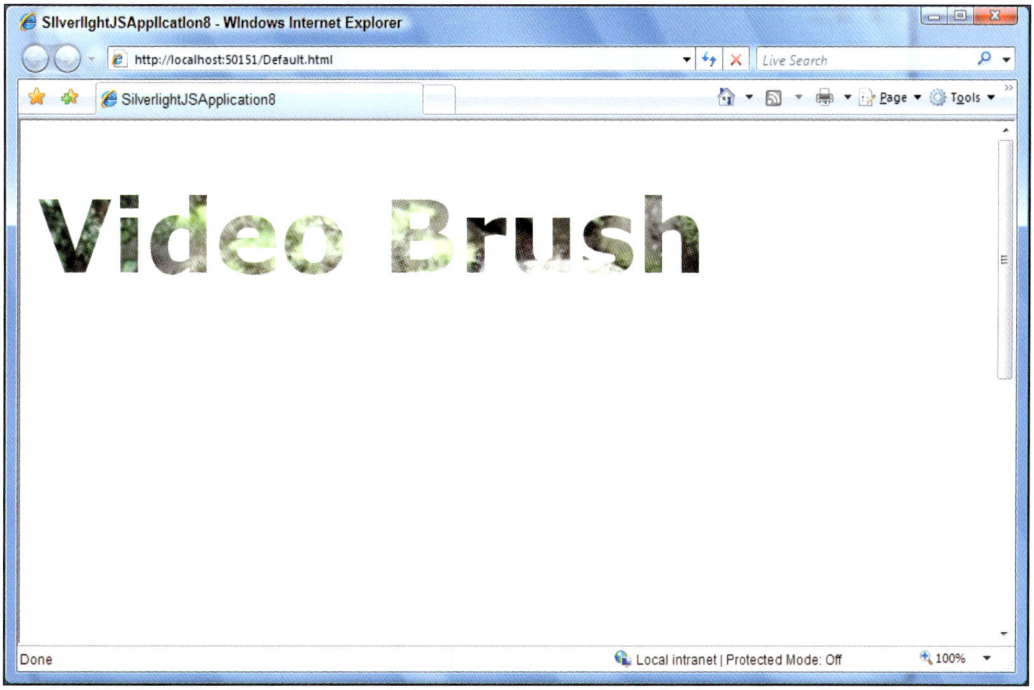

Figure 2-11

Creating Video Reflections

In many applications, video is not presented straight-on in a 2D space. Video and other objects are skewed and reflected to enhance the visual effects of the user interface. Using several of the techniques you have learned about so far in this chapter, you are equipped to do some more advanced XAML that creates a reflection on a rotated and skewed video. Figure 2-12 demonstrates a video that is reflecting and skewed.

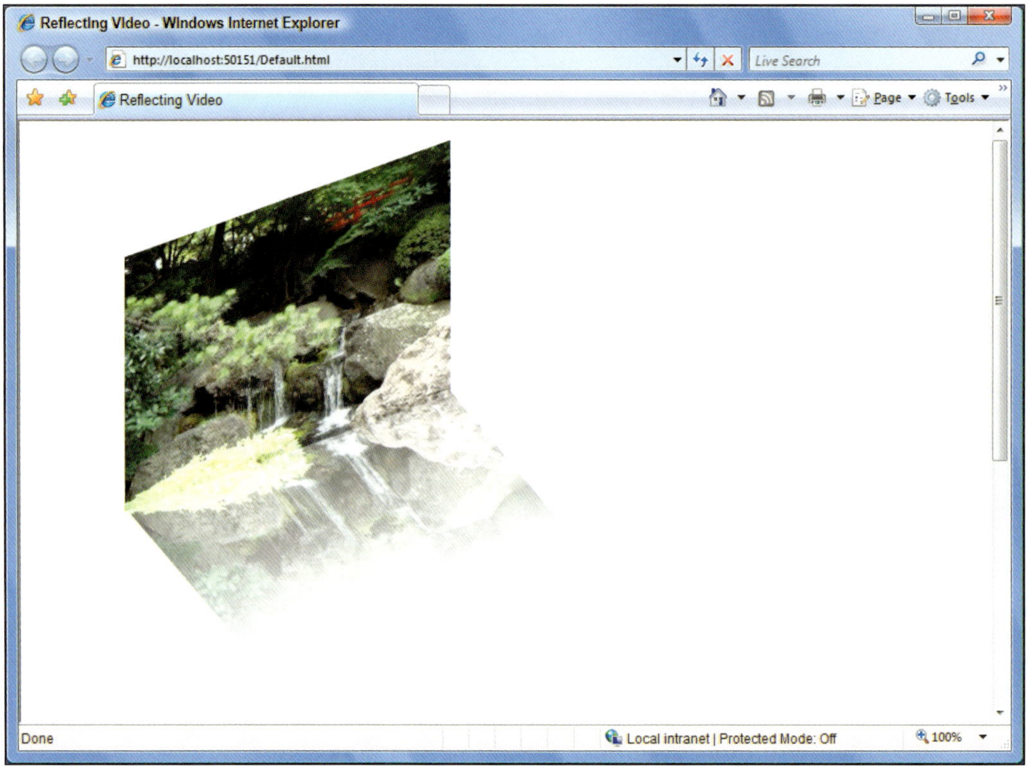

Figure 2-12

To accomplish what you see in Figure 2-12, examine the commented code in Listing 2-17.

Listing 2-17: Using Transforms, LinearGradientBrush, and Opacity to Reflect Video

```
<!-- Create the main video image -->
<Canvas Canvas.Left="86" Canvas.Top="68">
    <Canvas.RenderTransform>
        <TransformGroup>

            <!-- Skew and Scale the canvas -->
            <SkewTransform AngleY="-19" AngleX="0"
                           CenterX="0" CenterY="0"/>
            <ScaleTransform  ScaleY="1" ScaleX = "1"
                             CenterX="0" CenterY="0"/>
        </TransformGroup>
    </Canvas.RenderTransform>

    <!-- Add the MediaElement to the Canvas -->
    <MediaElement Source="watermarkers.wmv"
                  Width="300" Height="300" />
</Canvas>

<!-- Create the Canvas for the reflected video -->
```

Listing 2-17: *(continued)*

```
    <Canvas Canvas.Left="313" Canvas.Top="588">
        <Canvas.RenderTransform>

            <!-- Skew and Scale the canvas -->
            <TransformGroup>
                <SkewTransform  AngleY="19" AngleX="-41"
                                CenterX="0" CenterY="0" />

                <!-- Set the ScaleY to -1 to Flip the image -->
                <ScaleTransform ScaleY="-1" ScaleX="1"
                                CenterX="0" CenterY="0" />
            </TransformGroup>
        </Canvas.RenderTransform>

        <MediaElement Source="watermarkers.wmv"
                      Width="300" Height="300" Volume="0">

            <!-- Set an Opacity Mask on the Media Element -->
            <MediaElement.OpacityMask>
                <LinearGradientBrush
                    StartPoint="0,.25" EndPoint="0,1">
                    <GradientStop Offset="0.25"
                                  Color="#00000000"  />
                    <GradientStop Offset="1"
                                  Color="#CC000000"  />
                </LinearGradientBrush>
            </MediaElement.OpacityMask>
        </MediaElement>
    </Canvas>
```

The two important code blocks that make this happen are the `ScaleTransform` on the `Canvas` object that contains the second video and the `OpacityMask` applied to the second `MediaElement` object.

By setting the `ScaleY` property on the `ScaleTransform`, you are "flipping" the image, which is how a reflection would be rendered:

```
<ScaleTransform ScaleY="-1" ScaleX="1"
                CenterX="0" CenterY="0" />
```

If you consider how an object reflects against water, it has a trailing transparency. This is accomplished by applying the `OpacityMask` on the `MediaElement` object:

```
<MediaElement.OpacityMask>
    <LinearGradientBrush
        StartPoint="0,.25" EndPoint="0,1">
        <GradientStop Offset="0.25"
                      Color="#00000000"  />
        <GradientStop Offset="1"
                      Color="#CC000000"  />
    </LinearGradientBrush>
</MediaElement.OpacityMask>
```

Just like that, you can have enhanced rendering capabilities like reflections on media. The same concept can be applied to any object, including `VideoBrush`, `TextBlock`, and `Rectangle` objects.

Animating Silverlight Elements

One of the more impressive features of the WPF platform and now the Silverlight platform is the ability to animate any object. An animation can mean anything from an object fading into view or fading out of view, to a video flipping and rotating onto a form, to even a rolling ball or gear that repeats forever in the header of a page. For years, this was the lure to using Adobe Flash to create RIAs. Now, with Silverlight, you have the same exciting capabilities using XAML. When defining animations, you are building timelines and setting the behaviors of the timeline.

To get an idea of what you can do with animations and how the behaviors work, take a look at Listing 2-18. Here is a basic breakdown of what you do to create the animation:

- Create a basic `Rectangle`, with an `x:Name` property of `path1`.
- Create a Storyboard. Storyboards have properties such as `AutoReverse`, `BeginTime`, `Duration`, and `RepeatBehavior` that control the animation.
- Create a `DoubleAnimation` on the Storyboard with a target of the `path1 Rectangle` object you created.
- Create an `EventTrigger` on the `Canvas` object.
- Set the `EventTrigger` to fire in the `Canvas.Loaded` event, which tells this animation to start as soon as the canvas loads.

Listing 2-18: Creating an Animated Rectangle

```
<Canvas.Triggers>
    <EventTrigger RoutedEvent="Canvas.Loaded">
        <EventTrigger.Actions>
            <TriggerActionCollection>
                <BeginStoryboard>
                    <Storyboard BeginTime="0" Duration="Forever">
                        <DoubleAnimation
                             Storyboard.TargetName="path1"
                             Storyboard.TargetProperty="(Canvas.Top)"
                             From="0" To="700" AutoReverse="false"
                             BeginTime="0:0:0" Duration="0:0:2"
                             RepeatBehavior="1x"/>
                    </Storyboard>
                </BeginStoryboard>
            </TriggerActionCollection>
        </EventTrigger.Actions>
    </EventTrigger>
</Canvas.Triggers>

<Rectangle x:Name="path1" Opacity=".65" Fill="orange"
           Height="100" Width="100"
        RadiusX="10" RadiusY="10" />
```

It is difficult to demo animation in a book, but the result of the code in Listing 2-18 is the `Rectangle` moving across the screen, from 0 to 700 pixels, in a time period of 2 seconds, for 1 iteration or loop. In this case, the animation is a `DoubleAnimation`, which has `From`, `To`, and `By` properties that set the animation's behavior. Silverlight supports `Color`, `Double`, and `Point` animations, which correspond to the types of data they are animating. For example, the `ColorAnimation` will animate the `Color` property of an object over a specified time period. For each of the `Color`, `Double`, and `Point` animations, there are two categories of animation: From/To/By and Key Frame animation. Table 2-3 defines the animation categories.

Table 2-3: Animation Categories

Animation Category	Description
From/To/By	Animate using a start and destination value or by applying an offset to a start value.
Key Frame	Animate using more than two target values, and control an animation's interpolation method over a specified duration.

Many web sites have animations that loop forever, or restart after an event occurs. When you define your animation, you can set the `AutoReverse` or `RepeatBehavior` property to dictate the behavior of how an animation plays and ends. These properties are defined as follows:

- `AutoReverse` — Specifies whether a timeline plays backward after it reaches the end of its duration.
- `RepeatBehavior` — Specifies how many times a timeline plays.

Listing 2-19 demonstrates various implementations of using `AutoReverse` and `RepeatBehavior`.

Listing 2-19: Using AutoReverse and RepeatBehavior

```
<DoubleAnimation Storyboard.TargetName="path2"
                 Storyboard.TargetProperty="(Canvas.Left)"
                 From="0" To="400" AutoReverse="true"
                 BeginTime="0:0:0" Duration="0:0:4"
                 RepeatBehavior="1x"/>

<DoubleAnimation Storyboard.TargetName="path3"
                 Storyboard.TargetProperty="(Canvas.Top)"
                 From="0" To="200" AutoReverse="true"
                 BeginTime="0:0:0" Duration="0:0:8"
                 RepeatBehavior="5x"/>

<DoubleAnimation Storyboard.TargetName="path6"
                 Storyboard.TargetProperty="(Canvas.Left)"
                 From="0" To="600" AutoReverse="false"
                 BeginTime="0:0:0" Duration="0:0:2"
                 RepeatBehavior="Forever"/>
```

Chapters 3 and 4 get more in-depth on interacting with animations and how you can use Expression Blend to create rich animations.

Summary

In this chapter you gained the XAML knowledge you need to start writing Silverlight applications. Understanding layout and positioning and the types of objects you can render in Silverlight will prepare you for the more advanced chapters coming up. Remember that a main driver for Silverlight adoption is video and multimedia on the web, and using the video controls and animation capabilities, you can create rich, interactive applications for the web.

3

Designing Silverlight Applications Using Expression Blend 2

We've introduced Silverlight and XAML fundamentals in previous chapters, and by now you should be familiar with the basic building blocks available for building Silverlight applications. You've seen XAML used to define rectangles, shapes, brushes, and even animation and are probably wondering if you're going to be stuck hand-coding XAML for the rest of your days. Fortunately, the answer is no. Along with the introduction of WPF as a development platform, Microsoft introduced *Microsoft Expression Studio*, a suite of tools created for designers targeting Microsoft platforms.

Microsoft Expression Blend (Blend) is the tool in this suite used for designing application layouts, creating animation, and adding interactivity to your WPF or Silverlight applications. The initial release of Blend did not include support for Silverlight, because it was still not a public technology. So, in order to author Silverlight applications with Blend, you'll need to download and install the latest preview release of Blend 2, which adds new Silverlight 1.0 and 1.1 starter templates.

In this chapter, you:

- ❑ Get an introduction to the Blend interface
- ❑ See how to create artwork
- ❑ Create your first timeline
- ❑ Work with artwork created outside of Blend

It's time to get started!

Getting the Latest Blend 2 Preview

The Blend team posted the first public preview of Blend 2 in May, following Mix '07. They are continuing to post public previews until the final release.

Download the latest public preview from the Microsoft Expression web site:

```
www.microsoft.com/expression
```

The preview releases generally install as 30-day trials, but most releases let you try the software for a full 180 days with a serial number provided at the time of download.

Creating a New Silverlight Project

With the Blend 2 Preview installed, you should see the Create New Project dialog shown in Figure 3-1 when you start Blend. This dialog launches by default and presents a list of available project types you can use to get started.

Figure 3-1

The Create New Project dialog includes four starter templates for you to choose from:

- WPF Application
- WPF Control Library
- Silverlight Application (JavaScript)
- Silverlight Application (.NET)

Select the third option, Silverlight Application (JavaScript), customize your application name and location, and click OK.

Congratulations! You can now say you've created your first Silverlight 1.0 application in Blend. You can even hit F5 to run it. Your default web browser will be launched and your new (albeit empty) Silverlight app will run. This may seem a bit premature, but you can actually use this step to verify that you have the Silverlight player installed and ready for your new application.

The Silverlight Project Starter Template

Before digging into the Blend environment, take a quick look at what the starter template did behind the scenes. Just like Microsoft Visual Studio, Blend applications use a project file to store application settings. This project file ends with a `.csproj` extension and, among other things, includes the name of the project, a list of files in the project, and references to external assemblies that the project requires.

Select the Project tab to see the files added by the template (see Figure 3-2). You should see a C# Project icon followed by the name of the application you just created (I entered **StylingWithBlend**). Beneath the project name, you'll see an empty References folder, a `Default.html` file (with an accompanying `Default.html.js` file), a `Scene.xaml` file (with an accompanying `Scene.xaml.js` file), and a `Silverlight.js` file.

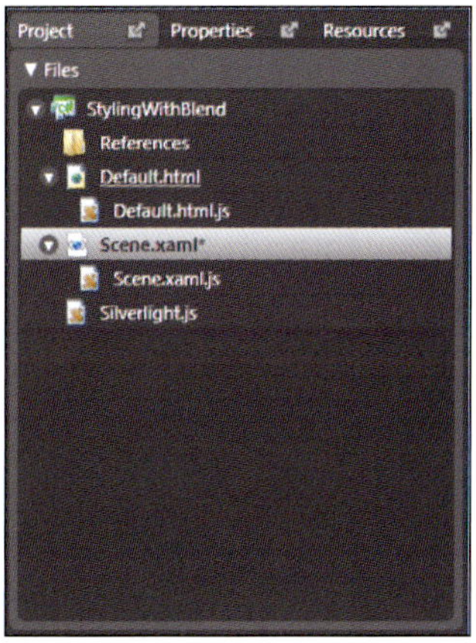

Figure 3-2

All of the files besides `Scene.xaml` take care of the behind-the-scenes work required to display a Silverlight control in a web page. You can take a look at the JavaScript and HTML created automatically by double-clicking the files you're curious about (hint: It should be all of them!), but know that currently Blend provides design time and code behind support only for XAML files, so double-clicking any files in your project besides `Scene.xaml` will result in that file being opened by the default application for that file type (for example, Microsoft Expression Web for `.html` files).

You can ensure that a particular file is opened in Visual Studio by right-clicking the file in the project tree (see Figure 3-3). You'll see the options Edit Externally (the default application launches) and Edit in Visual Studio.

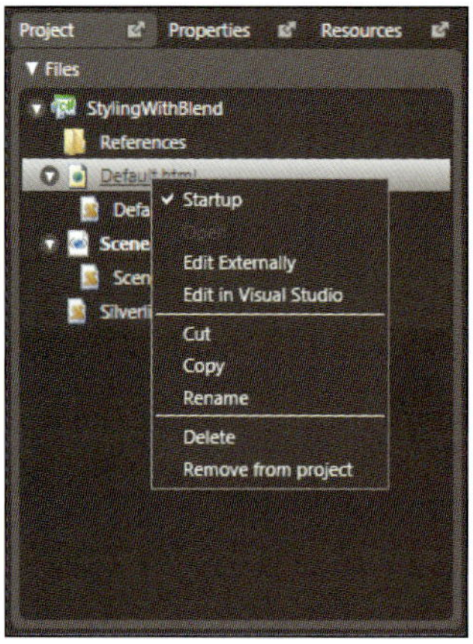

Figure 3-3

Blend Workspace Overview

The Blend workspace may at first look foreign to you, but whether you're a designer or a developer, I think you'll find areas that are familiar. And with a little patience you can master the areas that aren't. With that said, Blend is definitely a tool that targets designers and borrows more from existing design tools than it borrows from development tools. The Blend team even made sure that keyboard shortcuts are the same as they are in other design tools (where possible). This definitely eases the learning curve and makes the environment more familiar immediately (again, if you're a designer).

The default workspace is known as the Design Workspace. It is one of two predefined workspaces available on the Window menu on the main toolbar, the other being the Animation Workspace (see Figure 3-4). For most of this chapter, you'll work with the Design Workspace selected. You can toggle between the two now to see how the interface changes.

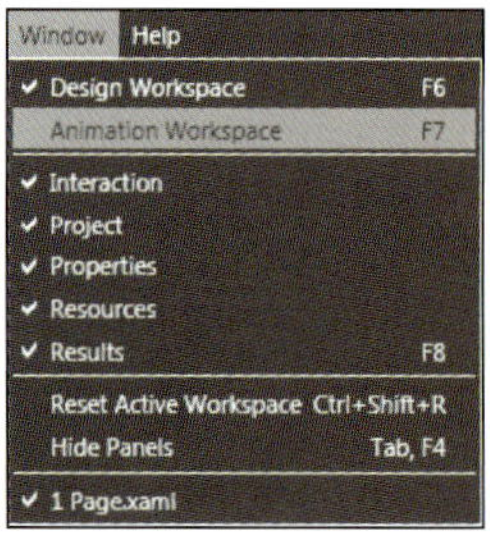

Figure 3-4

The Blend Panels

The Blend workspace is organized into a series of panels that provide resizing, limited docking, and collapsing. Panels that can be undocked can be identified by the small square and arrow icon in the panel header. (Refer back to Figure 3-2 and you can see this icon in the panel headers.) When a panel is undocked it can be freely moved around your screen and resized by pressing and dragging the lower right-hand corner of the panel. Re-dock the panel by clicking the same icon you used to undock the panel. All docked panels return to their predefined locations, so don't get frustrated when you can't completely reorganize your panels. Maybe we'll get that feature in future releases of Blend. You can switch to a minimal interface by hitting the Tab key. This will collapse all of the major panels into smaller Toolbox-style menus. Return to the default view by hitting the Tab key once again.

Toolbox

The Blend Toolbox lives on the left-hand side of the application and houses all of the tools you will use to move, resize, modify, and add new objects within your application. Some Toolbox entries include flyout menus that let you select from a list of similar tools. Figure 3-5 demonstrates how you can select the Rectangle, Ellipse, or Line tool from the Shape tools' flyout menu.

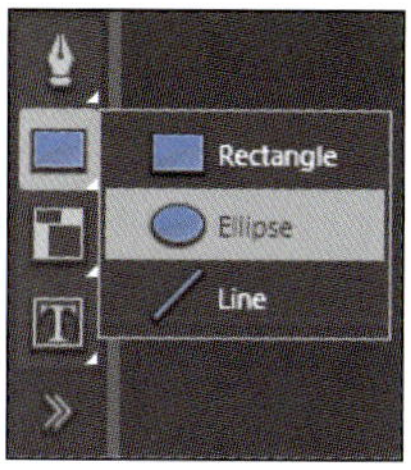

Figure 3-5

You can quickly identify Toolbox items that include a flyout by looking for the small arrow in the lower right-hand corner of the tool icon. Press and hold your left mouse button to access the additional tools.

Hover over each item with your mouse for a couple of seconds to get a tooltip that shows the tool's name, a brief description, and the keyboard shortcut. Figure 3-6 outlines the individual tools and highlights the tool groupings.

Interaction Panel

The Interaction panel can be found directly to the right of the Toolbox and is one of the locations where you'll spend most of your time in Blend. Two categories live in this panel:

- Triggers
- Objects and Timeline

We'll skip over the Triggers section for now but return to it later in the chapter to create your first animations.

The Object Tree

The Objects and Timeline area wears many hats but exists primarily to show you the elements on your canvas. If you're familiar with tools like Photoshop or Illustrator, this is similar to the Layers palette found in those tools. All of the elements on your canvas are displayed in a large tree view, allowing you to quickly navigate what may be a large amount of XAML behind the scenes. Figure 3-7 shows a Default Page canvas with no child elements.

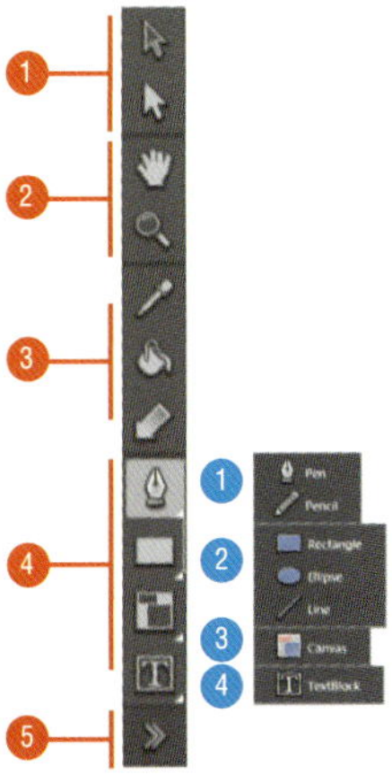

1. **Selection Tools:**
   Use the first arrow to select objects or second arrow to sub-select path points and nested objects within groups
2. **View Tools:**
   Use the hand to pan the artboard or the magnifying glass to zoom
3. **Brush tools:**
   Use the eyedropper and paintbucket together to select properties from one control and apply to another. The Brush Transform tool is used to edit gradient directions when you are editing a gradient brush.
4. **Object tools:**
   Select the type of object you want to create by choosing from the grouped controls in the Object tools category.
5. **Asset tools:**
   Access the Asset Library by clicking the double-arrow.
   The Asset library houses the Image control, the MediaElerr control and shows recently used assets.

1. Path tools: Pen, Pencil
2. Shape tools: Rectangle, Ellipse, Line
3. Layout panels: Canvas
4. Text controls: TextBox

Figure 3-6

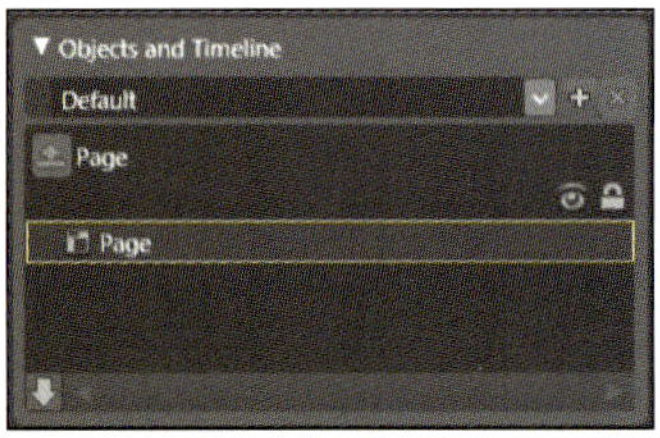

Figure 3-7

By default, the Silverlight template creates an empty root canvas for you with the name Page. You should see it listed as the single item in the Object tree. Go ahead and draw a rectangle on the canvas to see an additional item in the tree. You should now see a rectangle beneath Page as demonstrated in Figure 3-8. Pay attention to all of the information you have in the new line added for the rectangle you just created. There is a box icon representing the Rectangle object, the text [Rectangle], an eye icon, and a round circle icon.

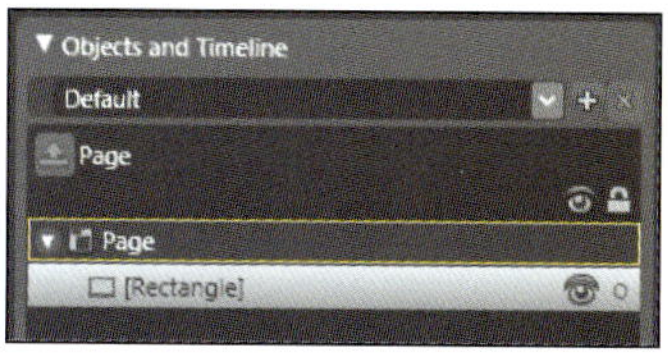

Figure 3-8

Blend includes specific icons for most items added to the design surface. If you pay attention to these early on and learn to identify them, you will save yourself extra work later when you're trying to figure out what type of control a specific element is. You now know what the icon for rectangles looks like, but this is one of the easier ones to remember.

Naming

Notice also the use of brackets around [Rectangle]. When an element has not been given a name, it is represented in the tree by its type surrounded by brackets. Page is not surrounded by brackets. Instead, it is the name given to a specific instance of the `Canvas` control. If you want to test this, right-click the rectangle in the tree and select View XAML. This will take you directly to the XAML for the selected rectangle. Add the following `x:Name` attribute to the `Rectangle` definition:

```
<Rectangle x:Name="myRect" Fill="#FFFFFFFF" Stroke="#FF000000" Width="100"
Height="53 />
```

Now switch back to Design view. You'll see myRect listed in the tree with no brackets, as demonstrated in Figure 3-9.

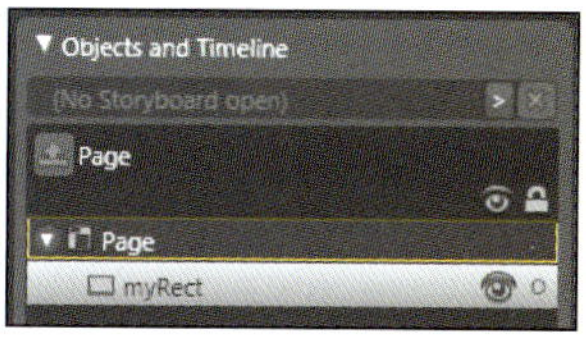

Figure 3-9

Hiding and Locking

You can toggle the visibility of items in the tree by clicking the eye icon. This will hide the element at design time but will not hide it at runtime. To hide elements at runtime, you'll have to set Opacity and/or Visibility properties on those elements. This eye icon is strictly intended for design-time assistance. For example, your layout will likely include elements that overlap each other. With a large number of elements on the screen, it can become difficult to select items in the background because of foreground elements. Hiding those foreground elements not only makes selection easier, it lets you focus on the task at hand.

In addition to hiding elements, you can also lock elements at design time to prevent you from moving them accidentally. Click the round icon next to the eye icon to lock elements. The icon will turn into a lock icon. Simply click it again to unlock. Try locking foreground elements so that you can select elements located in the background. This is a good alternative to hiding the foreground elements if you need to see everything on the screen. Again, this is a design-time aid and is not a setting that gets persisted when you compile and run your project.

Z-Index Order versus Markup Order

By default, items in the Object tree are arranged by *markup order*. This means items at the top of the tree appear earlier in XAML than the items further down the tree. The order in which items are added to XAML affects their position in the *Z-Index stack* (unless the Z-Index property is explicity set). The first item added to XAML is actually at the bottom of the Z-Index stack, with subsequent items added appearing in the foreground of their predecessors.

In most design programs, items at the top of the layer panel are in the foreground of items beneath them. When you are using markup order, it's just the opposite. Fortunately, Blend lets you toggle between markup order and Z-Index order, so you can choose the mode that works best for you. Figure 3-10 shows the footer of the Object panel. Click the arrow icon to toggle between markup order and Z-Index order.

Figure 3-10

Pay attention to the direction of the arrow and try to memorize which direction is which. This may sound like a minor thing, but I promise you'll thank me when you can glance and know that you're in Z-Index mode when the arrow is pointing up.

> *You can explicitly set the* `ZIndex` *property on items, which will override the default Z-Index ordering determined by the location of the item in XAML. This can be useful when you're updating the position of items dynamically, or adding and removing items dynamically via code behind.*

Timelines

We're going to skip the timeline aspect of the Objects and Timeline category for the moment. We cover timelines in the section "Creating and Understanding Timelines" later in the chapter.

Project Panel

You were introduced briefly to the Project panel (see Figure 3-11) when you created a Silverlight project using the Silverlight project template at the beginning of this chapter. The Project panel shows all of the files included in your current project. It is here where you can add, remove, rename, and move files within your project.

If you're familiar with Visual Studio, the Project panel should look familiar to you. It is essentially a simplified version of the Solution Explorer found there. For example, you won't find the ability to view hidden files or right-click ➪ Include in Project.

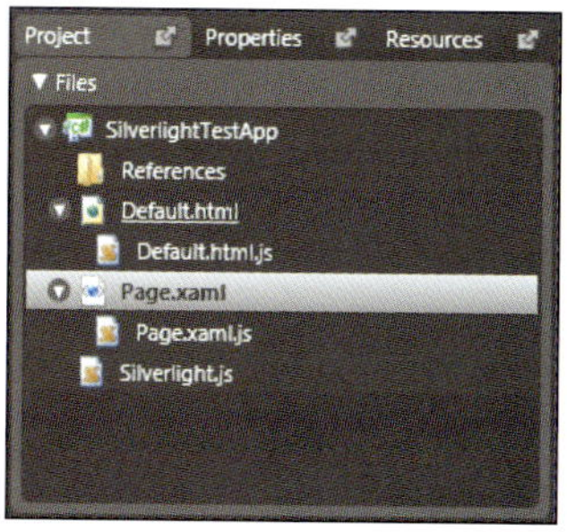

Figure 3-11

Adding Items to the Project

Add items to the project from within Blend by right-clicking the project name and selecting Add New Item, Add Existing Item, or Link to Existing Item from the context menu that appears (see Figure 3-12).

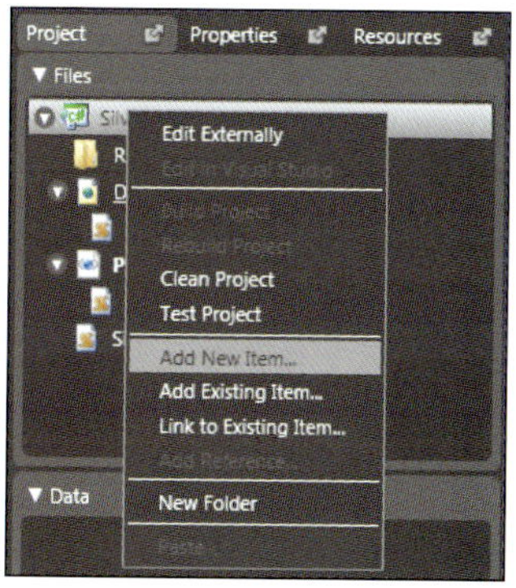

Figure 3-12

- **Add New Item** — When you select Add New Item, you'll see the dialog shown in Figure 3-13. Blend includes a single template named `Scene` that you can select from. `Scene` is a file that contains an empty `Canvas` control. When you click OK, a new file based on the `Scene` template will be added to your project with the filename you specify in the dialog.

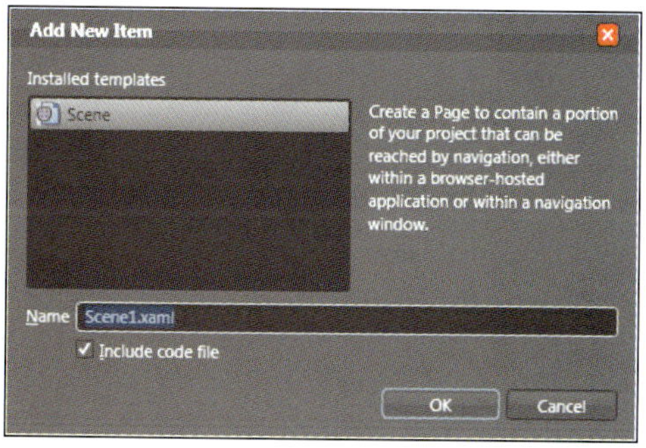

Figure 3-13

- **Add Existing Item** — When you select Add Existing Item from the context menu, a File Browser dialog will appear that lets you select a file from a location on your file system. Once you have selected the file, a copy of the file will be added to your project and will live within the project folder.
- **Link to Existing Item** — When you select Link to Existing Item, a reference to the file you select is added to your project but the file is not copied into your project folder.

Organizing Your Project

If you were paying attention earlier, you noticed a New Folder entry on the context menu shown in Figure 3-12. Use this option to add folders to your project for organization. Once you have created a new folder, you can move existing items into the folder simply by dragging the items in the Project panel to the destination folder. You can add new or existing items to a folder by right-clicking the folder itself. You will see a context menu similar to the one you saw when you right-clicked the project name.

Properties Panel

The Properties panel is docked with the Project panel and Resources panel when you start Blend. Click the Properties tab next to the Project tab (see Figure 3-14) to see its contents. The Properties panel exposes all of the properties of the currently selected object. If more than one object is selected, the intersection of the two objects' properties is shown, allowing you to set the properties shared by both objects.

Figure 3-14

The properties of the active object are grouped into the following categories: Brushes, Appearance, Layout, Common Properties, Text, Transform, and Miscellaneous. If you're not using a particular category or need additional vertical space, you can collapse a category by clicking the arrow next to its name.

Common Editors

Blend includes a set of common property editors that are type-specific. For example, all numeric properties share a unique editor that at first looks like a standard textbox. However, when you mouse over a numeric property field, such as Width, as in Figure 3-15, you will see a custom "crosshair" style cursor. Press and drag your mouse when you see this cursor and you can change the numeric value as if you were dragging a scrollbar. You'll grow to love this feature!

Figure 3-15

The other common editors include a combo box for properties that accept enumerated values, a checkbox for Boolean values, and standard textboxes for most other property types.

Some exceptions exist, however, and we'll look at those in detail momentarily.

The Marker System

The Properties panel exposes additional options for each property via a "marker system." These additional options are accessed by clicking the small marker located to the right of each property, as indicated in Figure 3-16.

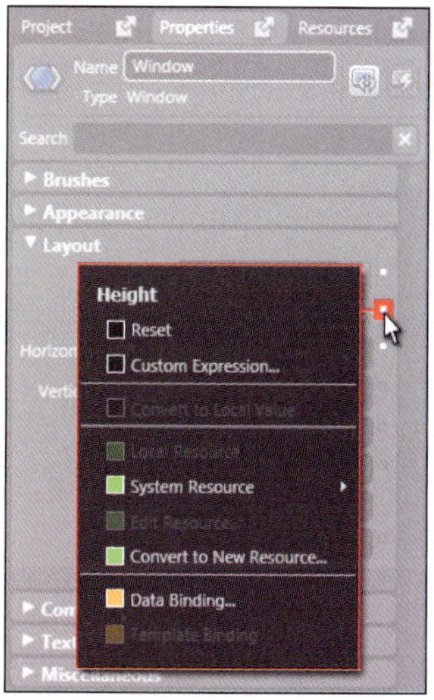

Figure 3-16

The first action listed on each property's submenu is always Reset. Any time you want to change a property's value back to its default value, click the marker and choose Reset. When a property value has been set, the marker will be colored white to indicate that a value other than the default value has been set. Change the value of an unset property and watch the marker color change just to verify.

Custom Property Editors

Some properties are more complex than simple numeric or text values and warrant custom editors. Brush properties fall into this category and thus received a significant custom property editor that we'll explore in depth. We'll also take a quick look at the Transform category, which contains custom editors for the RenderTransform and LayoutTransform properties.

Using the Brush Editor

Properties such as Fill, Background, Stroke, and Foreground all accept values of type Brush. Silverlight supports brushes of type SolidColorBrush, LinearGradientBrush, and RadialGradientBrush. A simple text field will obviously not work for this type of property. Enter the Brush editor, a tool that should look familiar to users of modern design programs. Figure 3-17 shows the Brush editor in Linear Gradient Editing mode.

Figure 3-17

In Figure 3-17, an ellipse is selected on the canvas whose Fill property is set to a LinearGradientBrush. Notice the list of brush properties at the very top of this category. You'll see the Fill, Stroke, and OpacityMask brush properties listed. You can tell that Fill is the active property because it's highlighted with a light gray background. Pay attention to two other details here also: the brush preview drawn adjacent to the property name, and the white marker directly next to the preview.

You can use the preview to glance and quickly determine the brush values that are applied to the currently selected object. The white box is known as a "marker" and is covered in "The Marker System" section earlier in the chapter. You can see that neither the Stroke nor the OpacityMask properties in Figure 3-17 have values set because their markers are both grayed out.

Applying a Brush Value

The Brush editor is divided into four tabs, one for each brush type available. Click the first tab to clear the brush value. Click the second tab to specify a SolidColorBrush, and click the third tab to specify a GradientBrush. The fourth tab is disabled in Silverlight projects but is used in WPF projects to apply brush resources.

Solid Color Brushes

When you specify a SolidColorBrush, the Brush editor interface appears as shown in Figure 3-18.

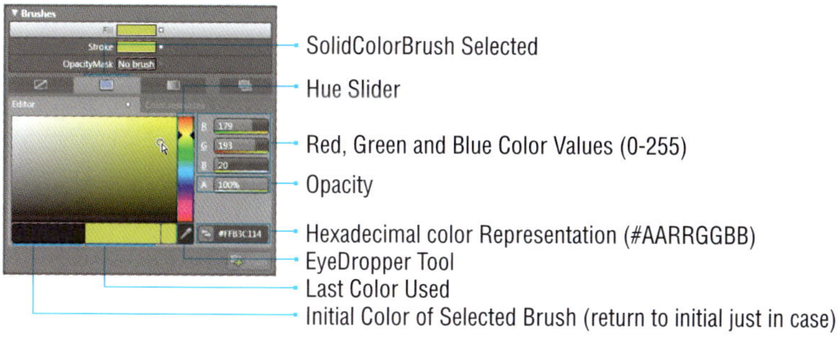

Figure 3-18

Although this editor may appear a little complicated at first glance, it is actually quite simple and just provides multiple ways to achieve the same task. You can quickly change the color by clicking anywhere in the large color area, indicated by the mouse cursor in Figure 3-18. Change the hue by dragging the Hue slider, or clicking anywhere along the hue range.

As you change the hue or choose different colors, the R, G, and B values will update accordingly. These are the Red, Green, and Blue color components of the selected color. Each component has a range from 0–255. The "A" entry listed beneath R, G, and B stands for Alpha (Transparency) and has a value range from 0%–100%, where 0 represents fully transparent and 100 represents fully opaque. You can also specify the color by typing in an #AARRGGBB hexadecimal representation. The hexadecimal box will accept RRGGBB values if you paste in from a paint program that doesn't include an Alpha value, so it's a quick way to bring over color values if you have them elsewhere.

Gradient Brushes

Click the third tab in the Brush editor to specify a Gradient Brush. By default, a LinearGradientBrush will be applied to your selected object. Silverlight supports two types of Gradient Brushes: LinearGradientBrush and RadialGradientBrush. You can toggle between these two gradient types by clicking either of the two Gradient Type buttons located in the lower-left corner of the editor (as shown in Figure 3-19).

The GradientBrush editor builds upon the SolidColorBrush editor by adding a gradient preview rectangle. The preview includes draggable swatches that represent Gradient stops. Simply click a swatch to make it the active swatch. In Figure 3-19, the right-most swatch is active, indicated by its black border.

- **Adding Stops** — Add additional Gradient stops by clicking anywhere in the preview rectangle that does not already include a stop.
- **Moving Stops** — Change the position and order of stops by pressing and dragging the target stop.
- **Deleting Stops** — Remove Gradient stops by dragging the stop down and away from the rectangle preview. Release when the stop disappears.

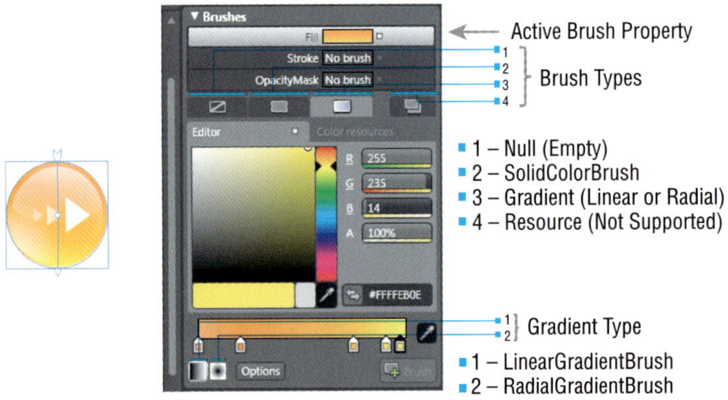

Figure 3-19

Precision Editing

When editing gradients that require extreme precision, such as the sharp highlight shown in Figure 3-20, you may find that the visual editor is not precise enough for you.

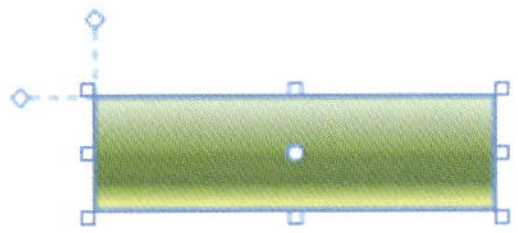

Figure 3-20

In Figure 3-21, the second stop from the left is actually two stops. Their offsets are so close that they appear to be a single stop. Achieving this level of precision is frustrating if not impossible using the editor itself. Fortunately, you can actually edit the Gradient stops in XAML. Jump directly to the XAML for your selected rectangle by right-clicking it in the Object tree and selecting View XAML from the context menu.

Figure 3-21

Listing 3-1 shows the XAML used to define the gradient shown in Figure 3-21.

Listing 3-1: Creating Sharp Gradients in XAML

```
<Rectangle
    Opacity="1"
    Canvas.Left="689"
    Canvas.Top="114"
    Width="128"
    Height="35">
```

Listing 3-1: *(continued)*

```
        <Rectangle.Fill>
            <LinearGradientBrush
                StartPoint="0.9334821701049805,0.05263148716517857"
                EndPoint="0.9334821701049805,0.9473685128348214">
                <LinearGradientBrush.GradientStops>
                    <GradientStopCollection>
                        <GradientStop
                            Color="#FFd3ddab"
                            Offset="0" />
                        <GradientStop
                            Color="#FF819d35"
                            Offset="0.49" />
                        <GradientStop
                            Color="#FF739221"
                            Offset="0.49" />
                        <GradientStop
                            Color="#FF678822"
                            Offset="0.79" />
                        <GradientStop
                            Color="#FFBBC749"
                            Offset="0.92" />
                        <GradientStop
                            Color="#FFdbde58"
                            Offset="1" />
                    </GradientStopCollection>
                </LinearGradientBrush.GradientStops>
            </LinearGradientBrush>
        </Rectangle.Fill>
    </Rectangle>
```

If you haven't edited gradients in XAML, Listing 3-1 may be a little daunting for you. It's actually quite simple, though. Just browse down to the `GradientStopCollection` and examine the list of `GradientStops`. Each `GradientStop` consists of a `Color` and `Offset` property. Both the second and third `GradientStop` have an Offset value of `"0.49"`, achieving a very sharp line in the resulting visual.

When two `GradientStops` *share the same* `Offset` *value, the Silverlight renderer relies on the order in which the* `GradientStops` *appear in XAML when drawing the gradient.*

Any time you find yourself having troubles getting your gradient to look exactly right, jump to the XAML and manually tweak the Offset values.

Using the Transform Editors

All controls in Silverlight have a RenderTransform property. The value of this property can be a single Transform-based object or a TransformGroup. By default, when a transform value is changed in Blend, a TransformGroup is automatically created and applied to the RenderTransform property. Transform values are applied to the base property settings of the active control.

The RenderTransform category provides a tabbed interface (see Figure 3-22) that allows you to set each of the transform types quickly using the default numeric editors. Individual tabs are exposed for the following transform types: Translate, Rotate, Scale, and Skew. There are two additional tabs, Center Point and Flip.

The Center Point tab actually maps to the RenderTransformOrigin property of the active control, and the Flip tab inverts the ScaleX and ScaleY values on the Scale tab.

Figure 3-22

Layout and Design in Blend

The Silverlight Canvas panel supports absolute positioning of elements. If you're coming to Silverlight from WPF, this means you have to say goodbye to your trusty grid and return to a fixed-sized, fixed-position world (for the most part). If you're coming to Silverlight with experience in other design applications, this setup should feel familiar to you. Basically, every element you draw on the design surface will have a height, width, X position, and Y position (see Figure 3-23).

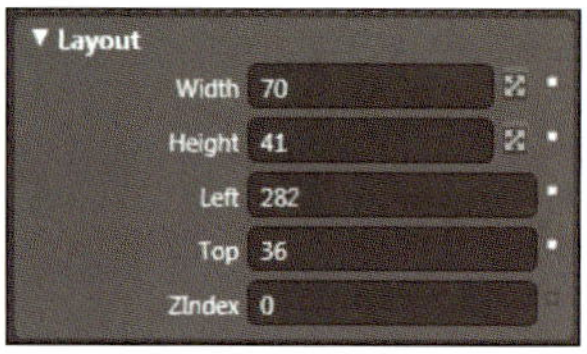

Figure 3-23

You have at your disposal a standard set of tools: a Path tool, a Line Tool, a Rectangle control, and an Ellipse control. This may not sound like a very rich list, but I think you'll find it pretty much has you covered. In addition to these path-based tools, you can also add Images and MediaElements, something I'll talk more about later.

The Design Surface

We're going to get started by taking a look at how the Design surface, the Properties panel, and the raw XAML all work together. When you make changes in any of these locations, the other areas are affected.

First, you'll create a new rectangle on the design surface and then update its properties in each of these three different places. Select the Rectangle tool (M) in the Toolbox. Create a new rectangle on the design surface by pressing your mouse at the starting point, dragging the rectangle to the desired size, and then releasing your mouse. Behind the scenes, Blend added a `Rectangle` element to the underlying XAML and set its corresponding `Canvas.Left`, `Canvas.Top`, `Height`, `Width`, `Fill`, `Stroke`, `RadiusX`, and `RadiusY` properties. Click the XAML tab (F12) to see what was just added:

```
<Rectangle Fill="#FF000000" Stroke="#FF000000" Width="123" Height="43"
Canvas.Left="32" Canvas.Top="67"/>
```

Try changing the `Canvas.Top` value in the XAML and then switch back to Design view (F11). You should see that the position of your rectangle has updated to reflect your changes. Experiment with the other properties by switching back and forth between Design and XAML view.

When you're ready to move on, make sure you're in Design view, and then select the Properties tab. With the rectangle selected, locate the Layout category on the Properties tab. You'll see Width, Height, Left, Top, and ZIndex properties. Click inside any of the fields and type in a new value. Hit Enter on your keyboard to commit the change. Both the design surface and the XAML have been updated to reflect your change. Just to reinforce the relationship between the design surface and XAML, switch to XAML view once again to verify the change.

Shape Tools

Figure 3-24 shows the three shape tools that you can select from the Blend Toolbox: the Rectangle, Ellipse, and Line. Both the Rectangle and Ellipse tools function in similar ways.

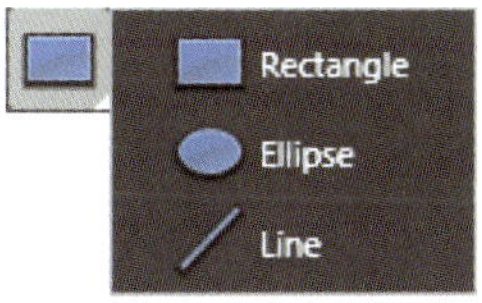

Figure 3-24

Rectangles and Ellipses

Simply select the tool, and then draw either a rectangle or an ellipse by pressing your mouse where you want the top-left corner to be. Then drag until you reach the desired shape and size.

If you want to create a perfect square or perfect circle, hold down the Shift key as you draw. Hold down the Alt key while drawing to set the point you first clicked as the center of the object, rather than the top-left corner.

You can quickly adjust the `CornerRadius` of rectangles on the design surface by dragging one of the two handles shown in Figure 3-25. As you drag the handles, the `RadiusX` and `RadiusY` properties are both updated. By default, these values are the same, ensuring a consistent rounding on both axes. You can override this by holding down the Shift key while you drag the handles.

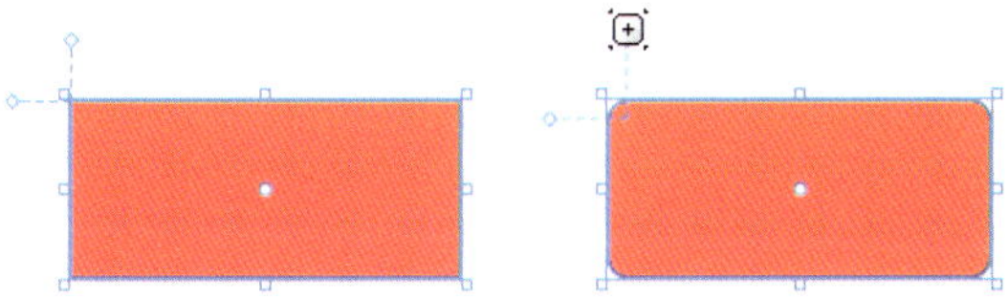

Figure 3-25

Lines

The Line tool in Blend lets you draw single straight lines, no more, no less. With the Line tool selected, simply press your mouse at the origin and drag to the desired length. Hold down the Shift key while you drag to "snap" the line to 15-degree intervals, giving you the ability to create perfectly horizontal or vertical lines. Behind the scenes, a `Path` object is created, the same object used by the Path tool and Pen tool.

Paths

In addition to the Line tool, Blend provides both the Pen tool and the Pencil tool, shown in Figure 3-26. Both of these tools are used to create open or closed paths that are much more complex than simple lines, rectangles, or ellipses.

Figure 3-26

The Pen Tool

Use the Pen tool to create illustrations much like you would in any illustration program (such as Adobe Illustrator or Corel DRAW). The Line tool only allowed you to define two points: a start point and an end point. The Pen tool lets you define an object with an infinite number of points. Start by selecting the Pen tool from the toolbox and then clicking anywhere on the design surface. Notice a blue dot is added to the canvas, indicating the starting point for your path. Click and release in a new location to create a straight line from the previous point to the new location. Click and drag your mouse to create a curve. When you're satisfied with your curve, release your mouse button and continue creating lines and curves until you are happy with your shape.

If you want to "close your path" move your mouse cursor back to the starting location of your path. A small square will appear in your cursor next to the Pen tool cursor. Click to close the path. If you don't want to close the path, either click the Pen tool again in the Toolbox or select any other tool in the Toolbox.

When a path is "closed," there will be no visible breaks in the stroke if a brush is applied to the Stroke property. Generally, paths are closed when the designer wants to apply a fill to them.

Like the other drawing tools, the behavior of the Pen tool can be altered by using the Shift key and the Alt key. Hold down the Shift key when you create line segments to force the line to snap to 15-degree intervals (just like the Line tool). When you create curved segments, the Shift key forces the tangent handles to snap to 15-degree intervals. Use the Alt key to edit the segments of your path while you're still defining it. This is useful if you need to move a point before defining the next point.

The Pencil Tool

Use the Pencil tool to draw on the canvas as if you were drawing with a pencil on a piece of paper. Blend converts your hand drawing to a path that can be edited with the sub-select tool, just like paths that are created using the Pen tool.

Combining Paths

Paths can be combined in Blend to create resulting objects that would be difficult to create by hand. For example, suppose you want a rectangle fill with a perfect circle cut out of it. Maybe you want a "sliver" shape similar to a cat's eye. These objects can easily be created by creating two starter objects then combining them using one of five Combine tools provided by Blend.

The Combine tools are accessed by clicking Object ➪ Combine from the main menu. From the Combine menu, you will find Unite, Divide, Intersect, Subtract, and Exclude Overlap. I'll step you through using Divide and you can experiment with the others on your own.

1. First, draw a rectangle on the canvas and then draw a circle directly on top of the rectangle.
2. Switch to the Selection tool, and using Shift on your keyboard, select both the rectangle and the circle you just created.
3. Now select Object ➪ Combine ➪ Subtract from the main menu to "punch" a circle out of the rectangle.

You now have a precise path that would have been quite difficult to create manually.

The order that objects appear in XAML affects the result of the combine operations. Since you drew the circle after drawing the rectangle, it was in the foreground of the rectangle. When the Subtract action was selected, the foreground shape was subtracted from the shape behind it. Try changing the order of objects before combining them to see how their order affects the outcome.

Adding Images

The Image control in Blend is not exposed in the main Toolbox. You have to open the Asset Library and check the "Show All Controls" checkbox as shown in Figure 3-27. Select Image to make it the active control. You can now draw an Image control on the canvas, just like you create a rectangle, or you can double-click the Image icon to add a default-sized image to the canvas.

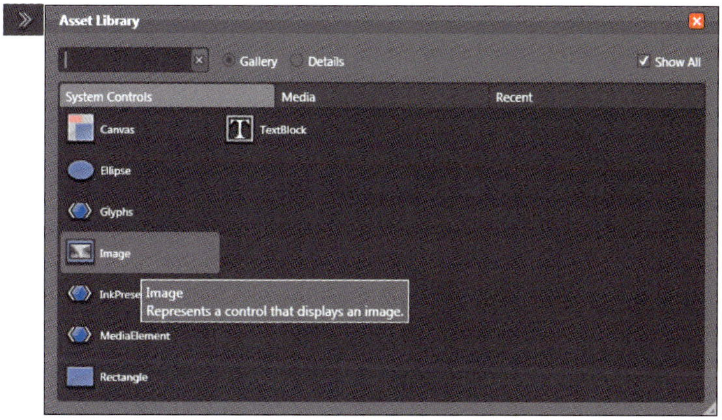

Figure 3-27

Setting the Image Source

Once you've added an Image control to the surface, you need to set its Source property using the Property panel. The Source property is found in the Common Properties category. If you've already added images to your project, those images should appear in the Source combo box. Figure 3-28 shows the ellipsis you can click to launch a file browser dialog. Once you've selected an image, that image will be added to your project.

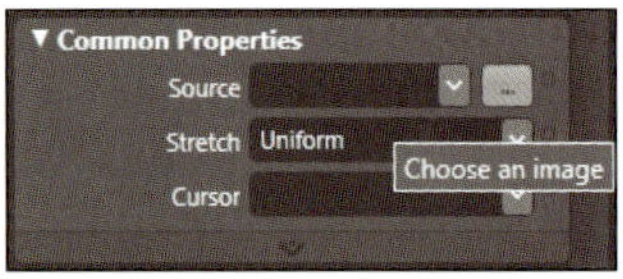

Figure 3-28

Adjusting the Image Size

Once you've set your Image source, you will probably want to adjust the image's size. By default, the Stretch property of Image is set to Uniform, as shown in Figure 3-28. This means that Silverlight will ensure the aspect ratio of your image is preserved, regardless of the actual size you set. If you want to display your image at its native size, Figure 3-29 highlights the Set to Auto buttons on the Width and Height properties.

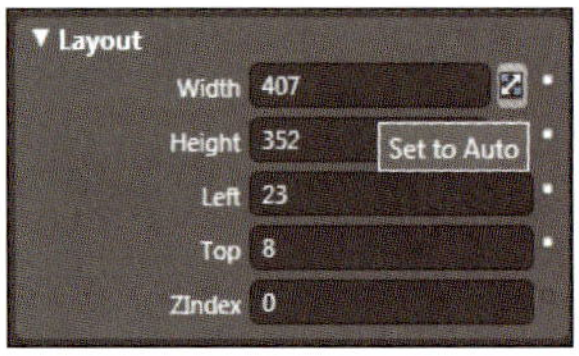

Figure 3-29

Adding MediaElements

The MediaElement control is used to add audio, video, or both to your application. Just like the Image control, the MediaElement control is not exposed directly on the toolbar in Blend. You will once again need to open the Asset Library and select MediaElement. (Be sure to check "Show All Controls.") Figure 3-30 highlights the MediaElement control in the Asset Library.

Setting the MediaElement Source

Once you've added a MediaElement to your canvas, you will need to set the Source property. Figure 3-31 shows the Media category, a new category that appears when a MediaElement control is selected. The Source property behaves the same on the MediaElement as it does on the Image. You can either click the ellipsis to import a new media file into your project, or you can use the combo box to select a media file that already exists in your project.

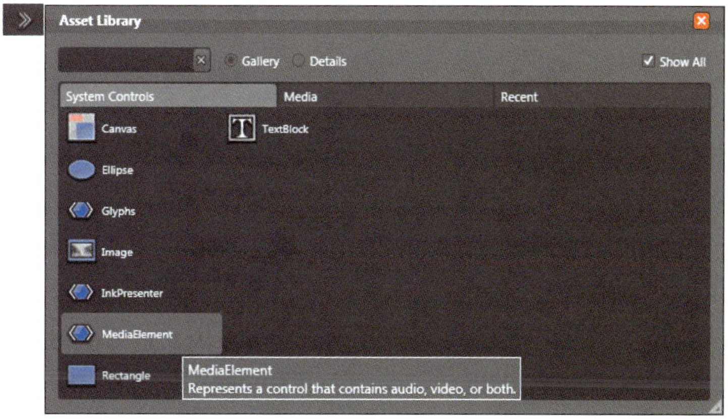

Figure 3-30

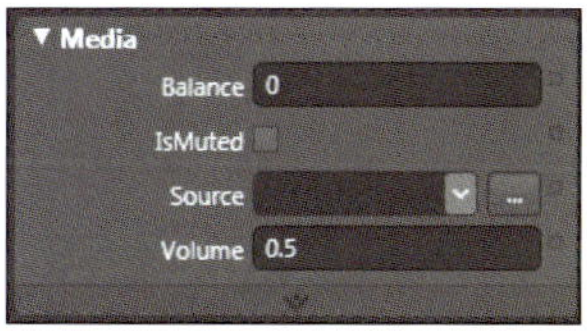

Figure 3-31

Controlling MediaElement Behavior

Blend does not expose very much control for the MediaElement. Most behavior, such as starting, stopping, or pausing, will be handled via JavaScript. Later chapters deal with this topic in more depth.

Creating and Understanding Timelines

Blend uses the concept of timelines to provide design-time support for Silverlight Storyboards. Silverlight Storyboards can contain a number of animation types not supported by Blend, such as DoubleAnimation and ColorAnimation. Blend provides support only for the animation types that end with UsingKeyFrames, such as DoubleAnimationUsingKeyFrames and ColorAnimationUsingKeyFrames. This may sound like a limitation at first, but the other non-UsingKeyFrames animations are more commonly used only when hand-coding XAML animations.

Using key frames for animations is an accepted practice across the board in design-related applications, whether the application targets video, 3D, audio, or web-based animation. A *key frame* represents a specific point in time and is usually represented as a point on a timeline, thus the category name *Objects and Timeline.*

Understanding Storyboards in Silverlight

A Silverlight Storyboard contains a collection of animations that each targets a specific property of a specific control. The animations do not add or remove elements from the base `canvas`; they just temporarily alter the property values of existing elements. If you create a new Storyboard and add a new rectangle to the canvas, that rectangle will be available to all Storyboards, not just the current Storyboard. The rectangle was added to the scene's base canvas and is not specific to the active Storyboard.

Creating a Timeline

Timelines in Blend are defined using the Storyboard Picker. Figure 3-32 shows the Storyboard Picker, launched by clicking the right-arrow button next to the line that reads "(No Storyboard open)."

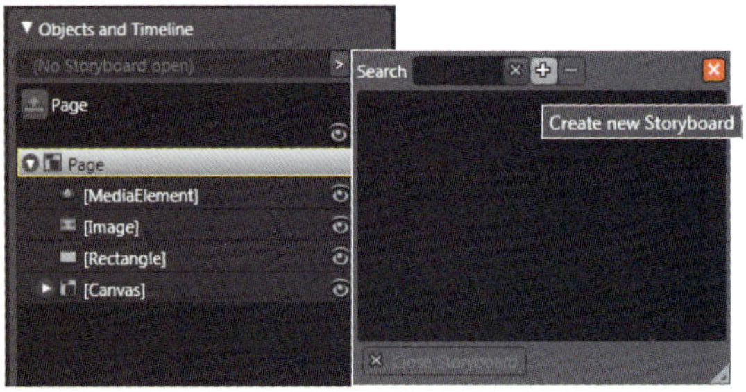

Figure 3-32

Create a new Storyboard by clicking the "plus" button. You'll see the Create Storyboard dialog shown in Figure 3-33.

Figure 3-33

You first need to name your Storyboard. The default value is Timeline1 and is acceptable for now. In a real application, you should give the Storyboard a more meaningful name, such as ShowMenu, HideMenu, or StartupTimeline. You are also given the option to create the Storyboard as a resource. Blend tells you that if you choose to create the Storyboard as a resource, you will have to control the Storyboard from code. If you don't select this option, the Storyboard will automatically play when the canvas loads. If you want to start and stop this animation based on user actions, you should check Create as a Resource.

After clicking OK, you should see a Timeline area directly to the right of the Object tree, as shown in Figure 3-34. Notice also that "Timeline1" appears where "(No Storyboard open)" appeared previously. This indicates that you are currently editing the Storyboard named Timeline1. You can exit the Storyboard by launching the Storyboard Picker and clicking the Close Storyboard button.

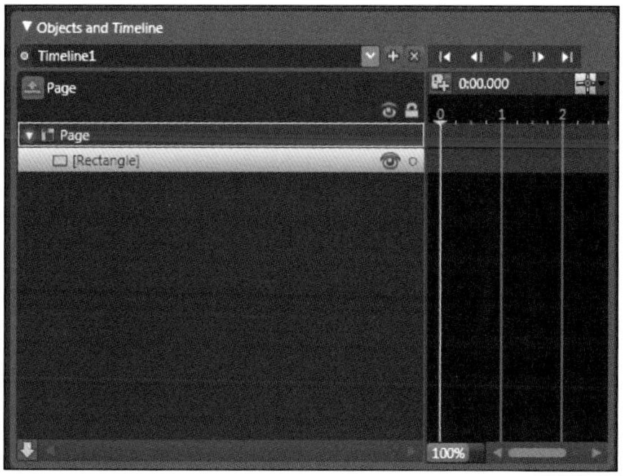

Figure 3-34

Earlier, when we covered the Objects and Timeline category in the Interaction panel, we skipped over the Timeline aspect. We focused on the Object tree itself and then moved on to the Property panel. You learned how to navigate the Object tree, select an object, and update its properties by using the Property panel. We're now going to take those same concepts and apply the idea of time to them.

Before digging into the details of the Timeline interface, you'll create a quick animation just to get you started (we're assuming you still have a single rectangle on the canvas). Drag the vertical yellow bar (the *playhead*) to the 1 second mark. Now select the rectangle on the canvas and change its position. Figure 3-35 shows the key frame indicator that appears when you change a property value. Drag the playhead from 1 to 0 and back — you should see the position of your rectangle animating on the canvas.

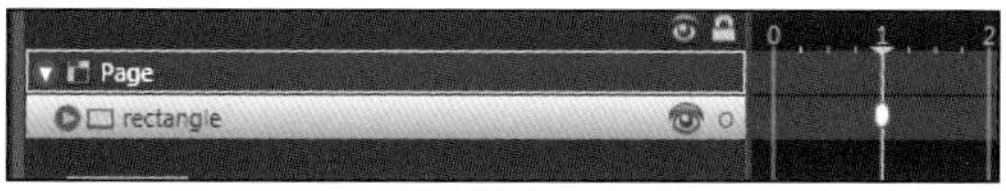

Figure 3-35

Now, expand the rectangle in the Object tree until you can expand it no further. You should see a new entry for RenderTransform. RenderTransform itself has a child named Translation, which in turn has two children, X and Y (see Figure 3-36).

Figure 3-37

So what's going on here? When you moved the rectangle, Blend applied a `TranslateTransform` to the rectangle and set the X and Y values of the translation to the amount that you moved the rectangle horizontally and vertically. You can see the exact values set by taking a look at the Transform property settings in the Property panel (see Figure 3-37).

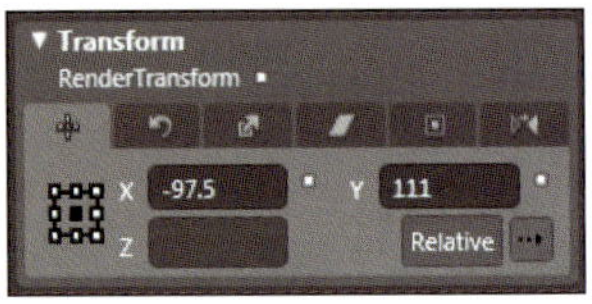

Figure 3-36

You may be wondering why the Left and Top properties weren't updated, and rightfully so. Truthfully, the Blend team had to make a choice because they could have actually set the Left and Top properties instead of applying a transform. (You can use the Property panel to type in new values for Top and Left and key frames will be added for those properties.)

The result of using a transform instead of explicitly setting the Left and Top properties is actually pretty cool. The `TranslateTransform` defines a change in position that is applied to the value set on the Default timeline. To test this, switch back to the Default timeline and change the position of the rectangle. Now switch back to Timeline1 and drag the playhead. The destination position has changed, but the *amount* of change has remained the same.

You'll really see the difference if you delete the RenderTransform key frame (click the oval key frame indicator at the RenderTransform level and hit the Delete key) and then change the values of Left and Top in the Property panel. Now return to the Default timeline once again, change the position of the rectangle, and return to Timeline1. When you drag the playhead this time, the destination position remains the same.

The default method employed by Blend will result in an animation that looks essentially the same when default positions are changed. If this is not the behavior you need, you can explicitly set the Left and Top values using the Property panel.

Keyframe Snapping

By default, as you drag the playhead it snaps to positions in intervals of 0.1 seconds (in other words, 10 intervals per second). You can disable snapping by clicking the icon in the top-right area of the Timeline editor, as shown in Figure 3-38. Figure 3-38 also shows the menu that appears when you click the drop-down arrow next to the Enable Snapping toggle button. This menu also lets you enable or disable snapping by toggling the first entry labeled "Snap." Click the second menu option, "Snapping...," to launch the dialog shown in Figure 3-39.

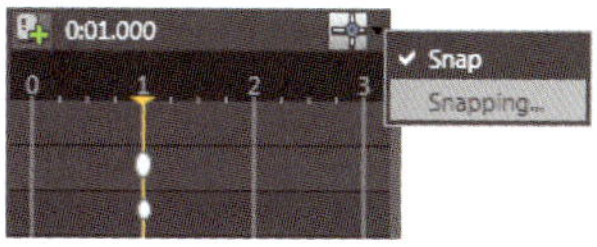

Figure 3-38

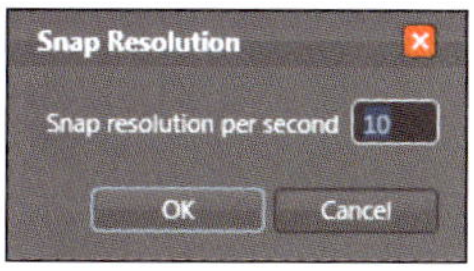

Figure 3-39

You can increase or decrease the level of precision of playhead snapping by changing the Snap Resolution per Second value. As previously indicated, the default is 10 intervals per second.

Easing

If you're not familiar with the term *easing*, I'm sure you're at least familiar with the end result. When easing is applied to a key frame, the animation either slows down or speeds up when approaching the key frame. Instead of a slicing the amount of change consistently at every moment in time, the amount of change is either increased or decreased depending on the type of easing chosen. Access the key frame easing menu by right-clicking a key frame, as shown in Figure 3-40.

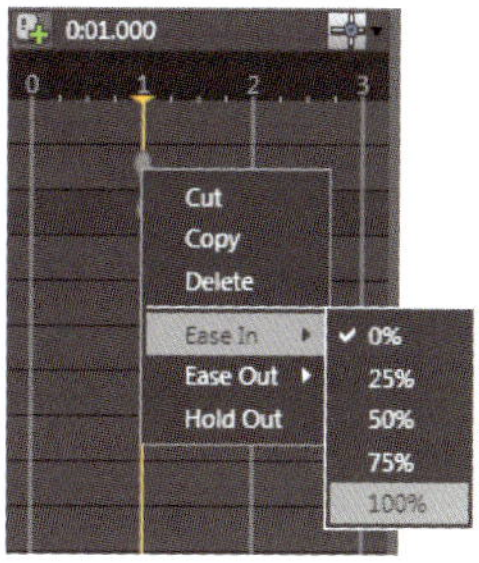

Figure 3-40

Select Ease In if you want the animation to slow down as the selected key frame is approached. Set an Ease Out value if you have a key frame after the current key frame and you want the animation to start slowly then increase in speed as the value moves toward the next key-framed value.

Timeline Summary

This section introduced you to the fundamentals of animation in Blend. It is now up to you to apply these fundamentals to your needs. You now know how to create and name Storyboards, animate elements, and define easing for key frames. Amazingly, rich visual effects are achieved by a combination of these simple techniques.

Working with Artwork Created Outside of Blend

You may be wondering why you would even need to work with artwork created outside of Blend, considering that Blend provides practically all of the tools you need to design a user interface. I think there are two clear answers to this question.

- One, most of you already have pre-existing artwork created in other applications that you would like to re-use.
- Two, many of you are already very familiar with your own design tools and can simply work faster in your design tool of choice.

Based on my experience, you will initially be inclined to export to XAML from your favorite tool, staying in your design comfort zone. Then, as you become more and more familiar with Blend, you will find yourself starting in Blend for most tasks and jumping back to your other program only for specialty design needs.

Designing with Blend/Silverlight in Mind

If you're doing the designing, exporting, and integrating yourself, you have the luxury (or responsibility) of designing with exporting in mind. This means you can anticipate the needs of your application layout and design so that achieving your intended results is as easy as possible. If you're a designer working in a third-party tool delivering artwork to a fellow developer using Blend, you can strengthen your work relationship by exporting your artwork in a way that makes the developer's job easier.

There are several questions you need to keep in mind when designing artwork:

- Are bitmaps acceptable? (If so, you can use all the effects you want.)
- Does the piece you're working on need to stretch? (Horizontally, vertically, or both?)
- Will pieces of the user interface animate? (Like panel backgrounds or buttons?)

We'll take a look at each of these scenarios and discuss certain techniques you can use that will make your life (or your co-workers' lives) easier.

Are Bitmaps Acceptable?

There are several factors that affect the answer to this question, many of which go beyond the scope of this book. However, we'll try to cover a few key scenarios here.

File Size

The first aspect, and possibly most obvious, of including bitmaps in your project is file size. Silverlight is a web-based platform, which means bandwidth is a very real concern. Even with growing numbers of broadband connections in homes, keeping the download footprint of your application to a minimum is still a necessary evil. There are times when the XAML required to represent your artwork could actually be larger than a representative bitmap, and if the other considerations listed next don't contradict your file size requirement, exporting your artwork as a bitmap may be the best option.

Scaling

At the heart of Silverlight is a high-performance, vector-based rendering engine. This means vector-based artwork, represented by XAML, can be rendered losslessly at virtually any size. If the artwork you are designing is intended to scale, exporting to bitmaps is not the way to go. When bitmaps are resized in the Silverlight player, you'll begin to see pixelation as the artwork increases in size and blurriness when the artwork decreases in size.

Dynamic Changes

Artwork in Silverlight applications can be updated dynamically at runtime. For example, you could change the brush that is used to paint the background of a button when the mouse moves over it. If the artwork you are creating will be used in this type of scenario, exporting as a bitmap is not an option.

Techniques That Require a Bitmap Export

Most design programs are platform-agnostic and export to a number of flattened file formats. When authoring for Silverlight, you have to consider the features of the Silverlight rendering engine. The following techniques are not supported by the Silverlight player and will require that you export your artwork as a bitmap. If exporting to bitmaps is not an option for your application, you can either scale back the visuals or re-craft your artwork using other techniques.

- **Effects** — Currently, the Silverlight player does not support live bitmap effects (such as drop shadows, blurs, glows, and so on), so any time you need to achieve these types of effects you will have to export your artwork as a bitmap.
- **Blending Modes** — If the visuals you're creating use Blending modes, (such as Screen, Add, Subtract, Saturation, and so on), you will have to export your artwork as a bitmap or choose alternative techniques. The Silverlight player does not currently include support for Blending modes.

Which Bitmap File Type Is Best?

If you find that you do have to include bitmaps in your project, your first step is to determine which file type is right for you. If you need to composite the bitmap with a transparent background, exporting as a 32-bit PNG with a transparent background is the best choice. If transparency isn't a requirement, finding the right balance between file size and quality is your next step. The same rules that apply to traditional web design apply here. If you're exporting a photo, a JPEG is the obvious choice. Just play with the quality settings until you achieve the right balance. If you're exporting artwork, experiment with JPEG quality and PNG bit depths until you reach a compromise that meets your needs. Most modern design applications provide live previews that help you find this quality/file size balance quickly.

Does the Piece You're Working on Need to Stretch?

The Silverlight player only provides support for a canvas panel, but that doesn't mean that your application can't provide a custom scaling solution. With that in mind, you need to consider whether the artwork you're working on needs to scale vertically, horizontally, or both. You need to anticipate how the artwork is going to scale and export your artwork accordingly. If you have rounded corners, how are you going to design so that the XAML you export behaves correctly? You will likely have to "slice" your artwork, much as traditional web designers would slice the artwork they export. Only, you'll have to create individual objects for each slice so that they can be represented as individual objects in XAML.

Will Pieces of the User Interface Animate?

When you start creating mockups for your application, initially you're primarily concerned with how the application is going to look. That's fine for the initial creative pass, but pretty quickly into your design process you need to consider how the different pieces of your application will interact. In the mockup artwork shown below in Figure 3-41, a chrome-like frame has been created that surrounds the "heart" of the application. When the Preferences button is clicked, a panel is intended to animate in from the bottom, filling the primary area of the application. When Preferences is clicked, I want a panel to slide in from the bottom, filling the main application area. In my initial mockup, the Preferences panel was actually drawn in the foreground of the chrome elements and sized to look as if it lived inside the chrome. In order to make this work in Blend, the Preferences panel will need to be a separate Canvas that contains all of the options I think are necessary. Because I want the panel to slide in from the bottom, the panel actually needs to be behind the chrome. I need to "punch" the chrome paths using my design tool (Adobe Fireworks CS3 in this example) so that the preferences panel is visible beneath the chrome.

Figure 3-41

If you as a designer don't consider how the application is going to behave, you'll end up with artwork in Blend that isn't functional. Regardless of the size team you're working on, it's important to establish open lines of communication between design and development. And if you're wearing both hats, design with interactivity in mind, and you'll save yourself lots of extra rework in the end.

Exporting to XAML in Other Tools

When I first started working with XAML (way back in the spring of 2005), I was pretty much stuck with Notepad and a handful of cobbled together converters and exporters. I would create artwork in Adobe Illustrator, save to an Illustrator SVG file, and then convert the SVG to XAML using the Xamlon SVG to XAML Converter. I would then hand-tweak the generated XAML and copy it into my application and cross my fingers. If things weren't quite right, I'd step through the process again... and again... and again....

Fortunately, things have matured considerably since then. There are now exporters and converters for a large number of design applications and file types. Mike Swanson, a technical evangelist at Microsoft, created a freely available Illustrator to XAML plug-in that many of us began using early on. During the summer of 2006, I spent my nights and weekends creating the Fireworks to XAML Exporter, a panel for

Adobe Fireworks that I still use in practically every WPF and Silverlight project. There are many other passionate people out there who have created similar plug-ins for their tools of choice, and we've provided the following list of those tools. We've also included in the list some commercial applications that you may need to help round out your toolset.

- **Microsoft Expression Design** (`www.microsoft.com/expression`) — Included in the Microsoft Expression Suite and available as a trial download. Supports WPF and Silverlight-specific XAML export.
- **Adobe Fireworks to WPF/XAML Exporter** by Grant Hinkson (`www.infragistics.com/design`) — A free extension for Adobe Fireworks CS3. This panel lets you copy XAML directly to the clipboard or save XAML to a file.
- **Adobe Illustrator to WPF/XAML Export Plug-In** by Mike Swanson (`www.mikeswanson.com/XAMLExport/`) — A free plug-in for Adobe Illustrator that adds XAML as an export format.
- **XamlXporter for Illustrator** by Pavan Podila (`www.codeplex.com/Wiki/View.aspx?ProjectName=xamlxporter`) — An open-source, C#-based exporter for Adobe Illustrator.
- **SWF2XAML: A Flash to XAML Conversion Tool** by Mike Swanson (`www.mikeswanson.com/SWF2XAML/`) — A free converter for Adobe Flash SWF files. Opens exported SWF files and converts each frame to XAML.
- **theConverted - SWF to XAML Edition** by Debreuil Digital Works (`http://theconverted.ca/`) — A commercial SWF to XAML converter.

Problems You May Encounter When Exporting

Most of the XAML exporters mentioned in the preceding section create XAML for the full-fledged WPF and not for Silverlight. And while XAML is XAML, the rendering engines behind WPF and Silverlight are not the same. As you learned in previous chapters, Silverlight 1.0 supports only a subset of the full WPF framework. The XAML created by some of these exporters may include controls not supported by the Silverlight player.

If you copy/paste the XAML into a Blend Silverlight project, you should see errors and be able to remove the rogue elements, but you may destroy the integrity of your design in the process. For example, the current version of the Fireworks to XAML Exporter exports grouped elements by wrapping the grouped elements with a Grid panel. This is actually how Blend provides grouping support as well. However, because Silverlight provides support only for the Canvas panel, you will need to convert all Grid instances to Canvases.

Doing this conversion manually is no picnic. You would have to translate `HorizontalAlignment`, `VerticalAlignment`, and `Margin` values to equivalent `Canvas.Top`, `Canvas.Left`, `Height`, and `Width` properties. And though it's certainly not rocket science to do the conversion, it *is* a form of science (of the mathematical variety) that will waste a considerable amount of your time.

Fortunately, I have another trick up my sleeve that will keep you moving right along! Even though Blend may not currently like your XAML, it's not because of Blend itself, but because of the Silverlight player. Open a new instance of Blend, and this time instead of selecting a Silverlight project, select the WPF Application template (see Figure 3-42).

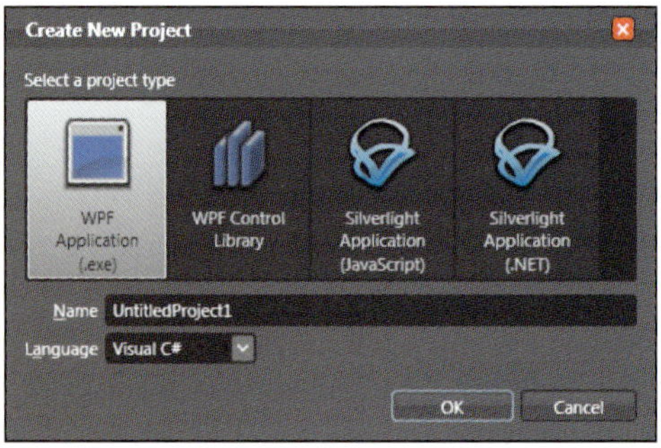

Figure 3-42

Now switch to XAML view and paste in your problematic XAML. Switch back to Design view and expand your object tree, identifying all Grids (or other unsupported panels). Right-click each one that you find and select Change Layout Type ➪ Canvas from the context menu that appears (see Figure 3-43).

Figure 3-43

Once you've changed all of the incorrect panels, copy and paste the XAML from this instance of Blend into your Silverlight project. Repeat this process until you've taken care of all of the problematic XAML. This is a process you can repeat for all unsupported elements, whether your XAML is the result of a non-Silverlight-aware exporter or the product of an existing WPF application.

Summary

This chapter introduced you to Blend 2 and walked you through the primary aspects of the Blend interface. You learned how to use the drawing tools, add Images, add MediaElements, and set properties using the Property panel. You created your first timeline and learned how to set easing values on individual key frames. You also saw how changes at design time affect the underlying XAML by switching back and forth between Design and XAML view.

You were introduced to a handful of third-party tools that allow you to export pre-existing artwork to XAML from tools other than Blend and were made aware of some challenges you may face when doing so. You should now be able to comfortably navigate Blend and explore its capabilities much further. Even if you're not a designer, don't be afraid to fire up Blend when you can't figure out how to target a particular property with a Storyboard. Find the right balance between Blend and Visual Studio and your development experience will be much, much better.

4

Coding Silverlight Applications with JavaScript and XAML

So far in this book you have seen how you can create highly interactive and graphically powerful applications using Silverlight, XAML, and media elements such as video. You have also looked at how you can use tools like Expression Blend to design compelling user experiences for your application. The examples you have seen have involved fairly static HTML and XAML markup that operates in a sandboxed Silverlight player embedded in a web browser. Although this in and of itself is useful, most real-world applications that you build will need to include much more interaction between the end user, the browser, and the Silverlight player. In a realistic Silverlight application you would want to manipulate the XAML elements programmatically, accessing and setting properties at runtime, and even reacting to events that occur in the Silverlight application. Thankfully, Silverlight 1.0 includes a rich programming model that allows you to develop sophisticated applications that seamlessly integrate into the browser and take full advantage of the Internet platform.

In this chapter, we'll cover:

- Creating the Silverlight player using JavaScript
- Accessing and manipulating XAML content loaded in the Silverlight player
- Creating and using Silverlight player events
- Accessing Storyboards programmatically
- Using the Silverlight Downloader object

As is the case with all the code samples in the book, the code samples in this chapter are available for download from `www.wrox.com`.

The JavaScript Programming Model

The primary means of working with the Silverlight player programmatically is through the use of JavaScript. This familiar and flexible programming language provides the primary programming model for Silverlight 1.0, allowing you to create rich, interactive applications that integrate smoothly into the existing browser DOM, and gives you the power to manipulate the Silverlight player with code, just as you would any other DOM element. The Silverlight player APIs are divided into two main objects:

- The `Content` object — The `Content` object contains properties and functions primarily related to the manipulation of the XAML content of the player.
- The `Settings` object — The `Settings` object contains properties and functions related to the settings of the Silverlight player object itself.

Additionally, as you will see later in the chapter, Silverlight even extends the concept of the DOM into the Silverlight player, allowing you to use JavaScript to reach directly into the Silverlight player to access individual XAML elements via a DOM-like model.

To get started looking at how you can use JavaScript to manipulate the Silverlight player, you need to first look at creating the player object using script.

Creating the Player Using JavaScript

In Chapter 1 you saw how you can create the Silverlight player using the standard HTML `object` or `embed` markup. Though this is a convenient way to quickly embed the Silverlight player in your web page, it does have some drawbacks and limitations.

- First, using markup only to embed the player in your web page may cause you to unintentionally lock some end users out of using your application. This is because of the way different browsers embed objects in a web page; some of them use the `<object />` tag, whereas others use the `<embed />` tag. Additionally, not every browser even supports embedding the Silverlight player.
- A second problem in using markup to embed the Silverlight player is the inability for you to determine if the Silverlight player is installed on the client, and if it is, if the version installed is the correct version for your application.

To solve these two problems, Silverlight includes the `Silverlight.js` helper library, which exposes functions that help you add the player to your web page using JavaScript. To get started adding the player to your web page, start with a simple web page like the one shown in Listing 4-1.

Listing 4-1: Simple Web Page Referencing the Silverlight Helper Library

```
<!DOCTYPE html PUBLIC "-//W3C//DTD XHTML 1.0 Transitional//EN"
"http://www.w3.org/TR/xhtml1/DTD/xhtml1-transitional.dtd">
<html xmlns="http://www.w3.org/1999/xhtml" >
<head>
    <title>Hello Silverlight World</title>
    <script type="text/javascript" src="Silverlight.js"></script>
```

Listing 4-1: *(continued)*

```
</head>
<body>
    <div id="mySilverlightHostElement" />
</body>
</html>
```

This listing demonstrates the default Visual Studio HTML `Page` template with two additions. First, a reference to the Silverlight JavaScript helper library, `Silverlight.js`, has been added using an HTML `<script>` tag:

```
<script type="text/javascript" src="Silverlight.js"></script>
```

Second, a `<div>` tag with the ID `mySilverlightHostElement` has been added to the HTML body. This element will serve as the parent element for the Silverlight player control:

```
<div id="mySilverlightHostElement" />
```

Now that the Silverlight helper library has been added to the page, you have access to the helper functions in the library. Using these functions, you can create a new Silverlight player control and insert it into the page, as shown in Listing 4-2. This listing extends Listing 4-1 by adding a new JavaScript function, and a bit of inline JavaScript.

Listing 4-2: Creating the Silverlight Object in the Web Page Using JavaScript

```
<!DOCTYPE html PUBLIC "-//W3C//DTD XHTML 1.0 Transitional//EN"
"http://www.w3.org/TR/xhtml1/DTD/xhtml1-transitional.dtd">
<html xmlns="http://www.w3.org/1999/xhtml" >
<head>
    <title>Hello Silverlight World</title>
    <script type="text/javascript" src="Silverlight.js"></script>
    <script type="text/javascript">
    <!--
    function createMySilverlightControl()
    {
        Silverlight.createObject(
            "",
            hostElement,
            "mySilverlightControl",
            {
                width:'300',
                height:'300',
                background:'#D6D6D6',
                version:'1.0'
            },
            {},
            null);
    }
    //-->
    </script>
</head>
```

(Continued)

Listing 4-2: *(continued)*

```
<body>
    <div id="mySilverlightHostElement" />

    <script type="text/javascript">
    <!--
        var hostElement = document.getElementById("mySilverlightHostElement");
        createMySilverlightControl();
    //-->
    </script>
</body>
</html>
```

If you dissect this listing, you will see that a new JavaScript function called `createMySilverlightControl` has been added to the page. This function contains the call to the `Silverlight.createObject` function, which creates the Silverlight player object and adds it to the host element. Later in the chapter, the specific capabilities of the `createObject` function are discussed, but for now, knowing that this function will create and add the object to the page is sufficient.

The second change in the page is the addition of two lines of inline JavaScript in the page body below the `<div>` tag. Because the browser loads the page serially, these lines of code will be executed as the page loads. The first line locates the Silverlight control's parent `<div>` element using the standard JavaScript `getElementById` function and assigns it to the `hostElement` variable. The second line calls the `createMySilverlightControl` function to create the Silverlight player.

That's all it takes to programmatically add the Silverlight control to your web page using JavaScript. As you can see in Figure 4-1, when you load the page in the browser the Silverlight player has been embedded in the web page.

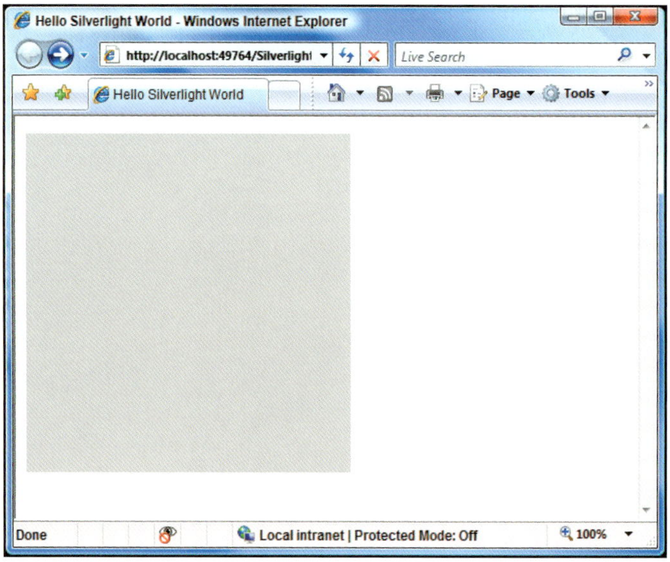

Figure 4-1

Using this technique to embed the Silverlight player in your web page allows you to leverage the built-in intelligence of the `Silverlight.js` helper library to more finely control the creation of the player control and to address the shortcomings of simply using HTML to embed the player objects that were discussed earlier in the chapter.

If you are interested, you can open up the `Silverlight.js` *file and examine exactly what the* `createObject` *function is doing. You will see that the function uses several internal functions to test for the existence of the correct version of the Silverlight player and ensures that the requesting browser supports embedding the Silverlight player. The library also includes functions for generating the appropriate HTML object embedding markup based on the requesting browser.*

If the conditions for embedding the Silverlight player in the page are not met, the appropriate message will be relayed to the end user; otherwise the library goes ahead and embeds the player in the page. Overall, because the `Silverlight.js` *helper library includes the additional intelligence of player, browser, and version detection, this allows you to give your end users a much better experience using your application.*

Refactoring the Silverlight Player Creation

Now that you have created a simple web page and programmatically added the Silverlight player, you should consider how you would refactor the page. Though having the `createMySilverlightControl` function in the page makes sense in this simple example, in a larger application you would probably want to keep that function in an external JavaScript file. Doing this allows you to reuse the same JavaScript throughout your web site as well as take advantage of browser caching to reduce the download weight of your web page. In fact, the default Silverlight template for Visual Studio 2005 automatically configures your project so that the creation of the Silverlight control is factored into its own script file.

Listing 4-3 shows the same web page from Listing 4-2, but the page has been refactored to reference a new JavaScript file, `Listing4-03.js`. This new file contains the same `createMySilverlightControl` function you used in prior examples.

Listing 4-3: Refactoring the Host Web Page to Reference an External JavaScript file

```
<!DOCTYPE html PUBLIC "-//W3C//DTD XHTML 1.0 Transitional//EN"
"http://www.w3.org/TR/xhtml1/DTD/xhtml1-transitional.dtd">
<html xmlns="http://www.w3.org/1999/xhtml" >
<head>
    <title>Hello Silverlight World</title>
    <script type="text/javascript" src="Silverlight.js"></script>
    <script type="text/javascript" src="Listing4-03.js"></script>
</head>
<body>
    <div id="mySilverlightHostElement" />

    <script type="text/javascript">
    <!--
        var hostElement = document.getElementById("mySilverlightHostElement");
        createMySilverlightControl();
    //-->
    </script>
</body>
</html>
```

Loading this page in the browser will result in the same behavior as the prior listing.

Dissecting the Silverlight.js Helper Library

Now that you have created your first Silverlight-enabled web page using JavaScript, you can take a closer look at the functions included in the `Silverlight.js` helper library. The `Silverlight.js` library exposes three functions you can use in your applications: the `createObject`, `createObjectEx`, and `isInstalled` functions. You can use these functions to help you optimize the embedding of the Silverlight player into your web page.

createObject and createObjectEx

The first two functions to look at (one of which you have already used) are the `createObject` and `createObjectEx` functions. As you have seen in prior examples, the `createObject` function is responsible for instantiating the Silverlight player object and inserting it into your web page. Just as you can specify Silverlight player initialization options using the HTML `<param>` tag when creating the player through markup, the `createObject` function allows you to provide function parameters to customize exactly how the Silverlight player object will be initialized.

The `createObjectEx` function performs the same basic behavior, but rather than using several separate function parameters, it uses a single JavaScript Object Notation (JSON) dictionary to package all of its parameters.

> *Although the examples in this chapter primarily demonstrate the use of the* `createObject` *function, the* `createObjectEx` *function could easily be substituted by simply refactoring the function parameters into a single JSON dictionary.*

The parameters of the `createObject` function are summarized in the following table:

Parameter	Description
`Source`	The source of the XAML the player should load initially. The parameter accepts a URL or a reference to an embedded XAML block and corresponds to the Silverlight player's `Source` property.
`Parent`	The ID of the HTML element that should serve as the Silverlight player's parent element in the browser DOM.
`ID`	The unique ID of the player element itself. You can access the Silverlight player in the browser DOM using this ID.
`Properties`	An array of initialization properties for the player. The properties allowed in this array are described later in the chapter.
`Events`	Control events that can be set at initialization time. Events available are `onLoad` and `onError`.
`initParams`	An array of user-defined initialization parameters.
`Context`	A unique identifier that can be passed into the `onLoad` event handler.

The XAML Source Parameter

The first parameter of the method tells the player what XAML to load. You can specify a URL that the player can access, as shown in Listing 4-4, which uses the `createObject` function to load the `HelloWorld.xaml` file from the Infragistics Labs' web site. The URL you specify can either be a fully qualified URL as shown in the listing or a relative URL.

Listing 4-4: Specifying the Silverlight XAML Content in the createObject Function

```
function createMySilverlightControl()
{
    Silverlight.createObject(
        "xaml/HelloWorld.xaml",
        hostElement,
        "mySilverlightControl",
        {
            width:'300',
            height:'300',
            background:'#D6D6D6',
            version:'1.0'
        },
        {},
        null);
}
```

The same script example can also be executed using `createObjectEx`, as shown in Listing 4-5.

Listing 4-5: Specifying the Silverlight XAML Content in the createObjectEx Function

```
function createMySilverlightControl()
{
    Silverlight.createObjectEx({
        source: "xaml/HelloWorld.xaml",
        parentElement: hostElement,
        id: "mySilverlightControl",
        properties: {
            width:'300',
            height:'300',
            background:'#D6D6D6',
            version:'1.0'
        },
        events: {},
        context: null});
}
```

The HelloWorld.xaml file contains a small example of XAML markup as shown here:

```
<Canvas Width="300" Height="300" x:Name="rootCanvas"
        xmlns="http://schemas.microsoft.com/client/2007"
        xmlns:x="http://schemas.microsoft.com/winfx/2006/xaml" >
    <TextBlock Text="Hello Silverlight World!" x:Name="myTextBlock" />
</Canvas>
```

As shown in Figure 4-2, running this example in the browser results in the Hello World text being displayed by the Silverlight player.

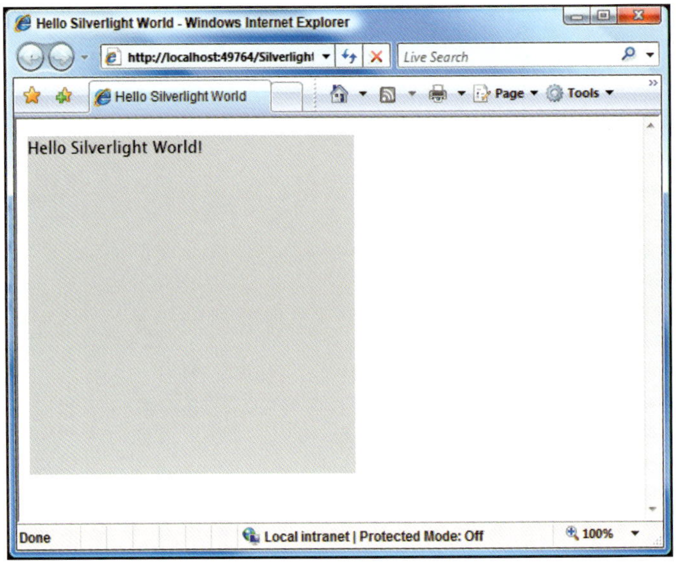

Figure 4-2

You can also provide to the source parameter the ID of an XAML script block embedded directly in the web page. In this technique, a block of XAML is embedded directly in the web page using a standard HTML `script` tag with the `type` attribute set to `text/xaml`. This is shown in Listing 4-6.

Listing 4-6: Creating Inline XAML Using the script Tag

```
<!DOCTYPE html PUBLIC "-//W3C//DTD XHTML 1.0 Transitional//EN"
"http://www.w3.org/TR/xhtml1/DTD/xhtml1-transitional.dtd">
<html xmlns="http://www.w3.org/1999/xhtml" >
<head>
    <title>Hello Silverlight World</title>
    <script type="text/javascript" src="Silverlight.js"></script>
    <script type="text/javascript" src="Listing4-07.js"></script>

    <script type="text/xaml" id="xamlContent"><?xml version="1.0"?>
      <Canvas Width="300" Height="300" x:Name="rootCanvas"
        xmlns="http://schemas.microsoft.com/client/2007"
        xmlns:x="http://schemas.microsoft.com/winfx/2006/xaml">
          <TextBlock Text="Hello Silverlight World!" x:Name="myTextBlock" />
      </Canvas>
    </script>

</head>
<body>
```

Listing 4-6: *(continued)*

```
        <div id="mySilverlightHostElement" />

        <script type="text/javascript">
        <!--
            var hostElement = document.getElementById("mySilverlightHostElement");
            createMySilverlightControl();
        //-->
        </script>

    </body>
    </html>
```

Once you have embedded the XAML content in the web page, you can reference it by specifying its ID as the value of the `createObject`'s `Source` parameter, as shown in Listing 4-7.

Listing 4-7: Specifying Inline XAML as the Silverlight Player Content

```
function createMySilverlightControl()
{
    Silverlight.createObject(
        "#xamlContent",
        hostElement,
        "mySilverlightControl",
        {
            width:'300',
            height:'300',
            background:'#D6D6D6',
            version:'1.0'
        },
        {},
        null);
}
```

Notice that when we reference the script block ID, it is prefaced with the "`#`" character. This indicates to Silverlight that the XAML source is an embedded script block, and it should attempt to locate the provided ID in the browser's DOM to find its XAML content.

Element and Parent IDs

Once you have specified the XAML to load into the Silverlight player, you next need to provide an HTML element ID in which the player will be parented. In the examples shown so far, the variable `hostElement` is provided as the value of this parameter. `hostElement` is a JavaScript variable that represents the HTML `<div>` element with the ID `mySilverlightHostElement`.

The next parameter required is a unique element ID. This ID is used to uniquely identify the Silverlight player in the browser's DOM and must follow the standard element ID rules. Later in your application, you can pass this ID to the standard JavaScript function `getElementById` to obtain a reference to the Silverlight player object.

Player Initialization Properties

The fourth parameter of the `createObject` function consists of an array of properties used to control how the player initializes. Some of the properties are used exclusively by the `Silverlight.js` helper library, whereas others correspond to properties exposed by the Silverlight player object or to properties exposed by its DOM element. The following table lists the initialization properties:

Property	Description
`width`	Defines the width of the Silverlight player element. The value can be defined as a fixed pixel value or as a percentage value. The default value is 0. Corresponds to the browser DOM's `Width` property.
`height`	Defines the height of the Silverlight player element. The value can be defined as a fixed pixel value, or as a percentage value. The default value is 0. Corresponds to the browser DOM's `Width` property.
`background`	Defines the background color of the player control. The default value is null, which is interpreted as white. Corresponds to the Silverlight object's `Settings.Background` property.
`isWindowless`	Determines if the player will be displayed as a windowless control in the browser. If the value is set to `true`, the color specified by the background becomes the alpha value for the control. The default value is `false`. Corresponds to the Silverlight object's `Settings.Windowless` property.
`frameRate`	Defines the maximum frames per second the control should render. The maximum frame rate is 64 frames per second. The default value is 24. Corresponds to the Silverlight object's `Settings.MaxFrameRate` property.
`inplaceInstallPrompt`	Determines if the in-place install prompt should be shown if the appropriate version of the Silverlight player is not installed on the client. The in-place install prompt differs from the standard install prompt by including links to the Silverlight license agreement and privacy information. Additionally, clicking the Silverlight logo immediately initiates the downloading of the Silverlight player. The standard dialog simply links the end user to the Silverlight download page. The default value is `false`. It is a violation of Microsoft licensing to remove or alter the wording, color, or location of the links in the in-place dialog.
`version`	Specifies the minimum version of the Silverlight player required to run the application. The Silverlight player will verify the specified version is installed prior to loading the player in the browser. If the minimum version is not available, the player will display the install dialog according to the value of the `inplaceInstallPrompt` property.

Property	Description
`ignoreBrowserVer`	Determines if Silverlight should not verify that the requesting browser type and version supports loading the Silverlight player control. The default value is `false`, meaning only supported browsers will load the player.
`enableHtmlAccess`	Determines whether the player content is allowed to access the content in the browser's DOM. The default value is `true`. Corresponds to the Silverlight object's `Settings.EnableHtmlAccess` property.

Though not all initialization properties required specification, the `Version` property must be specified in the `createObject`'s properties array parameter. Failure to provide this parameter will result in the `createObject` function raising a null value error.

Listing 4-8 demonstrates using the player initialization properties when creating the Silverlight player.

Listing 4-8: Specifying Silverlight Player Initialization Properties

```
function createMySilverlightControl()
{
    Silverlight.createObject(
        "xaml/HelloWorld.xaml",
        hostElement,
        "mySilverlightControl",
        {
            width:'300',
            height:'300',
            background:'#D6D6D6',
            isWindowless:false,
            framerate:'24',
            inplaceInstallPrompt:false,
            version:'0.9',
            ignoreBrowserVer:false,
            enableHtmlAccess:false
        },
        {},
        null);
}
```

Player Initialization Events

Although the Silverlight player object exposes several different events, which are discussed later in the chapter, there are two unique events that can be attached in the `createObject` function. The `onLoad` and `onError` events can have event handlers attached to them in the `createObject` function so that they can be raised during the control initialization.

Listing 4-9 demonstrates attaching event handlers to the `onLoad` and `onError` events in the `createObject` function.

Listing 4-9: Specifying Silverlight Player Initialization Events

```
function createMySilverlightControl()
{
    Silverlight.createObject(
        "xaml/HelloWorld.xaml",
        hostElement,
        "mySilverlightControl",
        {
            width:'300',
            height:'300',
            background:'#D6D6D6',
            version:'1.0'
        },
        {
            onError:onError,
            onLoad:onLoad
        },
        null);
}

function onLoad(control, userContext, sender)
{
    alert("The Silverlight control has successfully loaded.");
}

function onError(object, errorArgs)
{
    alert("An error occured loading the Silverlight player.");
}
```

In the listing, the `onLoad` event is raised once the Silverlight player has completed loading. Should the player encounter an error loading, the `onError` event is raised. You can test the `onError` event by changing the source property value to `http://labs.infragistics.com/wrox/silverlight1_0/chapter4/BadXaml.xaml`. This XAML file contains a malformed XAML fragment that causes an error to occur when the player attempts to load it.

Player initParams

In addition to the player-defined parameter types, the `createObject` function includes a specific parameter called `initParams` that allows you to provide the player with user-defined initialization parameters. Listing 4-10 demonstrates how you can provide `initParams` to the player using the `createObject` function.

Listing 4-10: Specifying initParams When Creating the Silverlight Player

```
function createMySilverlightControl()
{
    Silverlight.createObject(
        "xaml/HelloWorld.xaml",
        hostElement,
        "mySilverlightControl",
        {
            width:'300',
            height:'300',
            background:'#D6D6D6',
            version:'1.0'
        },
        {
            onLoad:onLoad
        },
        "The quick brown fox;jumped over the lazy dog",
        null);
}

function onLoad(control, userContext, sender)
{
    var params = control.initParams.split(";");

    var msg="";
    for(var i=0; i<params.length;i++)
    {
        msg += "Parameter " + i + ": " + params[i] + "\r\n";
    }

    alert(msg);
}
```

This example demonstrates providing the `createObject` function with an `initParam` value. In this case the value is a semicolon-delimited string. Once the player is initialized, the `onLoad` event is raised, and you can access the `initParams`, which in the example are simply displayed as the contents of a message box.

isInstalled

In addition to the `createObject` and `createObjectEx` functions, the `Silverlight.js` library also includes an `isInstalled` function, which allows you to manually check to see what version of the Silverlight player is installed. The function accepts as a parameter a specific version of Silverlight and returns a Boolean value indicating whether the version is installed. Using this function is shown in Listing 4-11.

Listing 4-11: Using the isInstalled Function to Detect Silverlight Versions

```
<script type="text/javascript">
<!--
    isInstalled = Silverlight.isInstalled("2.0.0.0");

    if (isInstalled)
    {
        var hostElement = document.getElementById("mySilverlightHostElement");
        createMySilverlightControl();
    }
    else
    {
        alert("You do not have the appropriate version of Silverlight installed.");
    }
//-->
</script>
```

This listing simply uses the `isInstalled` function to check to see if the client has version 2.0.0.0 of the Silverlight player installed. If it is available, the player is created, and if not, the end user is notified of the incorrect version.

Accessing the Silverlight Player Object

Once you have the Silverlight player embedded into your web page, you will want to begin to access the player object and use its APIs. Because the rest of this chapter focuses on using JavaScript to manipulate the Silverlight player and the XAML content it hosts, it's important to understand the ways that you can obtain a reference to the player object.

- The first and easiest way to do this is to get the reference from the browser's DOM using the standard `getElementById` function:

```
var control = document.getElementById("mySilverlightControl");
```

- If you are using Microsoft ASP.NET AJAX Extensions you could also use the shorthand `$get` function:

```
var control = $get("mySilverlightControl");
```

- Another way to get a reference to the player object is by using the `GetHost` function that is attached to every XAML element that is loaded in the Silverlight player control. This function comes in very handy when you are reacting to an event raised by the player. Although events are discussed in much greater detail later in the chapter, every event sends as part of its event handler the object that raised the event, which you can use to get the hosting Silverlight player object from:

```
function MyRectangle_onMouseEnter(sender, mouseEventArgs)
{
    var control = sender.getHost();
}
```

- In this example, the `sender` object would represent an XAML `Rectangle` element, which exposes the `getHost` function.

Accessing XAML Content

Now that you have looked at how you can use JavaScript to instantiate the Silverlight player in the browser, you can look at how you can use JavaScript to interact with the XAML loaded in the player. XAML content loaded in the Silverlight player is exposed through a hierarchical tree structure, similar in concept to the browser's DOM model. This hierarchical element structure allows you to easily navigate the XAML content and allows you to dynamically select, insert, and delete XAML elements in the player. Additionally, because element references returned by the `FindName` function are true representations of their underlying XAML objects, you can get and set properties in the element, including attached properties.

Locating XAML Content Elements

The primary means for locating elements in the player's XAML content is through the use of the `FindName` function. This simple function is exposed by every node in the element tree and allows you to find XAML elements based on the element's `x:Name` attribute value. The function restricts its search to the child elements of the element executing the `FindName` function.

Listing 4-12 demonstrates using the `FindName` function to locate an XAML rectangle.

Listing 4-12: Locating XAML Elements Using FindName

```
<!DOCTYPE html PUBLIC "-//W3C//DTD XHTML 1.0 Transitional//EN"
"http://www.w3.org/TR/xhtml1/DTD/xhtml1-transitional.dtd">
<html xmlns="http://www.w3.org/1999/xhtml" >
<head>
    <title>Hello Silverlight World</title>
    <script type="text/javascript" src="Silverlight.js"></script>
    <script type="text/javascript" src="Listing4-12.js"></script>
    <script type="text/javascript">
    <!--
    function getXamlText()
    {
        var control = document.getElementById("mySilverlightControl");
        var textBlock = control.content.FindName("myTextBlock");

        var inputText = document.getElementById("inputText");
        inputText.value = textBlock.Text;
    }

    function onLoad(control, userContext, sender)
    {
        document.getElementById("btnGetXamlText").disabled="";
    }
    //-->
    </script>
</head>
<body>
    <div>
        <input type="text" id="inputText" />
```

(Continued)

Listing 4-12: *(continued)*

```
        <button onclick="getXamlText();" id="btnGetXamlText"
            disabled="disabled">Get XAML Text</button>
    </div>

    <div id="mySilverlightHostElement" />
    <script type="text/javascript">
    <!--
        var hostElement = document.getElementById("mySilverlightHostElement");
        createMySilverlightControl();
    //-->
    </script>
</body>
</html>
```

In this listing, the HTML `<button>` element's `onclick` event calls the `getXamlText` function. This JavaScript function gets a reference to the Silverlight player and then uses the `FindName` function to locate the XAML `TextBlock` named `myTextBlock` loaded in the Silverlight element tree. In this case, because the search for the `TextBlock` needed to include the entire element tree, the example uses the `FindName` function attached to the player's `content` property.

When the `TextBlock` element is found, the function simply assigns its `Text` property to the HTML `<input>` element's value property.

One other small, but important thing to note in the example is the disabled state of the `<button>` element. By default the button is disabled because you do not want the user pressing the button before the Silverlight player has completed loading. If the user were able to do this, and the player's content had not completed loading, the `getXamlText` function could fail and cause an error. To solve this problem, the button is disabled by default, and its state changed in the Silverlight player's `onLoad` event.

Getting and Setting XAML Properties

If you refer back to Listing 4-12, you see that the Silverlight player's `FindName` function returns a reference to an XAML `TextBlock` element. The JavaScript then accesses the `TextBlock`'s `Text` property and assigns its value to an HTML `<input>` element:

```
var control = document.getElementById("mySilverlightControl");
var textBlock = control.content.FindName("myTextBlock");

var inputText = document.getElementById("inputText");
inputText.value = textBlock.Text;
```

This example demonstrates how, given a reference to an XAML object, you have the ability to access property values of that element, just as you would any other JavaScript object property.

Additionally, Silverlight not only allows you to read property values, but you can just as easily set property values using JavaScript, as shown in Listing 4-13.

Listing 4-13: Setting an XAML TextBlock Property Using JavaScript

```
function setXamlText()
{
    var control = document.getElementById("mySilverlightControl");
    var textBlock = control.content.FindName("myTextBlock");

    var inputText = document.getElementById("inputText");
    textBlock.Text = inputText.value;
}
```

This listing defines a new `setXamlText` function, which instead of the button's retrieving the `TextBlock`'s `Text` property and assigning it to the `<input>` element, the reverse happens; the value of the `<input>` element is assigned to the `TextBlock`'s `Text` property, again using the same standard JavaScript property setting syntax you are used to.

Finally, Silverlight also allows you to get and set two XAML functions: `getValue` and `setValue`. Though these functions are primarily used to access XAML attached properties, you are free to use them to access any element property. The functions are available on every XAML element object reference. Listing 4-14 demonstrates accessing the `TextBlock`'s `Canvas.Top` and `Canvas.Left` properties and setting them to new values.

Listing 4-14: Getting and Setting XAML Element Attached Properties Using JavaScript

```
<!DOCTYPE html PUBLIC "-//W3C//DTD XHTML 1.0 Transitional//EN"
"http://www.w3.org/TR/xhtml1/DTD/xhtml1-transitional.dtd">
<html xmlns="http://www.w3.org/1999/xhtml" >
<head>
    <title>Hello Silverlight World</title>
    <script type="text/javascript" src="Silverlight.js"></script>
    <script type="text/javascript" src="Listing4-13.js"></script>
    <script type="text/javascript">
    <!--
    function getTextPosition()
    {
        var control = document.getElementById("mySilverlightControl");
        var textBlock = control.content.FindName("myTextBlock");

        var canvasTop = document.getElementById("canvasTop");
        var canvasLeft = document.getElementById("canvasLeft");

        canvasTop.value = textBlock.getValue("Canvas.Top");
        canvasLeft.value = textBlock.getValue("Canvas.Left");
    }

    function setTextPosition()
    {
        var control = document.getElementById("mySilverlightControl");
        var textBlock = control.content.FindName("myTextBlock");

        var canvasTop = document.getElementById("canvasTop");
```

(Continued)

Listing 4-14: *(continued)*

```
            var canvasLeft = document.getElementById("canvasLeft");

            textBlock.setValue("Canvas.Top", canvasTop.value);
            textBlock.setValue("Canvas.Left", canvasLeft.value);
        }

        function onLoad(control, userContext, sender)
        {
            getTextPosition();

            document.getElementById("btnSetTextPosition").disabled="";
        }
        //-->
        </script>
    </head>
    <body>
        <div>
            <input type="text" id="canvasTop" value="20" />
            <input type="text" id="canvasLeft" value="20" /><br />
            <button onclick="setTextPosition();" id="btnSetTextPosition"
               disabled="disabled">Set Text Position</button>
        </div>

        <div id="mySilverlightHostElement" />
        <script type="text/javascript">
        <!--
            var hostElement = document.getElementById("mySilverlightHostElement");
            createMySilverlightControl();
        //-->
        </script>
    </body>
    </html>
```

This listing uses two JavaScript functions, `getTextPosition` and `setTextPosition`, to retrieve and change the XAML `textBlock` element's position. Also, as in Listing 4-12, the `<button>` element is disabled until the Silverlight player's `onLoad` event is raised, and the `getTextPosition` function is also not called until the player has completed loading.

Instantiating and Inserting XAML Elements

In addition to accessing and interacting with existing XAML objects loaded in the Silverlight player, you can also instantiate new XAML elements and attach them as children to existing elements. The Silverlight player includes the `CreateFromXaml` function, which accepts a string parameter containing an XAML snippet. The function parses the snippet and returns an element tree hierarchy that you can attach to an existing XAML object's `children` collection.

Listing 4-15 demonstrates instantiating a new XAML snippet and adding it to the existing canvas's collection of child elements.

Listing 4-15: Creating New XAML Elements Using JavaScript

```
<!DOCTYPE html PUBLIC "-//W3C//DTD XHTML 1.0 Transitional//EN"
"http://www.w3.org/TR/xhtml1/DTD/xhtml1-transitional.dtd">
<html xmlns="http://www.w3.org/1999/xhtml" >
<head>
    <title>Hello Silverlight World</title>
    <script type="text/javascript" src="Silverlight.js"></script>
    <script type="text/javascript" src="Listing4-13.js"></script>
    <script type="text/javascript">
    <!--
    function onLoad(control, userContext, sender)
    {
        var control = document.getElementById("mySilverlightControl");

        var textBlock = control.content.CreateFromXaml(
            "<TextBlock Text='Hello Again Silverlight World!' Canvas.Top='20' />");

        control.content.FindName('rootCanvas').children.add(textBlock);
    }
    //-->
    </script>
</head>
<body>

    <div id="mySilverlightHostElement" />
    <script type="text/javascript">
    <!--
        var hostElement = document.getElementById("mySilverlightHostElement");
        createMySilverlightControl();
    //-->
    </script>
</body>
</html>
```

In this example, the player is initiated with the same HelloWorld XAML used in prior examples. Once the player is loaded, its `onLoad` event is raised and in its event handler, a new string containing additional XAML markup, in this case a `TextBlock`, is created. This string is then passed into the Silverlight player's `CreateFromXaml` function, which parses the string and generates an element tree based on the snippet.

In this case, because the snippet you gave the function contains only the single element, the resulting tree contains a single element, the `TextBlock`. The element tree is then appended as a child element of the `rootCanvas` canvas, and as you can see in Figure 4-3, the additional `TextBlock` element now shows in the Silverlight player.

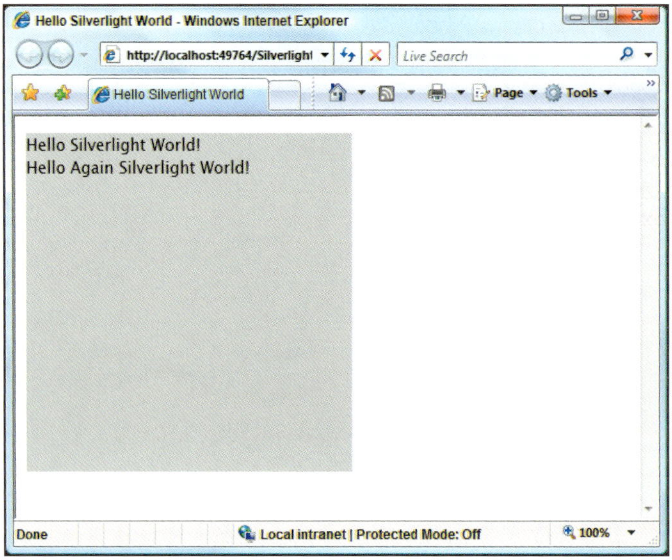

Figure 4-3

`CreateFromXaml` also allows you to pass in much more complex XAML snippets such as brushes, Storyboards, or even complex composite UIs such as XAML that represents a button. Keep in mind, though, that the snippet must be well-formed XML, containing a single root element. The following example demonstrates creating a complex `LinearGradientBrush` element using `CreateFromXaml` and assigning it to a rectangle's `Fill` property:

```
var sampleBrush = control.content.CreateFromXaml(
    "<LinearGradientBrush StartPoint='0,0' EndPoint='0,1'>" +
        "<LinearGradientBrush.GradientStops>" +
            "<GradientStopCollection>" +
                "<GradientStop Color='#FF56D460' Offset='0' />" +
                "<GradientStop Color='#FF56D460' Offset='1' />" +
            "</GradientStopCollection>" +
        "</LinearGradientBrush.GradientStops>" +
    "</LinearGradientBrush>",
    true);

rectangle.FindName("MyRectangle").Fill = sampleBrush;
```

In Listing 4-15, the `TextElement` that was added did not specify an `x:Name` attribute. Although this is perfectly legal to do, it does prevent you from using the `FindName` function later in your application to obtain a reference to the `TextBlock` should you want to change any of its properties. If you want to add the `x:Name` attribute, you also need to make sure you provide its required namespace declaration in your snippet, as shown in Listing 4-16.

Listing 4-16: Specifying the XAML x:Name Attribute

```
function onLoad(control, userContext, sender)
{
    var control = document.getElementById("mySilverlightControl");

    var textBlock = control.content.CreateFromXaml(
        "<TextBlock " +
            "xmlns:x='http://schemas.microsoft.com/winfx/2006/xaml' " +
            "x:Name='NewTextBlock' Text='Hello Again Silverlight World!' " +
             "Canvas.Top='20' />");


    control.content.FindName('rootCanvas').children.add(textBlock);
}
```

The reason you need to add the namespace is because the XAML parser called by the `CreateFromXaml` function parses the snippet independent of any other XAML that has be loaded in the Silverlight player. Therefore, without the declaration, the parser does not understand the x namespace and will fail to parse the snippet.

If you do specify the `x:Name` attribute on any element in your snippet, you also need to make sure that the names you give each element are unique in the XAML element hierarchy. This may be okay if you are adding the snippet only once, but if you want to add the snippet several times (for example, several different `TextBlock`s), you need to either give each instance of the snippet a unique name or set the nameScope parameter of `CreateFromXaml` to `true`, as shown here:

```
    var textBlock = control.content.CreateFromXaml(
        "<TextBlock " +
            "xmlns:x='http://schemas.microsoft.com/winfx/2006/xaml' " +
            "x:Name='NewTextBlock' Text='Hello Again Silverlight World!' " +
             "Canvas.Top='20' />",  true);
```

Note that if you set the nameScope attribute to `true`, Silverlight will automatically ensure that each element added in this scope gets a unique ID. This also means that you will not be able to access elements using the `FindName` method since their names will have been modified by Silverlight when being added to the element tree.

The Silverlight player also allows you to enumerate through the objects in the element hierarchy. As shown in previous examples, each element loaded in the player exposes a `children` collection that can be enumerated. For example, Listing 4-17 shows some sample XAML content that includes multiple `TextBlock`s that are all children of the parent `Canvas` element. Listing 4-18 shows how you can enumerate the `TextBlock`s in the XAML.

Listing 4-17: XAML Content with Multiple Child TextBlocks

```
<Canvas Width="300" Height="300" x:Name="rootCanvas"
    xmlns="http://schemas.microsoft.com/client/2007"
    xmlns:x="http://schemas.microsoft.com/winfx/2006/xaml">
    <TextBlock Canvas.Top="0" Text="The quick" x:Name="myTextBlock1" />
```

(Continued)

Listing 4-17: *(continued)*

```
    <TextBlock Canvas.Top="20" Text="brown fox" x:Name="myTextBlock2" />
    <TextBlock Canvas.Top="40" Text="jumped over" x:Name="myTextBlock3" />
    <TextBlock Canvas.Top="60" Text="the lazy" x:Name="myTextBlock4" />
    <TextBlock Canvas.Top="80" Text="dog." x:Name="myTextBlock5" />
</Canvas>
```

Listing 4-18: Using JavaScript to Enumerate XAML Elements

```
<!DOCTYPE html PUBLIC "-//W3C//DTD XHTML 1.0 Transitional//EN"
"http://www.w3.org/TR/xhtml1/DTD/xhtml1-transitional.dtd">
<html xmlns="http://www.w3.org/1999/xhtml" >
<head>
    <title>Hello Silverlight World</title>
    <script type="text/javascript" src="Silverlight.js"></script>
    <script type="text/javascript" src="Listing4-16.js"></script>
    <script type="text/javascript">
    <!--
    function onLoad(control, userContext, sender)
    {
        var control = document.getElementById("mySilverlightControl");
        var combo = document.getElementById("cboTextBlocks");

        // enumerate the children of the Canvas object.
        for (i = 0; i < control.content.root.children.count; i++)
        {
            combo.options[i] =
                new Option(
                    control.content.root.children.getItem(i).Name,
                    control.content.root.children.getItem(i).Name
                    );
        }

    }
    //-->
    </script>
</head>
<body>
    <div>
        <select id="cboTextBlocks"></select>
    </div>

    <div id="mySilverlightHostElement" />
    <script type="text/javascript">
    <!--
        var hostElement = document.getElementById("mySilverlightHostElement");
        createMySilverlightControl();
    //-->
    </script>
</body>
</html>
```

In this example, the XAML loaded during player initialization includes several `TextBlock` elements that are children of the root `Canvas` element. To enumerate through the children, a simple `for` loop is created that loops through all of the children of the Silverlight player's root element, in this case the `Canvas`. During each loop the `Text` of the `TextBlock` is added as a new option to the `<select>` element.

Examining Events in Silverlight

As with most modern development platforms, Silverlight includes a rich set of events that allow you to respond to changes in the player or elements of the player. Events are exposed by the Silverlight player and by individual XAML elements on the player's element tree. You can use these events to react to actions by the user, or other elements in the application.

Player Events

The Silverlight player exposes four events as described in the following table:

Event	Description
`onLoad`	Occurs after the XAML content has successfully loaded completely. Occurs after any specific XAML element's `Loaded` event, but before the page's JavaScript `onload` event. An `onLoad` handler cannot be attached once the player is initialized.
`onError`	Occurs when the Silverlight player encounters a general runtime error.
`onResize`	Occurs when the height or width of the Silverlight player plug-in changes. Will not occur if the player is in full screen mode, or in reaction to putting the player in full screen mode.
`onFullScreenChange`	Occurs whenever the `FullScreen` property of the Silverlight player changes.

As discussed earlier in the chapter, the `onLoad` and `onError` events can have handlers assigned by using the events' parameter of the `createObject` function. The function then assigns the supplied handlers appropriately. If no `onError` handler is provided, the `createObject` function assigns the default handler to the event.

```
Silverlight.createObject(
    "HelloWorld.xaml",
    hostElement,
    "mySilverlightControl",
    {
        width:'300',
        height:'300',
        background:'#D6D6D6',
        version:'1.0'
    },
```

```
        {
            onError:onError,
            onLoad:onLoad
        },
        null);
```

The `onError` event includes a special `errorEventArgs` parameter, which allows you to access information about the specific error that occurred. This parameter will provide you with one of three object types depending on the specific type of error: a generic `ErrorEventArgs` object, a `ParserErrorEventArgs` object if the XAML parser encountered an error, or a `RuntimeErrorEventArgs` object if the Silverlight runtime encountered an error. These objects, combined with the sender argument that indicates specifically which element raised the error event, allow you to create rich error handling routines for your application. Listing 4-19 demonstrates using the `errorEventArgs` to display a rich error information dialog.

Listing 4-19: Processing Silverlight Player Errors

```
function onError(object, errorArgs)
{
    var errMessage;

    switch (errorArgs.errorType)
    {
        case "ParserError" :
            errMessage =
                "A Silverlight parsing error occured in the file '" +
                errorArgs.xamlFile + "' at Line " + errorArgs.lineNumber +
                ", Character " + errorArgs.charPosition +
                ".\r\n\r\nError Element:" + errorArgs.xmlElement +
                "\r\nError Attribute: " + errorArgs.xmlAttribute;
            break;
        case "RuntimeError" :
            errMessage =
                "A Silverlight runtime occured" +
                "' at Line " + errorArgs.lineNumber +
                ", Character " + errorArgs.charPosition +
                " in method '" + errorArgs.methodName + "'";
            break;
        default:
            errMessage =
                "A generic Silverlight application error occured:\r\n\r\n" +
                errorArgs.errorMessage +
                "\r\n\r\nError Type: " + errorArgs.errorType +
                "\r\nErrorCode: " + errorArgs.errorCode;
            break;
    }

    alert(errMessage);
}
```

The player also exposes two other events that can prove useful in your application. The `onResize` and `onFullScreenChange` events allow you to respond to changes in the player size. Generally this is useful should you want to change the size and position of elements in the player based on its overall size, or in the case of the `onFullScreenChange` event, dynamically change the interface to allow the user to enter or exit full screen mode.

Unlike the `onLoad` and `onError` events, you can assign handlers to the `onResize` and `onFullScreenChange` events after the player has been initialized. The event handlers are assigned using two properties on the player's `content` object, as shown in Listing 4-20.

Listing 4-20: Attaching the Silverlight Player's FullScreenChange and Resize Events

```
function onLoad(control, userContext, sender)
{
    var control = document.getElementById("mySilverlightControl");

    control.content.onFullScreenChange=Control_onFullScreenChange;
    control.content.onResize = Control_onResize;
}

function Control_onFullScreenChange(sender, eventArgs)
{
    alert("Full Screen mode is now set to '" + control.content.fullScreen + "'");
}

function Control_onResize(sender, eventArgs)
{
    var control = document.getElementById("mySilverlightControl");

    alert("The Silverlight player size has changed to:" +
            " Width: " + control.content.actualWidth +
            ", Height: " + control.content.actualHeight;
}
```

In this example, the `onFullScreenChange` and `onResize` event handlers are provided to the event properties in the player's `onLoad` event by simply providing the handler method name as the value of each property.

XAML Element Events

The XAML elements contained in the Silverlight player can also expose events that you can connect handlers to in order to add a great deal of interactivity to your applications. Events range from generic mouse and keyboard events to events raised from specific elements such as the `MediaElement`.

Element Event Handler Declaration

XAML element events handlers can be assigned in two different ways in Silverlight. The first and easiest way to define an event handler is to simply add the specific event attribute directly to the XAML element and specify the name of the handling function as its value. In Listing 4-21, the `MyCanvas` element has its `MouseEnter` and `MouseLeave` event handlers defined.

Listing 4-21: Example MyCanvas.xaml Content

```
<Canvas
    xmlns="http://schemas.microsoft.com/client/2007"
    xmlns:x="http://schemas.microsoft.com/winfx/2006/xaml"
    Width="150" Height="55" Canvas.Top="20" Canvas.Left="20"
    Background="White" x:Name="MyCanvas"
    MouseEnter="MyCanvas_onMouseEnter" MouseLeave="MyCanvas_onMouseLeave">

    <Rectangle x:Name="MyCanvas_Rectangle" Stroke="#FF000000" Width="150"
    Height="55" RadiusX="5.5" RadiusY="5.5" Fill="#FF8E8E8E" />
    <TextBlock x:Name="MyCanvas_TextBlock" Canvas.Left="40" Canvas.Top="19"
    Text="Simple Button" TextWrapping="Wrap" FontFamily="Segoe UI" FontSize="12"
    FontWeight="Normal"/>
</Canvas>
```

In JavaScript you then simply define the corresponding handler functions, as shown in Listing 4-22:

Listing 4-22: Creating Silverlight Event Handlers in JavaScript

```
function createMySilverlightControl()
{
    Silverlight.createObject(
        "xaml/MyCanvas.xaml",
        hostElement,
        "mySilverlightControl",
        {
            width:'300',
            height:'300',
            background:'#D6D6D6',
            version:'1.0'
        },
        {},
        null);
}

function MyCanvas_onMouseEnter(sender, mouseEventArgs)
{
    sender.FindName("MyCanvas_Rectangle").Fill="#FFFFFFFF";
}

function MyCanvas_onMouseLeave(sender, mouseEventArgs)
{
    sender.FindName("MyCanvas_Rectangle").Fill="#FF8E8E8E";
}
```

Running this example, you should now see that when your mouse enters the canvas area, the `Fill` color of the `Rectangle` XAML element is changed. Move your mouse outside of the canvas bounds, and the color changes back to its original value. Remember that JavaScript is a case-sensitive language, so you need to make sure that the event handler function you create in JavaScript is the same character casing as the one defined in your XAML.

Although this method of assigning method handlers is easy and quick, it does mean that the handler function is statically assigned. If you need your application to be a bit more dynamic in nature, you might consider the second method of handler assignment, the `addEventListener` function. This function is available on every XAML element reference and allows you to use JavaScript to dynamically add event listeners to elements in the player. Additionally, there is a corresponding `removeEventListener` function that allows you to remove the handler. Listing 4-23 demonstrates using the `addEventHandler` function to connect mouse event handlers to a `Canvas` element. Note that the event definitions should be removed from the XAML file if you are choosing to add the event handlers through JavaScript.

Listing 4-23: Attaching Event Handlers in JavaScript

```
function createMySilverlightControl()
{
    Silverlight.createObject(
        "xaml/MyCanvas.xaml",
        hostElement,
        "mySilverlightControl",
        {
            width:'300',
            height:'300',
            background:'#D6D6D6',
            version:'1.0'
        },
        {
            onLoad:onLoad
        },
        null);
}

function onLoad(sender, eventArgs, context)
{
    var canvas = sender.content.FindName('MyCanvas');

    var canvasenter = canvas.addEventListener("mouseenter","MyCanvas_onMouseEnter");
    var canvasleave = canvas.addEventListener("mouseleave","MyCanvas_onMouseLeave");
}

function MyCanvas_onMouseEnter(sender, mouseEventArgs)
{
    sender.FindName("MyCanvas_Rectangle").Fill="#FFFFFFFF";
}

function MyCanvas_onMouseLeave(sender, mouseEventArgs)
{
    sender.FindName("MyCanvas_Rectangle").Fill="#FF8E8E8E";
}
```

The `addEventHandler` function returns a reference to the event handler that you can later provide to the `removeEventHandler` function in order to remove the event listener.

Keyboard and Mouse Input

Silverlight allows a rich set of keyboard and mouse events to be raised by elements in the player. These events are useful for reacting to actions made by the end user of the application. The following table describes the available keyboard and mouse events.

Event	Description
`KeyDown`	Occurs when a key is pressed while the content has focus.
`KeyUp`	Occurs when a key is released while the content has focus.
`MouseEnter`	Occurs when the mouse enters the bounding area of an element.
`MouseLeave`	Occurs when the mouse leaves the bounding area of an element.
`MouseMove`	Occurs when the mouse moves within the bounding area of an element.
`MouseLeftButtonDown`	Occurs when the left mouse button is pressed within the element's bounding area.
`MouseLeftButtonUp`	Occurs when the left mouse button is released within the element's bounding area.

There are several important things to know about the keyboard events in Silverlight, and the next few sections discuss these.

Keyboard Event Notification

First, in order to receive keyboard events from the browser, the Silverlight player must be the focused object in the web page. Once it gets focus, it is still dependent on the browser to pass keyboard events to it. Because the browser is ultimately the first to learn of keyboard events, it may choose to handle the events itself and not pass them to the Silverlight player. For example, in Firefox the Ctrl+D keyboard combination triggers the command to add a Bookmark. Because the browser is handling the keyboard events in this case, the Silverlight player does not receive any notification of the events.

You can find a list of keyboard shortcuts for Firefox and Internet Explorer here: `http://www.mozilla.org/support/firefox/keyboard`.

Operating System Specific Keys

Second, the keyboard event arguments include two properties that can help you identify the specific key that raised the event.

- The `KeyEventArgs.Key` property returns a value from the Silverlight `Key` enumeration. This enumeration represents the available portable key codes in Silverlight. *Portable key codes* represent a subset of key codes that are common across platforms.

- The `KeyEventArgs.PlatformKeyCode` property returns the platform-specific key code. The *platform-specific key code* represents the key code value returned by the operating system currently executing the Silverlight application.

You can find out more information about platform-specific key codes by visiting the following web sites:

- **Windows Key Codes** — `http://msdn2.microsoft.com/en-us/library/ms645540`
- **Mac Key Codes** — `http://developer.apple.com/documentation/carbon/reference/keyboardlayoutservices/toc.html`

Remember that certain key codes are not portable. One example of this is the Scroll Lock key code, which is available only on the Windows platform. In this case, the `Key` property would return 255, the value for `Unknown`, and the `PlatformKeyCode` would return the key code 145.

Keyboard Events and Full Screen Mode

When the Silverlight player is put into full screen mode, all keyboard events are disabled, except those key strokes that would return the player to embedded mode. This is done primarily for security purposes to prevent end users from unintentionally entering sensitive information.

Implementing Keyboard Events

Now that you have reviewed some of the important issues around using the keyboard events in Silverlight, you can begin to look at how you can implement keyboard events in your application. As with other events, you can add event handlers by either defining the handlers directly in the XAML or by using the `addEventListener` function. One important difference between keyboard events and other events is that currently, Silverlight only allows keyboard events handlers to be attached to the root `Canvas` element in the XAML content. Listing 4-24 demonstrates attaching `KeyDown` and `KeyUp` event handlers to a `Canvas` element in XAML.

Listing 4-24: Attaching Keyboard Event Handlers in XAML

```
<Canvas
    xmlns="http://schemas.microsoft.com/client/2007"
    xmlns:x="http://schemas.microsoft.com/winfx/2006/xaml"
    KeyDown="MyCanvas_onKeyDown" KeyUp="MyCanvas_onKeyUp">

        <TextBlock x:Name="MyCanvas_TextBlock"  Canvas.Left="40" Canvas.Top="19"
            Text="Simple Button" TextWrapping="Wrap" FontFamily="Segoe UI"
            FontSize="12" FontWeight="Normal"/>

</Canvas>
```

Listing 4-25 demonstrates handling those events in JavaScript. In this case, the `KeyDown` handler checks to see if the key combination Shift+Y has been pressed, and if so, changes the `TextBlock`'s `Foreground` property. The `KeyUp` event handler simply returns the `Foreground` color to its original value.

Listing 4-25: Handling Keyboard Events in JavaScript

```
function createMySilverlightControl()
{
    Silverlight.createObject(
        "xaml/MyCanvasKeyUpDown.xaml",
        hostElement,
        "mySilverlightControl",
        {
            width:'300',
            height:'300',
            background:'#D6D6D6',
            version:'1.0'
        },
        {},
        null);
}

function MyCanvas_onKeyDown(sender, keyEventArgs)
{
    if ((keyEventArgs.shift) && (keyEventArgs.key==54)) {
        var textBlock = sender.GetHost().content.FindName("MyCanvas_TextBlock");
        textBlock.Foreground="White";
    }
}

function MyCanvas_onKeyUp(sender, keyEventArgs)
{
        var textBlock = sender.GetHost().content.FindName("MyCanvas_TextBlock");
        textBlock.Foreground="Black";
}
```

When adding keyboard events, the event handler parameters include the `keyEventArgs`. This special event arguments object includes information on what key was pressed (as previously discussed), as well as special properties for detecting the Shift and Ctrl keys. As shown in the previous example, having separate properties for Shift and Ctrl keys allows you to detect specific key combinations.

Handling Mouse Input

In addition to keyboard events, Silverlight provides five mouse events that you can add to your application. Adding mouse events to your application is similar to adding keyboard events; however unlike the keyboard events, mouse event handlers can be attached to any UI element in your XAML. As with the keyboard events, you have the choice of specifying the event handlers directly in the XAML or using Silverlight's `addEventListener` function. Listing 4-26 demonstrates the usage of the five mouse events in a simple XAML file.

Listing 4-26: Attaching Mouse Event Handlers in XAML

```
<Canvas Width="300" Height="300" x:Name="rootCanvas"
    xmlns="http://schemas.microsoft.com/client/2007"
```

Listing 4-26: *(continued)*

```
        xmlns:x="http://schemas.microsoft.com/winfx/2006/xaml" >

        <Rectangle Canvas.Left="10" Canvas.Top="10" Width="75"
            Height="75" Fill="Red" x:Name="MyRectangle1"
            MouseEnter="MyRectangle1_MouseEnter" MouseLeave="MyRectangle1_MouseLeave"/>

        <Rectangle Canvas.Left="95" Canvas.Top="10" Width="75" x:Name="MyRectangle2"
            Height="75" Fill="White" MouseMove="MyRectangle2_MouseMove" />

        <TextBlock Canvas.Left="95" Canvas.Top="40" Width="75" x:Name="MyTextBlock"
            FontSize="12" />

        <Rectangle Canvas.Left="180" Canvas.Top="10" Width="75"
            Height="75" Fill="Blue" x:Name="MyRectangle3"
            MouseLeftButtonDown="MyRectangle3_MouseLeftButtonDown"
            MouseLeftButtonUp="MyRectangle3_MouseLeftButtonUp"  />
    </Canvas>
```

In the JavaScript file, shown in Listing 4-27, corresponding event handler functions have been created. The `MouseEnter` and `MouseLeave` handlers simply change their associated `Rectangle` element's `Fill` property, the `MouseMove` handler updates the `TextBlock` text with the current mouse coordinates, and the `MouseLeftMouseButton` and `MouseLeftButtonUp` handlers change their associated `Rectangle`'s `Fill` property.

Listing 4-27: Handling Mouse Events in JavaScript

```
function MyRectangle1_MouseEnter(sender, mouseEventArgs)
{
    sender.Fill="Green";
}

function MyRectangle1_MouseLeave(sender, mouseEventArgs)
{
    sender.Fill="Red";
}

function MyRectangle2_MouseMove(sender, mouseEventArgs)
{
    sender.GetHost().content.FindName("MyTextBlock").Text=
        "X: " + mouseEventArgs.getPosition(null).x +
        ",Y: " + mouseEventArgs.getPosition(null).y;
}

function MyRectangle3_MouseLeftButtonDown(sender, mouseEventArgs)
{
    sender.Fill="Yellow";
}

function MyRectangle3_MouseLeftButtonUp(sender, mouseEventArgs)
{
    sender.Fill="Blue";
}
```

When you run the example, you can see that moving your mouse over the left rectangle causes its color to change, moving your mouse over the center causes the coordinate text to change, and left-clicking the right rectangle causes its color to change.

All five mouse events provide the same `mouseEventArgs` object as part of their event handler. The object allows you to determine what the current mouse position is, as well when the Ctrl or Shift keys are pressed.

The `MouseMove` event also includes a feature unique to itself called Event Bubbling. *Event Bubbling* simply means that events bubble from the lowest child in the element hierarchy up until they reach the root element. To illustrate this, consider the XAML in Listing 4-28.

Listing 4-28: MouseMove Event Bubbling XAML

```
<Canvas
  xmlns="http://schemas.microsoft.com/client/2007"
  xmlns:x="http://schemas.microsoft.com/winfx/2006/xaml"
  Width="640" Height="480"
  Background="OldLace"
  MouseMove="onCanvasMouseMove"
  Loaded="onLoaded">

  <Rectangle
    x:Name="RectA"
    MouseMove="onRectMouseMove"
    Width="100" Height="100" Fill="PowderBlue" />

  <Rectangle
    x:Name="RectB"
    MouseMove="onRectMouseMove"
    Width="100" Height="100" Fill="Gold"
    Canvas.Top="50" Canvas.Left="50" Opacity="0.5" />

  <TextBlock x:Name="statusTextBlock" Canvas.Top="180" />

</Canvas>
```

In this example, the `Rectangle`s are positioned as child elements to the `Canvas`. While each element has the `MouseMove` event defined, and the two `Rectangle` elements each use the same `MouseMove` event handler, the `Canvas` defines its own handler. The JavaScript in Listing 4-29 defines the event handler functions for the XAML.

Listing 4-29: Handling Bubbled MouseMove Events in JavaScript

```
var statusTextBlock;

function createMySilverlightControl()
{
    Silverlight.createObject(
        "xaml/EventBubbling.xaml",
```

Listing 4-29: *(continued)*

```
            hostElement,
            "mySilverlightControl",
            {
                width:'300',
                height:'300',
                background:'#D6D6D6',
                version:'1.0'
            },
            {},
            null);
    }

    function onLoaded(sender) {
        statusTextBlock = sender.findName("statusTextBlock");
    }

    function onCanvasMouseMove(sender, mouseEventArgs)
    {
        var msg = "x:y = " + mouseEventArgs.getPosition(null).x + ", " +
            mouseEventArgs.getPosition(null).y;
        //statusTextBlock.text = "Canvas: " + msg;
    }

    function onRectMouseMove(sender, mouseEventArgs)
    {
        var msg = " x:y = " + mouseEventArgs.getPosition(null).x + ", " +
            mouseEventArgs.getPosition(null).y;
        statusTextBlock.text = sender.name + msg;
    }
```

When you first run this example you will notice that as you move your mouse over each `Rectangle`, the text in the `TextBlock` changes letting you know which `Rectangle` is raising the `MouseMove` event. Because the `RectB` has a higher Z-Index than `RectA`, it is the element that raises the `MouseMove` event where the two elements overlap.

When you move your mouse out of the rectangles the `TextBlock` stops updating, but this is not because the event is not being raised. In fact if you uncomment the second line in the `Canvas` `MouseMove` event handler you will indeed see that the event is being raised. You will also notice that the `TextBlock` now only shows that the `Canvas` `MouseMove` event is being raised, but again this is not true. In reality all of the elements are raising their `MouseMove` events, but because the events bubble from the child elements (the `Rectangles`) to the parent (the `Canvas`), the `Canvas` always overwrites the `TextBlock` contents. You can see bubbling even more clearly by placing breakpoints in each function. The `Rectangle`'s `MouseMove` handler will break first, then the `Canvas`'s `MouseMove` handler.

Even in very complex element hierarchies with many nested elements, the `MouseMove` events would continue to bubble up the element hierarchy to the root element.

Mouse Capture

Silverlight includes another mouse input feature called Mouse Capture. *Mouse Capture* allows a single element to raise mouse events even after the mouse cursor has its borders, which can be very useful to implement drag-and-drop operations. Mouse Capture can be enabled on an element if the mouse is over the Silverlight player, if no other Silverlight object has captured the mouse, if no other non-Silverlight object has captured the mouse, and if the left mouse button is pressed.

To enable Mouse Capture on an element, you simply call the `captureMouse` function of the element:

```
function MyButton_onMouseLeftButtonDown(sender, eventArgs)
{
    sender.captureMouse();
}
```

The `captureMouse` function will return a Boolean value indicating whether or not the capture has been enabled. Once Mouse Capture has been enabled, all Silverlight mouse events will be redirected to that element. To end the Mouse Capture you can use the `releaseMouseCapture` function.

Listing 4-30 demonstrates using the Mouse Capture to implement a simple drag-and-drop operation in a Silverlight application. This sample uses a new XAML file, `DragAndDrop.xaml`.

Remember that you can download all the relevant code samples for the book from `www.wrox.com`.

Listing 4-30: Implementing Drag and Drop in Silverlight

```
var leftoffset;
var topoffset;

function createMySilverlightControl()
{
    Silverlight.createObject(
        "xaml/DragAndDrop.xaml",
        hostElement,
        "mySilverlightControl",
        {
            width:'300',
            height:'300',
            background:'#D6D6D6',
            version:'1.0'
        },
        {
            onLoad:onLoad
        },
        null);
}

function onLoad(sender, eventArgs, context)
{
    var canvas = sender.content.FindName('MyCanvas');

    canvas.addEventListener("mouseleftbuttondown","MyCanvas_onMouseLeftButtonDown");
    canvas.addEventListener("mouseleftbuttonup","MyCanvas_onMouseLeftButtonUp");
    canvas.addEventListener("mousemove","MyCanvas_onMouseMove");
```

Listing 4-30: *(continued)*

```
}

function MyCanvas_onMouseLeftButtonDown(sender, mouseEventArgs)
{
    leftoffset = mouseEventArgs.getPosition(null).x -
        sender.getValue("Canvas.Left");
        topoffset = sender.getValue("Canvas.Top") - mouseEventArgs.getPosition(null).y;

    sender.captureMouse();
}

function MyCanvas_onMouseLeftButtonUp(sender, mouseEventArgs)
{
    sender.releaseMouseCapture();
}

function MyCanvas_onMouseMove(sender, mouseEventArgs)
{
    if (sender.captureMouse())
    {
        sender.setValue("Canvas.Left", mouseEventArgs.getPosition(null).x-leftoffset);
        sender.setValue("Canvas.Top", mouseEventArgs.getPosition(null).y+topoffset);
    }
}
```

In this example, when the left mouse button is pressed on the canvas, the event handler calculates the offset between the left edge of the canvas and the current mouse position. The offset between the top edge of the canvas and the current mouse position is also calculated. These values will be used to reposition the canvas as the mouse moves across the player.

Once the offsets are calculated, the `CaptureMouse` function is called, enabling Mouse Capture on the canvas event. This means that all mouse events that occur in the Silverlight player will be redirected to the canvas. When the mouse is moved, the `MouseMove` event is raised, and the canvas is repositioned based on the new mouse coordinates and the offsets calculated in the `MouseLeftButtonDown` event handler.

Finally, once the drag is completed and the left mouse button is released, the `MouseLeftButtonUp` event is raised by the canvas, and the Mouse Capture is released.

Running the example, you will see that you can now click and drag the canvas around the player.

Accessing Storyboards Programmatically

Silverlight includes the capability to animate XAML objects by using Storyboards. Creating animations using Storyboards is discussed in depth in Chapters 2 and 3, but Silverlight also allows you to programmatically access Storyboards to run, pause, or stop them, which you will see in this section.

To demonstrate how you can control Storyboard animations in Silverlight using JavaScript, you can use the XAML code in Listing 4-31.

Listing 4-31: A Sample XAML Storyboard Animation

```
<Canvas
    xmlns="http://schemas.microsoft.vcom/client/2007"
    xmlns:x="http://schemas.microsoft.com/winfx/2006/xaml"
    Width="640" Height="480" x:Name="MyCanvas">

    <Canvas.Resources>
        <Storyboard x:Name="MoveRectangleResource">
            <DoubleAnimationUsingKeyFrames BeginTime="00:00:00"
                Storyboard.TargetName="rectangle" Storyboard.TargetProperty="
                (UIElement.RenderTransform).
                (TransformGroup.Children)[3].
                (TranslateTransform.X)">
                <SplineDoubleKeyFrame KeyTime="00:00:00" Value="0"/>
                <SplineDoubleKeyFrame KeyTime="00:00:00.4000000" Value="101"/>
                <SplineDoubleKeyFrame KeyTime="00:00:00.8000000" Value="197"/>
            </DoubleAnimationUsingKeyFrames>
            <DoubleAnimationUsingKeyFrames BeginTime="00:00:00"
                Storyboard.TargetName="rectangle" Storyboard.TargetProperty="
                (UIElement.RenderTransform).
                (TransformGroup.Children)[3].
                (TranslateTransform.Y)">
                <SplineDoubleKeyFrame KeyTime="00:00:00" Value="0"/>
                <SplineDoubleKeyFrame KeyTime="00:00:00.4000000" Value="-40"/>
                <SplineDoubleKeyFrame KeyTime="00:00:00.8000000" Value="172"/>
            </DoubleAnimationUsingKeyFrames>
            <DoubleAnimationUsingKeyFrames BeginTime="00:00:00"
                Storyboard.TargetName="rectangle" Storyboard.TargetProperty="
                (UIElement.RenderTransform).
                (TransformGroup.Children)[2].
                (RotateTransform.Angle)">
                <SplineDoubleKeyFrame KeyTime="00:00:00" Value="0"/>
                <SplineDoubleKeyFrame KeyTime="00:00:00.4000000" Value="64.387"/>
                <SplineDoubleKeyFrame KeyTime="00:00:00.8000000" Value="167.698"/>
            </DoubleAnimationUsingKeyFrames>
        </Storyboard>
    </Canvas.Resources>

    <Rectangle RenderTransformOrigin="0.5,0.5" x:Name="rectangle"
               Width="192" Height="100" Fill="#FFFF9595"
               Stroke="#FF000000" Canvas.Left="58" Canvas.Top="105">
        <Rectangle.RenderTransform>
            <TransformGroup>
                <ScaleTransform ScaleX="1" ScaleY="1"/>
                <SkewTransform AngleX="0" AngleY="0"/>
                <RotateTransform Angle="0"/>
                <TranslateTransform X="0" Y="0"/>
            </TransformGroup>
        </Rectangle.RenderTransform>
    </Rectangle>
```

Listing 4-31: *(continued)*

```
    <Rectangle x:Name="begin"
    MouseLeftButtonUp="begin_onMouseLeftButtonUp" Fill="Blue"
               Height="23" Width="75" Canvas.Top="10" Canvas.Left="10" />
    <Rectangle x:Name="pause"
    MouseLeftButtonUp="pause_onMouseLeftButtonUp" Fill="Blue"
               Height="23" Width="75"  Canvas.Top="10" Canvas.Left="95" />
    <Rectangle x:Name="stop"
    MouseLeftButtonUp="stop_onMouseLeftButtonUp" Fill="Blue"
               Height="23" Width="75"  Canvas.Top="10" Canvas.Left="180" />
    <Rectangle x:Name="resume"
    MouseLeftButtonUp="resume_onMouseLeftButtonUp" Fill="Blue"
               Height="23" Width="75"  Canvas.Top="10" Canvas.Left="265" />

    <TextBlock Text="Begin"  Height="23" Width="75"
Canvas.Top="10" Canvas.Left="10" />
    <TextBlock Text="Pause"  Height="23" Width="75"
Canvas.Top="10" Canvas.Left="95" />
    <TextBlock Text="Stop"  Height="23" Width="75"
Canvas.Top="10" Canvas.Left="180" />
    <TextBlock Text="Resume"  Height="23" Width="75"
Canvas.Top="10" Canvas.Left="265" />

</Canvas>
```

The XAML defines a basic Storyboard that animates the first rectangle's `TransformGroup`. It also includes a series of `Rectangle` and `TextBlock` elements that serve as the buttons in this example.

In order to control the Storyboard you need to call the appropriate functions on the element. The element exposes functions that allow you to begin, pause, resume, and stop the animation. To control the animation in the previous listing, the JavaScript connects the `MouseLeftButtonUp` event to each rectangle "button" in the example. In each event handler, a different animation control function is called. Listing 4-32 shows the JavaScript.

Listing 4-32: Controlling Storyboards Using Mouse Events

```
function createMySilverlightControl()
{
    Silverlight.createObject(
        "xaml/Storyboards.xaml",
        hostElement,
        "mySilverlightControl",
        {
            width:'640',
            height:'480',
            background:'#D6D6D6',
            version:'1.0'
        },
        {
        },
        null);
```

(Continued)

Listing 4-32: *(continued)*

```
}

function begin_onMouseLeftButtonUp(sender, mouseEventArgs)
{
    sender.getHost().content.FindName('MoveRectangleResource').Begin();
}

function pause_onMouseLeftButtonUp(sender, mouseEventArgs)
{
    sender.getHost().content.FindName('MoveRectangleResource').Pause();
}

function stop_onMouseLeftButtonUp(sender, mouseEventArgs)
{
    sender.getHost().content.FindName('MoveRectangleResource').Stop();
}

function resume_onMouseLeftButtonUp(sender, mouseEventArgs)
{
    sender.getHost().content.FindName('MoveRectangleResource').Resume();
}
```

The Storyboard also exposes properties you can use to autoreverse the animation, control its begin time and duration, or change the Storyboard's repeat behavior.

Using the Downloader Object

Besides the player and element objects included with Silverlight, there is an additional object called the Downloader that can prove to be very useful in the disconnected web environment in which Silverlight lives. The Downloader allows you to initiate AJAX-style callbacks to the server to load additional XAML, image files, or any other resource that can be retrieved via an HTTP `GET` request and consumed by Silverlight. The object utilizes the existing `XMLHttpRequest` object exposed by modern web browsers, and because of this, requests are executed asynchronously.

To get started using the Downloader object you use the Silverlight player's `createObject` method. This method accepts an `objectType` parameter and returns an instantiated object of that type. In Silverlight 1.0 the only object available for creation is the Downloader object.

```
function onLoaded(sender) {
    var downloader = sender.GetHost().createObject("downloader");
}
```

Once the object has been created, you can use its properties and functions (which are similar to those available on the `XMLHttpRequest` object) to initiate requests and process the results.

First, the `Open` function allows you to define the HTTP action that will be used to retrieve the data from the server. In Silverlight 1.0 the only supported value is `GET`, which indicates the object should use the HTTP `GET` action. Its second parameter is the Universal Resource Identifier (URI) that you want to retrieve.

Due to the requirements for developing secure web-based applications, there are a number of restrictions on the value you can provide for the URI parameter:

- The URI value must be a relative URI because the Downloader object does not support downloading cross-domain content.
- You cannot explicitly define the protocol that should be used to retrieve the content. The downloader object will, however, detect if its host web page has been loaded using HTTPS and will attempt to retrieve the resource using the HTTPS protocol.
- The URI may not contain any backslashes (\), although forward slashes (/) are permitted.
- The FILE (`file://`) protocol is not supported by the Downloader object.

Once you have added the `Open` function, you simply need to call the `Send` function to execute the request.

Listing 4-33 demonstrates using the Downloader to asynchronously download an image from the server and assign it to an element in the XAML content.

Listing 4-33: Using the Downloader Object to Retrieve an Image

```
function onLoad(sender, eventArts, context)
{
    var downloader = sender.createObject("downloader");

    downloader.addEventListener("downloadprogresschanged",
    downloader_DownloadProgressChanged);
    downloader.addEventListener("completed",downloader_Completed);
    downloader.addEventListener("downloadfailed",downloader_DownloadFailed);


    downloader.open("GET","images/GreenSeaTurtle.jpg");
    downloader.send();
}

function downloader_DownloadProgressChanged(sender, eventArgs)
{
    var textBlock = sender.GetHost().content.FindName("myTextBlock");
    textBlock.Text = sender.downloadProgress.toString();
}

function downloader_Completed(sender, eventArgs)
{
    var textBlock = sender.GetHost().content.FindName("myTextBlock");
    textBlock.Text = "The download has completed.";
}

function downloader_DownloadFailed(sender, eventArgs)
{
    var textBlock = sender.GetHost().content.FindName("myTextBlock");
    textBlock.Text = "The download has failed.";

}
```

This example leverages three Downloader events that you can use to monitor the download progress: `DownloadProgressChanged`, `DownloadFailed`, and `Completed`.

- The `DownloadProgressChanged` event is raised by the Downloader object whenever the downloaded content increases by .05 percent or more. You can use this event to create download progress bars or to pause the execution of your application while the resource is downloading. The listing uses the event to update a `TextBlock` with the value of the `DownloadProgress` property.
- The `DownloadFailed` event is raised by the Downloader when the download completes but has not returned any content.
- The `Completed` event is raised when the download of the specified content has completed.

In both the `DownloadFailed` and `Completed` event, it is a good practice to verify the status of the download. In both cases, you would want to use the Downloader object's `Status` and `StatusText` properties to help verify that the download has succeeded or failed, and in the event of a failure, why it failed.

- The `Status` property will return the HTTP return code from the server once the request has completed. For a successful request, the `Status` will return code 200. A complete list of HTTP server codes is available at `http://msdn2.microsoft.com/en-us/library/aa384325.aspx`.
- The `StatusText` property returns a text description of the `Status` code. In the case of code 200, the `StatusText` property would return "OK."

Once you have verified that the download was completed successfully you will most likely want to access the resource that was just downloaded. The Downloader object provides a way to do this with the `ResponseText` property and the `GetResponseText` function.

The `ResponseText` property allows you to retrieve the raw text content of a request. This is useful if you have downloaded textual content such as text-based user data, additional JavaScript code, or perhaps an XAML snippet. Listing 4-34 demonstrates the use of the `ResponseText` property to retrieve some JavaScript code, which is then evaluated by the JavaScript `eval` function.

Listing 4-34: Using the Downloader Object's ResponseText Property

```
function onLoad(sender, eventArts, context)
{
    var downloader = sender.createObject("downloader");

    downloader.addEventListener("downloadprogresschanged",
    downloader_DownloadProgressChanged);
    downloader.addEventListener("completed",downloader_Completed);

    downloader.open("GET","Sample.js");
    downloader.send();
}

function downloader_DownloadProgressChanged(sender, eventArgs)
{
```

Listing 4-34: *(continued)*

```
        var textBlock = sender.GetHost().content.FindName("myTextBlock");
        textBlock.Text = sender.downloadProgress.toString();
    }

    function downloader_Completed(sender, eventArgs)
    {
        if (sender.status=200)
        {
            var response = sender.ResponseText;
            eval(response);
        }
    }
```

The GetResponseText function allows you to retrieve content that has been compiled as part of a ZIP package. To use the GetResponseText function you simply provide the part name you want to retrieve as the function parameter. Downloading and accessing content in ZIP packages is discussed in greater detail in the next section.

Downloading Packages

One interesting way to use the Silverlight Downloader object is to have the object download a single package of content that includes multiple text, image, and media resources. Creating content packages, which are simply ZIP files, can improve the performance of your application by allowing you to take advantage of the ZIP compression of data and allowing you to download multiple application resources as a single content source.

Silverlight provides several specialized methods for dealing with package content that allow you to specify the specific part (or filename) of the package that you want to access or assign as the source of an element.

Listing 4-35 demonstrates accessing content contained in a package. In this case the package is a single ZIP file that contains an XAML file, a JavaScript file, and an image.

Listing 4-35: Downloading Packages Using the Downloader Object

```
    function onLoad(sender, eventArts, context)
    {
        var downloader = sender.createObject("downloader");

        downloader.addEventListener("downloadprogresschanged",
        downloader_DownloadProgressChanged);
        downloader.addEventListener("completed",downloader_Completed);

        downloader.open("GET","PackagedContent.zip");
        downloader.send();
    }

    function downloader_DownloadProgressChanged(sender, eventArgs)
```

(Continued)

Listing 4-35: *(continued)*

```
{
    var textBlock = sender.GetHost().content.FindName("myTextBlock");
    textBlock.Text = sender.downloadProgress.toString();
}

function downloader_Completed(sender, eventArgs)
{
    if (sender.status=200)
    {
        var response = sender.GetResponseText("PackagedScript.js")
        eval(response);

        var xaml = sender.GetHost().content.createFromXamlDownloader(
            sender, "PackagedXaml.xaml");

        var image = xaml.FindName('MyImage');
        image.SetSource(sender,"GreenSeaTurtle.jpg");

        sender.GetHost().content.FindName('rootCanvas').children.add(xaml);

    }
}
```

The next few sections discuss what's going on in this listing.

Text Content

In this example, once the `Completed` event has been raised and the Downloader's status verified, the first item retrieved from the package is the JavaScript file. The file is accessed by using the `GetResponseText` function and passing the JavaScript filename into the function's part parameter:

```
var response = sender.GetResponseText("PackagedScript.js")
eval(response);
```

The result is a string that represents the contents of the JavaScript file, which is then passed to the standard JavaScript `eval` function for execution by the application.

XAML Content

Next the application retrieves the XAML file from the package. In this case, because the content is XAML, the application uses the `createFromXamlDownloader` function to retrieve the XAML. This handy function takes a part name to determine which asset of the package to retrieve and automatically attempts to parse the content into an XAML element hierarchy.

```
var xaml = sender.GetHost().content.createFromXamlDownloader(sender,
"PackagedXaml.xaml");
```

Using this function can offer some performance benefits over saving the content to a variable and using the `CreateFromXaml` function.

Image and Media Content

Finally, the application retrieves the image file from the package. In this case the application uses the `CreateFromXaml` function that was discussed earlier in the chapter to generate a new `Image` XAML element. Once the element has been created the application uses the image's `SetSource` function to assign the image file as its source.

```
var image = xaml.FindName('MyImage');
image.SetSource(sender,"GreenSeaTurtle.jpg");
```

The `SetSource` function requires that you provide it the Downloader object that references the package and the name of the part in the package you want to set as the element's source. The `SetSource` function is available on the `Image`, `MediaElement`, and `ImageBrush` XAML elements.

Once the `Image` has had its source assigned, the XAML snippet is added to the Silverlight player's existing content.

Downloading Fonts

Finally, another use for the Downloader object is to download fonts used by the application to the client. Because Silverlight allows you to create highly stylized interfaces for your applications, often you will use unique fonts to help define your interface. Unfortunately, you cannot depend on all of your end users having those specific fonts on their system, and Silverlight does not currently automatically embed font data into the application. Fortunately, you can use the Downloader object to solve this problem and simply download the specific fonts needed by your application to the client. Downloading fonts is done using the same techniques described earlier in the chapter, and they can be downloaded individually or as part of a package. Once the font has been downloaded, you can use the `textBlock`'s `setFontSource` to indicate to the `textBlock` what font it should apply.

Listing 4-36 demonstrates downloading a font and using the `setFontSource` with a `textBlock` element.

Listing 4-36: Downloading Fonts Using the Downloader Object

```
function onLoad(sender, eventArts, context)
{
    var downloader = sender.createObject("downloader");

    downloader.addEventListener("downloadprogresschanged",
    downloader_DownloadProgressChanged);
    downloader.addEventListener("completed",downloader_Completed);

    downloader.open("GET","BASKVILL.TTF");
    downloader.send();
}

function downloader_DownloadProgressChanged(sender, eventArgs)
{
    var textBlock = sender.GetHost().content.FindName("myTextBlock");
    textBlock.Text = sender.downloadProgress.toString();
```

(Continued)

Listing 4-36: *(continued)*

```
}

function downloader_Completed(sender, eventArgs)
{
    if (sender.status=200)
    {
        var textBlock = sender.GetHost().content.FindName('myTextBlock');
        textBlock.setFontSource(sender);
        textBlock.fontFamily = "Baskerville Old Face";
        textBlock.fontSize=24;
        textBlock.text = "Baskerville Old Face";

    }
}
```

Note that fonts applied using the `setFontSource` function must be TrueType or Open Type fonts and must end in the TTF file extension. Once the font has been set on the `textBlock`, you simply set the element's `fontFamily` property as shown in the previous example.

Using JavaScript and the MediaElement

Chapter 2 introduced you to using the `MediaElement` element to embed video and audio media into a Silverlight and discussed the various attributes available on the element you can use to control its look and feel and some of its behavior. But when writing real-world applications that use the `MediaElement`, you will want to give your users a more interactive experience, allowing them to control the media playing by starting, stopping, and pausing playback, or changing the current play position. Additionally, you will want your application to respond to the events raised by the element so that you can provide the application user with feedback, such as how much of the media has been downloaded, when its playback state changes, or even when embedded elements like markers have been reached.

To get started programming against the `MediaElement`, you can use the XAML shown in Listing 4-37.

Listing 4-37: Simple MediaElement XAML Content

```
<Canvas
    xmlns="http://schemas.microsoft.com/client/2007"
    xmlns:x="http://schemas.microsoft.com/winfx/2006/xaml"
    Width="640" Height="480" x:Name="rootCanvas">

    <MediaElement Source="water.wmv" x:Name="myMediaElement" />

</Canvas>
```

This simple XAML file includes a single `MediaElement` whose source is a small Windows media file. Once you have this implemented, you can begin to add some additional markup and JavaScript to allow your application users to control the player. Begin by adding some additional XAML to the canvas. The

XAML defines three new rectangles and three new `TextBlocks` that will serve as the `MediaElement`'s control buttons.

```
<Rectangle x:Name="play" Height="75" Width="75" Canvas.Left="10" />
<Rectangle x:Name="pause" Height="75" Width="75" Canvas.Left="95" />
<Rectangle x:Name="stop" Height="75" Width="75" Canvas.Left="180" />
```

Now that you have the buttons defined, you can use JavaScript to add event handlers in which you can place commands to control the `MediaElement`. Listing 4-38 demonstrates this JavaScript.

Listing 4-38: Controlling the MediaElement through JavaScript

```
function createMySilverlightControl()
{
    Silverlight.createObject(
        "xaml/MediaElements.xaml",
        hostElement,
        "mySilverlightControl",
        {
            width:'300',
            height:'300',
            background:'#D6D6D6',
            version:'1.0'
        },
        {
            onLoad:onLoad
        },
        null);
}

function onLoad(sender, eventArgs)
{
    sender.content.FindName('play').addEventListener(
        "mouseleftbuttonup",play_onMouseLeftButtonUp);
    sender.content.FindName('pause').addEventListener(
        "mouseleftbuttonup",pause_onMouseLeftButtonUp);
    sender.content.FindName('stop').addEventListener(
        "mouseleftbuttonup",stop_onMouseLeftButtonUp);
}

function play_onMouseLeftButtonUp(sender, mouseEventArgs)
{
    sender.getHost().FindName('myMediaElement').play();
}

function pause_onMouseLeftButtonUp(sender, mouseEventArgs)
{
    sender.getHost().FindName('myMediaElement').pause();
}

function stop_onMouseLeftButtonUp(sender, mouseEventArgs)
{
    sender.getHost().FindName('myMediaElement').stop();
}
```

In this example, a MouseLeftButtonUp event handler is attached to each rectangle. Each handler calls one of the basic MediaElement playback functions: Play, Pause, and Stop.

Using DownloadProgressChanged and BufferingProgressChanged Events

Although this basic functionality is nice, there are some drawbacks to this basic example. First, as was discussed in Chapter 2, the MediaElement uses progressive download and buffering to allow the video to begin playback before the complete media file has been downloaded, but the example provides no visual queue to the end users to inform them about the progressive download or buffering progress.

Thankfully, the MediaElement exposes the DownloadProgressChanged and BufferingProgressChanged events, which allow you to receive notifications from the MediaElement when the DownloadProgress or BufferingProgress values change. Listing 4-39 demonstrates using the DownloadProgressChanged and BufferingProgressChanged events to provide progress information to the end user.

Listing 4-39: Tracking the MediaElement's Buffer and Download Progress

```
function myMediaElement_onBufferingProgressChanged(sender, eventArgs)
{
    sender.getHost().content.FindName('BufferProgress').Text =
    "Buffer Progress: " +
        sender.bufferingProgress.toString();
}

function myMediaElement_onDownloadProgressChanged(sender, eventArgs)
{
    sender.getHost().content.FindName('DownloadProgress').Text =
    "Download Progress: " +
        sender.downloadProgress.toString();
}
```

This example uses the event handlers, which are being attached in the onLoad event, to push the download and buffering progress values into two TextBlocks in the application.

Once the media source has downloaded and buffered sufficiently (as dictated by the BufferTime property), the MediaElement attempts to validate and open the media. If the element was unable to locate the media source URI or determines that the media source is not a supported format, the MediaFailed event will be raised, allowing you to properly handle media failures.

If the MediaElement successfully validates and opens the media, it will read in the media headers and raise the MediaOpened event. Additionally, if the MediaPlayer's AutoPlay property is set to true, the element will begin to play the media.

In addition to signaling the start of media playback, the MediaOpened event signals the availability of metadata information about the media source. Information such as embedded media attributes and the natural duration of the media become available once the MediaOpened event is raised. The Natural

`Duration` property corresponds to the natural length of the media and is useful for including playback information in your user interface.

During all of these changes in the MediaPlayer, from downloading and buffering to executing the play, pause, and stop commands, the player keeps track of its current state and exposes it through its `CurrentState` property. You can use this property to add capabilities such as disabling the command buttons while the media is opening or closed, or even providing a simple status indicator to your end users. The element even makes it easy to detect changes in its state by raising the `CurrentStateChanged` event. The use of this event is shown here:

```
function myMediaElement_onCurrentStateChanged(sender, eventArgs)
{
    sender.getHost().content.FindName('CurrentState').Text = sender.CurrentState;
}
```

Working with Markers

Another very useful feature of the Silverlight `MediaElement` is its ability to detect and raise events in response to markers embedded in the media. Adding markers to your media using Expression Encoder was introduced in Chapter 2. The `MediaElement` exposes the embedded markers through its Markers collection. This collection is populated when the media is opened, so you have immediate access to all markers embedded in the media. Using the collection you can allow application users to jump to marker positions within the media.

In addition to the markers exposing the Markers collection, as the `MediaElement` plays the media, it will raise the `MarkerReached` event when it encounters a Marker embedded in the stream. You can use this event to alter you application's user interface based on the contents of the Marker. Listing 4-40 demonstrates the use of the `MarkerReached` event to change the value of a `TextBlock` in the application to the value of the marker.

Listing 4-40: Attaching and Reacting to the MarkerReached Event

```
function onLoad(sender, eventArgs)
{
    sender.content.FindName('play').addEventListener(
        "mouseleftbuttonup",play_onMouseLeftButtonUp);
    sender.content.FindName('pause').addEventListener(
        "mouseleftbuttonup",pause_onMouseLeftButtonUp);
    sender.content.FindName('stop').addEventListener(
        "mouseleftbuttonup",stop_onMouseLeftButtonUp);

    sender.content.FindName('myMediaElement').addEventListener(
        "markerreached",myMediaElement_onMarkerReached);

}

function play_onMouseLeftButtonUp(sender, mouseEventArgs)
{
    sender.getHost().content.FindName('myMediaElement').Play();
```

(Continued)

Listing 4-40: *(continued)*

```
}

function pause_onMouseLeftButtonUp(sender, mouseEventArgs)
{
    sender.getHost().content.FindName('myMediaElement').Pause();
}

function stop_onMouseLeftButtonUp(sender, mouseEventArgs)
{
    sender.getHost().content.FindName('myMediaElement').Stop();
}

function myMediaElement_onMarkerReached(sender, markerEventArgs)
{
    if (markerEventArts.Type=="")
    {
        sender.getHost().content.FindName('MarkerText').Text =
            markerEventArgs.Marker.Text;
    }
}
```

The `MarkerReached` event includes a special `markerEventArgs` object, which provides you with the specific `TimelineMarker` object that was reached in the media. Using this object you can access the marker details such as the marker `Type` (marker or script command), `Text`, and `Time`. In the previous example, the `MarkerReached` event handler verifies that the marker is a Windows media marker and then sets the `Text` of a `TextBlock` to the value of the marker's `Text`.

Summary

This chapter attempted to show you how powerful Silverlight 1.0 combined with JavaScript can be in allowing you to create rich, highly interactive web-based applications. This chapter began with a deep dive into adding the Silverlight player object to your web page using JavaScript and the `createObject` function. You examined all of the parameters available to you that help you define the initialization behavior of the Silverlight player, including XAML source, initialization properties, and initialization events. The `onLoad` and `onError` events were discussed, and the `errorEventArgs` object was dissected showing you how to easily add rich error handling support to your application.

Next, the mouse and keyboard events were reviewed. Examples showing you how you can add event handlers like the mouse and keyboard event handlers to your application using either XAML or JavaScript were shown. Additionally, the chapter showed how you can use the five mouse events to create complex and interactive applications using Silverlight. The Silverlight Downloader object was examined, showing you how you can asynchronously retrieve additional application resources from the server such as JavaScript files, XAML snippets, and media like images and videos.

Finally, the chapter reviewed some of the available options for dealing with Storyboard animations and the `MediaElement` XAML control through JavaScript, including starting and stopping the animation and media and reacting to `MediaElement` events.

5

Using Silverlight with ASP.NET

The nice thing for ASP.NET developers is that using Silverlight 1.0 with ASP.NET is a very familiar paradigm. Essentially, the only difference between using Silverlight with ASP.NET and normal ASP.NET development is that instead of using HTML for the presentation, you're going to use XAML. In some ways, chiefly for rich, animated, cross-browser UIs, this is a great benefit; in others, chiefly in receiving input, due to the limited objects available in Silverlight, it is certainly a restriction.

The key to creating a great Silverlight application in ASP.NET is in recognizing where it is better to use Silverlight (XAML) and where it is better to use ASP.NET (HTML). I've already alluded to a key guideline that can help you choose; namely, if you need textual data input, you're best off sticking with standard ASP.NET and, consequently, HTML input controls. The tricky part comes in choosing when both HTML and XAML would work, and of course, that will vary from project to project, but Table 5-1 contains some suggested guidelines.

Table 5-1: Silverlight-ASP.NET Scenario Analysis

Requirement/Scenario	Silverlight	ASP.NET
Rich or Deep Navigation/Menus	This is an area where Silverlight really shines. Users like interactive and responsive navigational tools, and because Silverlight provides reliable cross-platform interactive features via animations, transforms, and vector graphics, it is a great choice for all but the most basic navigation.	Using a blend of JavaScript and CSS, nowadays, you can create pretty rich navigational experiences, but even the best-written menu controls can have problems with varying browser support for CSS and JavaScript. In addition, even the richest DHTML menus pale next to a well-designed, Silverlight-based menu.

(Continued)

Table 5-1: *(continued)*

Requirement/Scenario	Silverlight	ASP.NET
Rich Textual Document Display	Because Silverlight 1.0 is very limited in terms of text support, it's not a good choice for this scenario. The `TextBlock` has very limited formatting capabilities compared with HTML and CSS. Further, most web assets are stored using HTML, so some transformation would have to take place.	ASP.NET, as a server-side technology, doesn't have a lot to offer in this scenario. However, it is built on HTML and CSS, so it more naturally supports rich textual document display for the web. Most CMS systems are using HTML and CSS, including SharePoint, so ASP.NET is the way to go for this scenario until Silverlight gets better text support.
Flexible Layout	Silverlight 1.0 (and 1.1 as of this writing) only has the `Canvas` element for layout, which is based on an absolute positioning scheme. Because of this, it is very limited in terms of layout, so most applications should not use Silverlight as the primary layout mechanism.	Because ASP.NET has been evolving with web standards for several years, it can take advantage of all of the layout mechanisms in HTML and CSS such as tables/grids, absolute positioning, and flow layout. There are few, if any, layouts that cannot be relatively easily achieved using these, so ASP.NET should remain the primary layout mechanism until Silverlight gets more layout options.
Textual Data Input	Silverlight has no native textual input mechanisms, so it isn't really an option for this scenario.	ASP.NET has all of the long-tested and used input mechanisms in HTML, so it is the choice for this scenario.
Rich Media	This is the single scenario where Silverlight 1.0 shines brightest (and the primary scenario targeted by its developers). With its support for MP3, WMV, and WMA, including HD and the great features for playback and bandwidth maximization, it is the choice for rich media.	In itself, ASP.NET has no support to speak of for rich media. Prior to Silverlight, your choices were mostly between using Windows Media Player, Flash, QuickTime, or Real Media. Flash seems to be the player of choice for broadest reach in web media, though each format/player has things to recommend it. Silverlight takes the promise of Flash's reach and greater quality and combines them, so it should be the choice for rich media going forward.

Table 5-1: *(continued)*

Requirement/Scenario	Silverlight	ASP.NET
Data Binding	Silverlight has no data binding mechanisms. Control developers could, with effort, emulate data binding, but in most scenarios, this would be more trouble than it is worth. Unless the data bound to is rich media, you're just asking for trouble.	This is one of ASP.NET's greatest features, and it is only getting better with the new LINQ support, dynamic language support, and scaffolding. For all but the most basic, rich media-oriented scenarios, ASP.NET is the choice hands down.
Rich Interactive Browsing	Because of its use of vector graphics, transforms, and animations, Silverlight is a great choice for applications that have minimal user input (for example, clicking around to browse) and the need to display media and visuals in a richer way than feasible in DHTML.	Thanks to modern browser support of CSS, JavaScript, and out-of-band callbacks, it is possible to create very rich applications using ASP.NET, but the complications involved in these make the costs for creating and maintaining such applications burdensome. It may be a better option to use Silverlight for this scenario.
Web-based Gaming	Silverlight, like Flash, provides a decent platform to create some kinds of games and other entertainment-oriented materials. This is basically extending the Rich Interactive Browsing scenario for the purposes of entertainment.	It is very difficult to create games using just DHTML, so Silverlight is a better option for this scenario.
Data Visualization	The key win Silverlight can provide for data visualization over other standard web options is the potential for greater interactivity and the communication of trending through animations.	Though there are data visualization controls that can reach a decent level of communication through the generation of static images and AJAX for interactivity, Silverlight has greater potential in this area, particularly when you get to the post-1.0 release that includes the client-side CLR.

As you reviewed the scenarios, you probably started to form a mental map of where Silverlight is strong and where it isn't. You probably derived that, generally speaking, ASP.NET should still be used as the primary web application development platform and that Silverlight should be used within ASP.NET applications where things like rich media and rich interactivity (such as in navigation) are needed. That's a good general way to think about using Silverlight with ASP.NET.

You may find that you can bend the rules as your expertise with Silverlight, XAML, and JavaScript increase because with effort you can emulate the areas where basic Silverlight tooling is weak. Whether or not you take that effort will depend on your situation, but it is safe to say that Silverlight 1.0 usage should be limited and targeted in web applications and be thought of as a compliment to ASP.NET, not a replacement. Whether or not this remains true for Silverlight 1.1 and beyond is yet to be seen, but it does have the potential to eventually become the next web platform.

For now, though, we remain grounded in today's realities, and the rest of this chapter discusses in more depth how you can use Silverlight together with ASP.NET:

- First, we look at creating custom ASP.NET controls for Silverlight.
- Then we look at how ASP.NET AJAX and Silverlight work together.
- Finally, we discuss how you can apply this knowledge to create dynamic user interfaces.

Creating Custom Controls

In this section, we cover the ins and outs of creating custom ASP.NET controls for Silverlight. It's important to note that a custom control, in terms of Silverlight 1.0, means an ASP.NET custom control. Of course, other server-side technologies can be used for the same purposes, but the context here is ASP.NET. As noted earlier, because Silverlight 1.0 is essentially an XAML interpreter/player, creating a custom control for Silverlight is much the same as creating a custom control for standard ASP.NET (using HTML).

A key difference is that because you likely won't be using a Silverlight control to collect input, you don't have to be concerned so much with view state and postback processing; however, you'll still want to use view state to persist any property changes across postbacks that do occur. But that's simple enough for anyone who has built an ASP.NET custom control before.

For an example, we're going to look at a basic Silverlight media player control. It's worth noting that the ASP.NET Futures to be released sometime after ASP.NET 3.5 includes such a control (the Media control) because it is indeed the most common scenario expected with Silverlight 1.0. ASP.NET Futures also includes a general Xaml control to simplify putting arbitrary XAML on your page. We're going to roughly mirror the approach of the Media control (ours will be simplified) as an example of how to build ASP.NET custom controls for Silverlight 1.0. Because at time of publishing Visual Studio 2008 is not yet released and because people will likely continue using Visual Studio 2005 for some time, we're going to use Visual Studio 2005 in our samples here.

Setting Up the Project

The first thing you'll do is create a new class library. You could simply stuff the code required for a custom control into your web site or web application project (WAP), but using a web site means you can't easily package it for use in other applications and using a WAP means you'd need to distribute the whole web application assembly just to share the control. So that's why we're starting with a class library.

1. In the File menu, choose New ➪ Project... as in Figure 5-1.

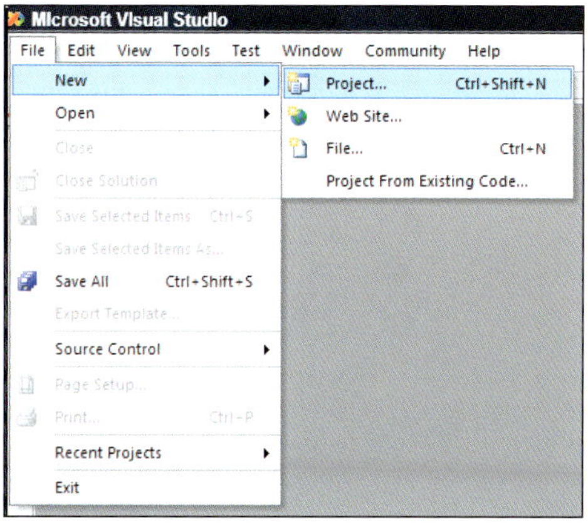

Figure 5-1

2. In the dialog that displays, choose Visual C# (or Visual Basic if you prefer) and select Class Library from the list of project templates. Give it whatever name you like; we're using `Wrox.Silverlight1_0.Controls` (Figure 5-2) because we could later build a 1.1 library. (So just using `Wrox.Silverlight.Controls` could cause naming collisions if we have the same controls for 1.1.)

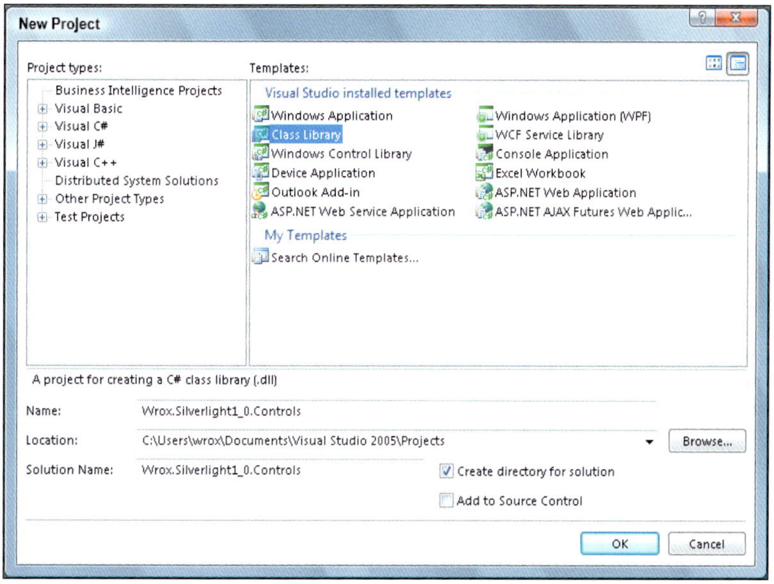

Figure 5-2

3. Now that you have a basic class library, delete the standard `Class1` file in the project, right-click the project in Solution Explorer (View ➪ Solution Explorer if you don't see it), and choose Add ➪ Add New Item... (Figure 5-3).

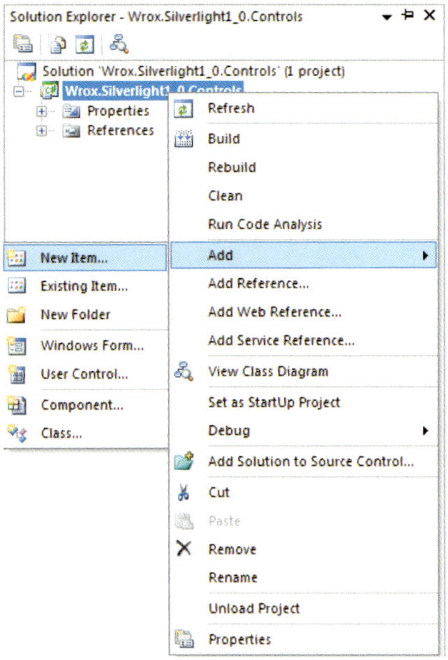

Figure 5-3

4. In the dialog that displays, choose Web Custom Control from the list of item templates and give it the name that you desire (Figure 5-4). Because we're doing a base XAML control, we'll call it Xaml. Then click Add. At this point, Visual Studio will create the new class in its own class file, add references to `System.Drawing` and `System.Web`, and open the new class file in the IDE.

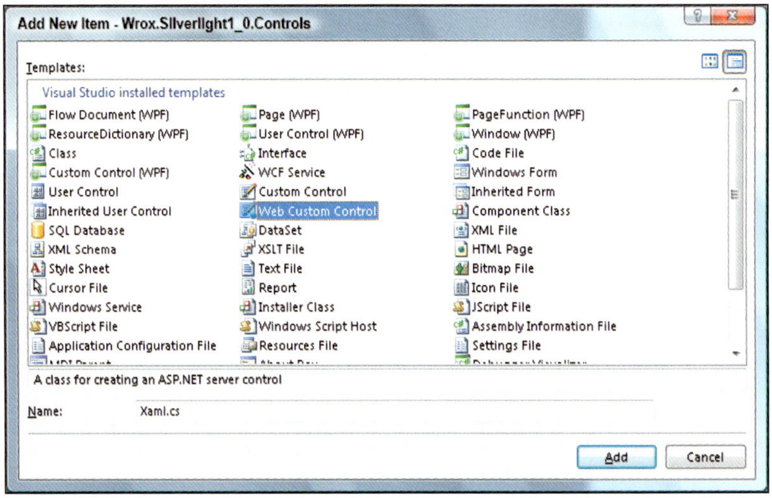

Figure 5-4

At this point, you'll have a basic custom ASP.NET control that looks like Listing 5-1.

Listing 5-1: New Xaml Web Custom Control

```
using System;
using System.Collections.Generic;
using System.ComponentModel;
using System.Text;
using System.Web;
using System.Web.UI;
using System.Web.UI.WebControls;

namespace Wrox.Silverlight1_0.Controls
{
    [DefaultProperty("Text")]
    [ToolboxData("<{0}:Xaml runat=server></{0}:Xaml>")]
    public class Xaml : WebControl
    {
        [Bindable(true)]
        [Category("Appearance")]
        [DefaultValue("")]
        [Localizable(true)]
        public string Text
        {
            get
            {
                String s = (String)ViewState["Text"];
                return ((s == null) ? String.Empty : s);
            }

            set
            {
                ViewState["Text"] = value;
            }
        }

        protected override void RenderContents(HtmlTextWriter output)
        {
            output.Write(Text);
        }
    }
}
```

The nice thing about using the Web Custom Control template is that it sets you up with the basics and gives you a simple example on implementation. Of course, as with any template, you're going to have to delete most of it, but it does give you a good idea of the basics of creating an ASP.NET custom control.

Okay, so now you have everything in place to start developing your Silverlight 1.0 control. There are a few things, as you've seen in previous chapters, that you need to get Silverlight onto a web page, and that's what we'll focus on first because once you get that in place, you can focus on what makes this particular control better.

We're going to bake these basic Silverlight control features first into a base Xaml control and then have our MediaPlayer derive from it (which is precisely what the ASP.NET Futures' approach is doing). Once the new Xaml control is released, the recommended approach would be to derive from it as the starting point for your custom controls. We'll try to mirror its public interface so that it is easy to switch when it is released.

Adding the Silverlight JavaScript Library

The next thing you're going to do is add the Silverlight JavaScript library. This will likely be found in any number of places on your hard drive if you've been doing any Silverlight development thus far. In Chapter 1, for example, if you created the project using the Silverlight template, you can grab the `Silverlight.js` file from that project. It's also in the SDK directory if you have that installed.

1. Wherever you get it from, what we suggest is creating a `Client` directory in your project (right-click the project and choose Add ➪ New Folder, giving it the name "Client"). Then right-click that folder and choose Add ➪ Existing Item... as in Figure 5-5. In the Add Existing Item dialog that comes up, you'll need to change the Files of Type drop-down list to All Files to find the JavaScript file.

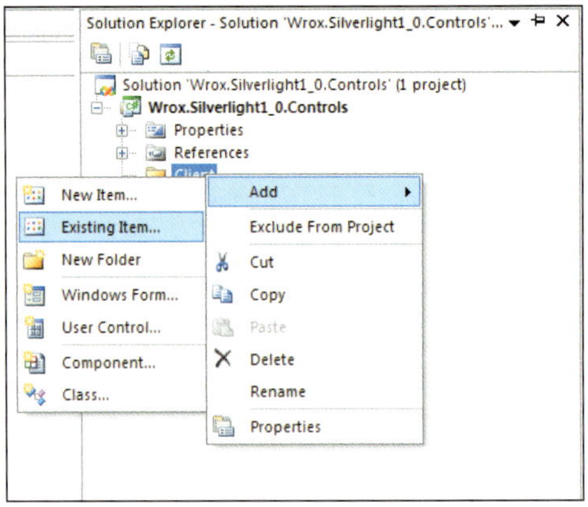

Figure 5-5

2. The next thing you need to do is mark the JavaScript file as embedded. You do this by right-clicking the `Silverlight.js` file and choosing Properties. This will bring up the Properties grid so that you can then select Embedded Resource from the Build Action drop-down list (see Figure 5-6).

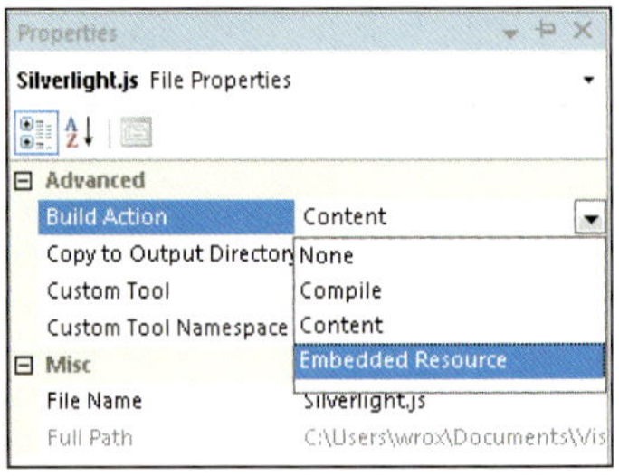

Figure 5-6

3. With ASP.NET 2.0, you can now use the nifty `WebResource` attribute to easily reference and retrieve embedded resources in ASP.NET assemblies, so the next step is to add this attribute. Because it is an assembly-level attribute, you can pretty much add it anywhere, but for this example stick it in `AssemblyInfo` because that's where most of them are already. So just open the `AssemblyInfo` file, as in Figure 5-7.

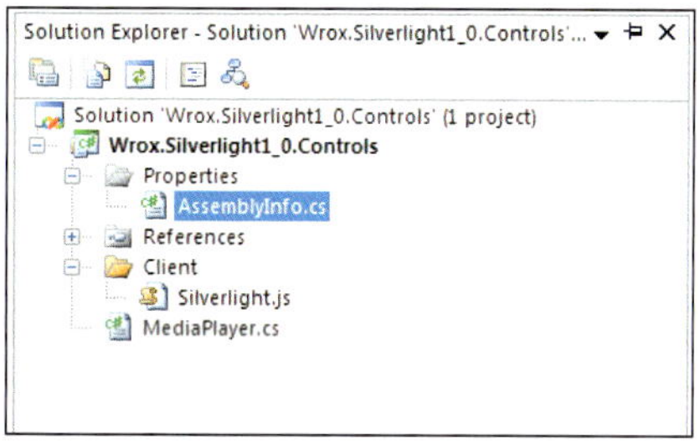

Figure 5-7

In `AssemblyInfo`, the first thing to do is add a `using` statement (Imports in VB) to make it easier to add more web resources later should you choose to:

```
using System.Web.UI;
```

Then at the bottom of the file, add the following:

```
// Client Resources
[assembly: WebResource("Wrox.Silverlight1_0.Controls.Client.Silverlight.js",
  "application/x-javascript")]
```

The `WebResource` attribute takes the location of the embedded resource, which is the full namespace (including directories) plus the filename. Because the project namespace is `Wrox.Silverlight1_0.Controls` and you put the file in the `Client` folder, the full embedded resource namespace is `Wrox.Silverlight1_0.Controls.Client`, and you just add `.Silverlight.js` to that because it is the name of the file in the folder. The second parameter is the MIME content type. It's important to set this because ASP.NET will use this to tell browsers (via the content type header) what kind of content it is sending when this resource is requested.

4. The next step is more of a developer convenience, though it can certainly help in maintainability. You're going to add a static class that handles registering client-side resources with ASP.NET, so right-click the `Client` folder and choose Add ➪ New Item..., select the Class item template, and specify Resources as the class name, as in Figure 5-8. Click Add to finish.

The default Class item template declares the class without an accessibility modifier, so the first thing to do to the `Resources` class is add `public static` to make it public and static (Shared in VB):

```
public static class Resources
```

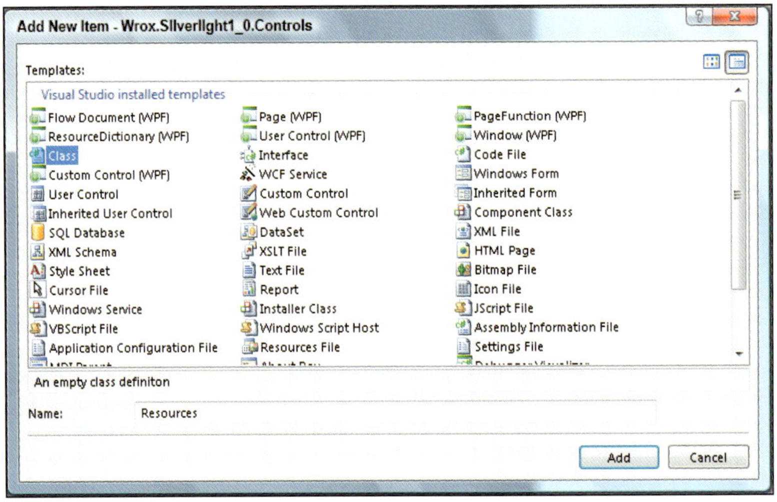

Figure 5-8

5. You'll probably also want to add an XML comment describing what the class is for, which you can do in Visual Studio by putting the cursor above the type or type member and typing a triple-slash (///); in VB it is a triple-tick ('''). Doing this will cause Visual Studio to expand out a snippet that has all of the XML comment stuff for that type or member. In this example the comment looks like this:

```
/// <summary>
/// This class centralizes client resource management.
/// </summary>
public static class Resources
```

You'll notice these throughout this implementation because for class libraries it is a best practice to include XML comments so that consumers of the library get your comments in IntelliSense, and they can also be used to generate API documentation using tools like NDoc, Visual Studio, and Sandcastle.

6. Next you'll add two nested static classes to group related constants. The first one is called `Keys`, and it will hold constants for all known embedded resource paths. Right now, you only have one, so it'll look like this (remember, this is nested inside of the `Resources` class):

```
#region Keys
/// <summary>
/// Groups known client resource keys.
/// </summary>
public static class Keys
{
    /// <summary>
    /// Silverlight library embedded resource.
    /// </summary>
    public const string SilverlightLibrary =
        "Wrox.Silverlight1_0.Controls.Client.Silverlight.js";
}
#endregion
```

Note the use of the #region ... #endregion. This is just for maintainability and readability. The only key you're defining thus far is the SilverlightLibrary key, and you see the path is the same one from earlier that you used to register your web resource using the WebResource attribute. You'll go back later and refactor that to use this constant, but while you're here, add constants for your content types:

```
#region Content Types
/// <summary>
/// Groups known/used MIME content types.
/// </summary>
public static class ContentTypes
{
    /// <summary>
    /// The Javascript MIME content type.
    /// </summary>
    public const string Javascript =
        "application/x-javascript";
}
#endregion
```

Following the YAGNI (You Ain't Gonna Need It) architectural principle, you're not going to try to exhaustively define every content type — just the ones you know you need. Right now, that's just JavaScript.

7. Now that you have both of these in place, you can go back and refactor the WebResource attribute to use these so that you are centralizing your use of literal strings. To do this, open the AssemblyInfo file again, add a using statement to the top, and replace the literals with the new constants:

```
using Wrox.Silverlight1_0.Controls.Client;
...
// Client Resources
[assembly: WebResource(Resources.Keys.SilverlightLibrary,
  Resources.ContentTypes.Javascript)]
```

There, now you have a nice, clean refactoring.

8. Now you need to add a convenience method. Well, you don't have to, but hey, convenience is nice, right? So back in the Resources class, add the following method (also, use/import the System.Web.UI namespace for the Page parameter):

```
#region RegisterClientScriptResource
/// <summary>
/// Registers the given client script resource with
/// the given page if not already registered.
/// </summary>
/// <param name="page">The page to register with.</param>
/// <param name="key">The client-script resource identifier.</param>
/// <remarks>The <i>key</i> should be the full embedded resource
path.</remarks>
public static void RegisterClientScriptResource(Page page, string key)
{
    if (!page.ClientScript.IsClientScriptIncludeRegistered(
    typeof(Resources), key))
    {
```

```
            page.ClientScript.RegisterClientScriptInclude(key,
                page.ClientScript.GetWebResourceUrl(typeof(Resources), key));
        }
    }
    #endregion
```

That will make registering your client script resources easier. All you have to do now to add new client script resources is to add them to the project, mark them as embedded, add a key, and add the `WebResource` attribute. Sure, it is a tiny bit more work now, but you'll see it helps later.

Adding Xaml Control Properties

Finally! We're back to our original goal, which is to create a custom Silverlight control. You now have the Silverlight library embedded. The next thing you're going to do is add some properties that will expose the functionality you're looking for in the Silverlight control.

First, delete the autogenerated `Text` property; you're not going to need that on this control, and you can go ahead and delete the `RenderContents` method as well — you'll add what you need to render later. The first and most important property to add is `XamlUrl`:

```
/// <summary>
/// Gets or sets the URL to the associated XAML.
/// </summary>
[DefaultValue("")]
[UrlProperty]
[Bindable(true)]
[Category("Appearance")]
[Description("The URL to the associated XAML.")]
public virtual string XamlUrl
{
    get
    {
        return ((this.ViewState["XamlUrl"] as string) ?? string.Empty);
    }
    set
    {
        this.ViewState["XamlUrl"] = value;
    }
}
```

First, you see the XML comment and then a few attributes that help usability in the designer. The `DefaultValue` attribute is used to determine if the current value is different from the default (and thus it'll show bold in the property grid). The `UrlProperty` attribute lets the designer know this property contains a URL string. The `Bindable` attribute specifies that the property is typically used in binding. The `Category` attribute is what the property grid uses to group control properties into categories, and the `Description` attribute is used to display a description in the property grid. The getter and setter implementations are standard custom control practices:

1. Use the `ViewState` state bag to store serializable control values that should be kept across postbacks.
2. When getting values from view state, if the value is null, return a non-null default.

All of your properties will follow these practices. Before moving on to those, you should update the `DefaultProperty` attribute on the class to `XamlUrl` and add an XML comment for the class:

```
/// <summary>
/// This class encapsulates the client-side Silverlight
/// object's properties and facilitates declaration.
/// </summary>
[DefaultProperty("XamlUrl")]
[ToolboxData("<{0}:Xaml runat=server></{0}:Xaml>")]
public class Xaml : WebControl
```

Listing 5-2 shows one-to-one mappings between the actual Silverlight object's properties and your control. You do this to make it easy to control the Silverlight object properties using your custom control. (Again, we're following the ASP.NET Futures public interface here to make it easy to port to it when it is released.) First, use/import System.Drawing for the `Color` property.

Listing 5-2: Xaml Control Properties

```
/// <summary>
/// Gets or sets whether or not the Silverlight
/// control functions in its own Window or as part
/// of the browser Window.
/// </summary>
/// <remarks>Use Windowless if you need to overlay
/// browser DOM objects on top of the Silverlight
/// control.</remarks>
[DefaultValue(false)]
[Category("Appearance")]
[Browsable(true)]
[Description("Whether or not the Silverlight control functions in its own Window or
as part of the browser window.")]
public virtual bool Windowless
{
    get
    {
        object o = this.ViewState["Windowless"];
        return (o != null) ? (bool)o : false;
    }
    set
    {
        this.ViewState["Windowless"] = value;
    }
}

/// <summary>
/// Gets or sets the background color of the
/// Silverlight control.
/// </summary>
[DefaultValue(typeof(Color), "")]
[Category("Appearance")]
[Browsable(true)]
[Description("The background color of the Silverlight control.")]
```

(Continued)

Listing 5-2: *(continued)*

```
public Color SilverlightBackColor
{
    get
    {
        object o = this.ViewState["SilverlightBackColor"];
        return o != null ? (Color)o : Color.Empty;
    }
    set
    {
        this.ViewState["SilverlightBackColor"] = value;
    }
}

/// <summary>
/// Gets or sets whether or not the Silverlight
/// control can get access to the HTML DOM.
/// </summary>
[DefaultValue(true)]
[Category("Behavior")]
[Browsable(true)]
[Description("Whether or not the Silverlight control can get access to the HTML
DOM.")]
public virtual bool EnableHtmlAccess
{
    get
    {
        object o = this.ViewState["EnableHtmlAccess"];
        return (o != null) ? (bool)o : true;
    }
    set
    {
        this.ViewState["EnableHtmlAccess"] = value;
    }
}

/// <summary>
/// Gets or sets the maximum number of frames
/// to render per second.
/// </summary>
/// <remarks>If not set, this uses the Silverlight
/// control's default.</remarks>
[DefaultValue(0)]
[Category("Behavior")]
[Browsable(true)]
[Description("The maximum number of frames to render per second.")]
public virtual int MaxFramerate
{
    get
    {
        object o = this.ViewState["MaxFramerate"];
        return o != null ? (int)o : 0;
    }
```

Listing 5-2: *(continued)*

```
        set
        {
            this.ViewState["MaxFramerate"] = value;
        }
    }

    /// <summary>
    /// Gets or sets the lowest version of Silverlight that is
    /// compatible with the specified XAML (and associated script).
    /// </summary>
    [DefaultValue("")]
    [Category("Behavior")]
    [Browsable(true)]
    [Description("The lowest version of Silverlight that is compatible with the
    specified XAML (and associated script).")]
    public virtual string MinimumSilverlightVersion
    {
        get
        {
            return ((this.ViewState["MinimumSilverlightVersion"] as string) ??
            string.Empty);
        }
        set
        {
            this.ViewState["MinimumSilverlightVersion"] = value;
        }
    }

    #region Client-Side Handlers
    /// <summary>
    /// Gets or sets the client-side Javascript handler for errors
    /// in the Silverlight control.
    /// </summary>
    [DefaultValue("")]
    [Bindable(true)]
    [Category("Behavior")]
    [Description("The client-side Javascript handler for errors in the Silverlight
    control.")]
    public virtual string OnClientXamlError
    {
        get
        {
            return ((this.ViewState["OnClientXamlError"] as string) ?? string.Empty);
        }
        set
        {
            this.ViewState["OnClientXamlError"] = value;
        }
    }

    /// <summary>
    /// Gets or sets the client-side Javascript handler for
```

(Continued)

Listing 5-2: *(continued)*

```
/// when the Silverlight control has loaded.
/// </summary>
[DefaultValue("")]
[Bindable(true)]
[Category("Behavior")]
[Description("The client-side Javascript handler for when the Silverlight control
has loaded.")]
public virtual string OnClientXamlLoaded
{
    get
    {
        return ((this.ViewState["OnClientXamlLoaded"] as string) ?? string.Empty);
    }
    set
    {
        this.ViewState["OnClientXamlLoaded"] = value;
    }
}
#endregion
```

That's the grunt work you have to do to empower consumers to control the Silverlight control declaration using your custom control properties. Now for the final step: adding an implementation to render the control declaration using the configured properties.

Rendering the Xaml Control

There are a number of approaches you could take to render what is needed to create a Silverlight control instance on the client. As of this writing, the ASP.NET Futures control renders the actual `object` or `embed` tag (depending on the browser's support for ActiveX). In this implementation, we're going to follow the generally recommended practice of using the JavaScript library's `createObjectEx` method. The end result should be the same, though in some browsers using the JavaScript approach is actually better because it will bypass the "Click to activate control" message.

The key trickiness in this approach is that the `createObjectEx` method wants an HTML element (via the `parentElement` parameter) that it uses as the "host" for the Silverlight object — it sets the parent element's `innerHTML` property to the generated Silverlight object HTML to instantiate the Silverlight control. Though you could likely rig things up where using `document.write` would work to write the HTML out as the page renders, doing so would likely require you to embed the Silverlight library script directly. This means the library wouldn't cache and also seems a bit hacky.

Rather than do that, go with the more familiar approach for those using the Silverlight `createOjbectEx` method, which is requiring the specification of a containing `DIV`. For this, you must add the `ParentElementID` property:

```
/// <summary>
/// Gets or sets the parent element client-side identifier.
/// </summary>
/// <remarks>If not set, this control will automatically render
/// a DIV where this control is in the page and set its ID to be
```

```
    /// this control's ClientID plus "_Host" to host the control.</remarks>
    [DefaultValue("")]
    [Category("Appearance")]
    [Description("The parent element client-side identifier.")]
    public virtual string ParentElementID
    {
        get
        {
            return ((this.ViewState["ParentElementID"] as string) ?? string.Empty);
        }
        set
        {
            this.ViewState["ParentElementID"] = value;
        }
    }
```

As you can see here, you can actually make it a tad easier so that you don't always have to specify a surrounding `DIV`. As the XML remarks say, if no `ParentElementID` is specified, the control will automatically render a host `DIV` (using the control's `ClientID` plus `"_Host"` as the `DIV`'s client ID). You'll see that implementation later in the overriding of the `Render` method. The thing to note here is that the end result of using this control versus the ASP.NET Futures version will be the same (if you don't specify the `ParentElementID`), that is, it will just work and render the control where you put it on the page. Most consumers have no need to manually specify the `ParentElementID`, but it is there should they want to.

The real workhorse of this control is the method that builds the script needed to create the Silverlight control using the `createObjectEx` method. We've named this method `GetDeclarationScript`, and it's shown in Listing 5-3.

Listing 5-3: Generating the Object Creation Script

```
    /// <summary>
    /// Gets a script block that will create a Silverlight control on the client
    /// based on the current properties of this control.
    /// </summary>
    /// <returns>A script block that will create a Silverlight control on the client
    /// based on the current properties of this control.</returns>
    /// <remarks>This will automatically be added to the start script
    /// blocks for the page in the pre-render phase.</remarks>
    public string GetDeclarationScript()
    {
        System.Text.StringBuilder sb = new StringBuilder();
        sb.AppendLine(@"<script type=""text/javascript"">");
        sb.AppendLine(@"Silverlight.createObjectEx({");
        sb.AppendLine(@"    source: '" +
            this.ResolveClientUrl(this.XamlUrl) + "',");
        sb.AppendLine(@"    parentElement: document.getElementById('" +
            (this.ParentElementID.Length > 0 ? this.ParentElementID : this.ClientID
                + "_Host") + "'),");
        sb.AppendLine(@"    id: '" + this.ClientID + "',");
        sb.AppendLine(@"    properties: {");
        if (this.Width.Value > 0)
            sb.AppendLine(@"        width: '" + this.Width.ToString() + "',");
```

(Continued)

Listing 53: *(continued)*

```
        if (this.Height.Value > 0)
            sb.AppendLine(@"        height: '" + this.Height.ToString() + "',");
        sb.AppendLine(@"        version: '" + this.MinimumSilverlightVersion + "',");
        if (this.SilverlightBackColor != Color.Empty)
            sb.AppendLine(@"        background: '" +
                ColorTranslator.ToHtml(this.SilverlightBackColor) + "',");
        sb.AppendLine(@"        isWindowless: '" +
            this.Windowless.ToString().ToLower() + "'");
        sb.AppendLine(@"    },");
        sb.AppendLine(@"    events: {"); // null on the events will use the script
        default
        sb.AppendLine(@"        onError: " + (this.OnClientXamlError.Length > 0 ?
            this.OnClientXamlError : "null") + ",");
        sb.AppendLine(@"        onLoad: " + (this.OnClientXamlLoaded.Length > 0 ?
            this.OnClientXamlLoaded : "null"));
        sb.AppendLine(@"    }");
        sb.AppendLine(@"});");
        sb.AppendLine(@"</script>");
        return sb.ToString();
    }
```

Without going through each line individually, you can see the ultimate goal is to build out a JavaScript block that calls the Silverlight library's `createObjectEx` method, passing in the parameters that map to the property settings on the control. Where possible, you defer to the Silverlight library defaults so that you minimize differences between using this server control and setting up the call to `createObjectEx` yourself as so many of the examples instruct you to do. As the XML remarks note, this will be called from the `OnPreRender` override, which you should add as follows:

```
    /// <summary>
    /// Sets up the client script registrations.
    /// </summary>
    /// <param name="e">Event args.</param>
    protected override void OnPreRender(EventArgs e)
    {
        base.OnPreRender(e);
        // ensure that the silverlight library is registered
        Client.Resources.RegisterClientScriptResource(
            this.Page, Client.Resources.Keys.SilverlightLibrary);
        // ensure that this instance's script is registered
        if (!this.Page.ClientScript.IsStartupScriptRegistered(
            typeof(Xaml), this.ClientID))
        {
            this.Page.ClientScript.RegisterStartupScript(
                typeof(Xaml), this.ClientID,
                this.GetDeclarationScript(), false);
        }
    }
```

Now you see where all that work you did in setting up the client `Resources` class comes in — you simply call `RegisterClientScriptResource` and give it the constant key you set up, and it ensures that the Silverlight library is registered on the page. This means that any other controls you develop can do the same thing, and it'll ensure the resource is registered only once.

The other thing you're doing here is adding the dynamically generated call to `createObjectEx` as a startup script block for the page. Note that you're doing the check to see if it already registered; this is on the off chance that something calls this method more than once — you only want to register it once.

Now, you're almost there. Due to the aforementioned trickiness, you also need to override `Render` to see if you need to render a host `DIV` for the control:

```
/// <summary>
/// Renders the control to the given writer.
/// </summary>
/// <param name="writer">Writer to render to.</param>
protected override void Render(HtmlTextWriter writer)
{
    // if no parent identifier is supplied, we create
    // our own host for the control that will render where
    // this control is in the server-side control hierarchy
    if (this.ParentElementID.Length == 0)
    {
        writer.AddAttribute(HtmlTextWriterAttribute.Id,
            this.ClientID + "_Host");
        writer.RenderBeginTag(HtmlTextWriterTag.Div);
        writer.RenderEndTag();
    }
}
```

As the comments note, if a `ParentElementID` is not set, you simply render an empty `DIV` with the client ID that you set up in `GetDeclarationScript`.

The last thing you do for completeness is override `CreateControlCollection` to return an empty collection just to prevent any goofiness with child controls being added to this control:

```
/// <summary>
/// Gets an <see cref="EmptyControlCollection"/>.
/// </summary>
/// <returns>An <see cref="EmptyControlCollection"/>.</returns>
protected override ControlCollection CreateControlCollection()
{
    return new EmptyControlCollection(this);
}
```

That's it! You now have a working Xaml control that you can use in your ASP.NET pages or user controls by simply adding a registration and using it like so:

```
<%@ Register TagPrefix="wroxAg" Namespace="Wrox.Silverlight1_0.Controls"
Assembly="Wrox.Silverlight1_0.Controls" %>
...
<wroxAg:Xaml runat="server" ID="MySilverlight" SilverlightBackColor="Aqua"
Width="100" Height="100" />
```

This is the most basic usage. Of course, for it to be useful at all, you'll need to create some XAML and point it at that XAML using the `XamlUrl` property.

Although the control is now usable to generically create a Silverlight control on a page, we want to go ahead and take it to the next step, because most of this was just laying the foundation for your custom controls that actually do something more than declare Silverlight. We explore this in the section entitled "Creating Dynamic User Interfaces with Silverlight and ASP.NET" later in the chapter. In the next section, we show how to incorporate AJAX into your custom controls.

Using ASP.NET AJAX with Silverlight

As has been mentioned elsewhere, ASP.NET AJAX is an extension to the ASP.NET 2.0 Framework; in fact, its proper name is ASP.NET 2.0 AJAX Extensions. The purpose of the server-side extensions is to make it easier to AJAX-enable existing controls as well as to empower developers to create new AJAX-enabled controls and pages. What you're going to do here is extend your own Xaml control to use ASP.NET AJAX and add some functionality that exemplifies how it can be used in conjunction with Silverlight.

Refactor into a ScriptControl

The first step to adding ASP.NET AJAX to your control is to add a reference to the `System.Web.Extensions` library, which is installed as part of the ASP.NET 2.0 AJAX Extensions that you can download from `ajax.asp.net`. Once installed, you simply right-click the project and choose Add Reference... as in Figure 5-9.

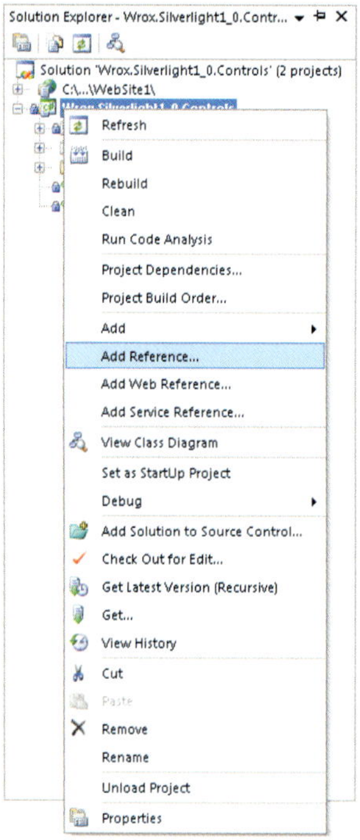

Figure 5-9

Be sure to select version 1.0.61025.0 (Figure 5-10). If you've installed Visual Studio 2008, ASP.NET Futures (May 2007 or later), or .NET Framework 3.5, you might see a version 2.0.0.0 (or later). Because this is not released as of this writing, we're going with the 1.0.61025.0 version. After .NET 3.5 is released, if you want to use it, you won't have to install ASP.NET 2.0 AJAX Extensions separately and can instead just use the 2.0 version of `System.Web.Extensions`. In either case, the code you write to use it won't change.

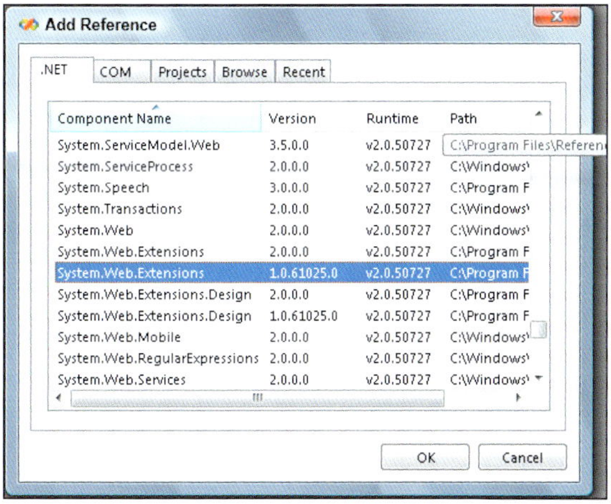

Figure 5-10

Now that you've referenced `System.Web.Extensions`, you simply have to refactor your base class on the Xaml control to be `ScriptControl` in the `System.Web.UI` namespace, instead of `WebControl`. This will add some core functionality (chiefly registering the control with the page's `ScriptManager`) as well as ensure there is a `ScriptManager`. You can also implement `IScriptControl`, if you don't want to use the built-in stuff for `WebControl` or have some other constraint that prevents you from changing your base class, but because in this example you're already deriving from `WebControl`, you may as well just change it to derive from `ScriptControl` and save a little trouble:

```
public class Xaml : ScriptControl
```

Because you're already using the `System.Web.UI` namespace, this is easy enough. `ScriptControl` has a couple of abstract methods on it that you can either manually implement or use the smart tag in Visual Studio to generate the method stubs. If you do the latter, you should now have the following added to your class:

```
protected override IEnumerable<ScriptDescriptor> GetScriptDescriptors()
{
    throw new Exception("The method or operation is not implemented.");
}

protected override IEnumerable<ScriptReference> GetScriptReferences()
{
    throw new Exception("The method or operation is not implemented.");
}
```

Adding Client-Oriented Properties

You need to implement these methods, but before doing so, you need to set up some other stuff that you'll use in them. In order to keep as close to the Xaml control and to provide a further foundation to deriving controls, you need to add a few more properties:

1. First, you add a `ClientType` property to enable inheritors to specify a client control type that provides some client-side functionality or information:

```
/// <summary>
/// Gets or sets the client/Javascript type for this control.
/// </summary>
public virtual string ClientType
{
    get
    {
        return ((string)this.ViewState["ClientType"]) ??
            (this.DefaultClientType ?? string.Empty);
    }
    set
    {
        this.ViewState["ClientType"] = value;
    }
}

/// <summary>
/// Gets the default client/Javascript type for this control.
/// </summary>
/// <remarks>Inheritors should typically override this to
/// provide a client type that relates to their server-side type.</remarks>
protected virtual string DefaultClientType
{
    get
    {
        return "Wrox.Silverlight1_0.Controls.Xaml";
    }
}
```

2. The next thing you want to do is empower developers to easily associate requisite scripts with the control, so to do this, you add a `Scripts` collection property:

```
ScriptReferenceCollection _scripts = null;
/// <summary>
/// Gets the collection of scripts associated with this instance.
/// </summary>
[PersistenceMode(PersistenceMode.InnerProperty)]
[Category("Behavior")]
public ScriptReferenceCollection Scripts
{
    get
    {
        if (this._scripts == null)
        {
            this._scripts = new ScriptReferenceCollection();
```

```
            }
            return this._scripts;
        }
    }
```

The `PersistenceMode` attribute lets you tell ASP.NET that consumers declare the property inside of the control tag. The usage of this property will be equivalent to the `Scripts` property of the `ScriptManager` and have much the same effect; it is just a nifty way to allow consumers to group scripts with the controls they're related to.

3. The last bit of refactoring you need to do is to go ahead and call `base.Render` because `ScriptControl` does some AJAX magic in that method, so here's the new `Render` method:

```
/// <summary>
/// Renders the control to the given writer.
/// </summary>
/// <param name="writer">Writer to render to.</param>
protected override void Render(HtmlTextWriter writer)
{
    // if no parent identifier is supplied, we create
    // our own host for the control that will render where
    // this control is in the server-side control hierarchy
    if (this.ParentElementID.Length == 0)
    {
        writer.AddAttribute(HtmlTextWriterAttribute.Id,
            this.ClientID + "_Host");
        writer.RenderBeginTag(HtmlTextWriterTag.Div);
        base.Render(writer);
        writer.RenderEndTag();
    }
    else
        base.Render(writer);
}
```

Because the container control will have its HTML programmatically replaced by the Silverlight library, it doesn't really matter what it renders. (It renders the default `<span>` tag for the curious.) The important thing is that the AJAX magic takes place. If you wanted to, you could override the `TagKey` property to control the tag that was rendered, but as we said, in this case, it doesn't matter.

Creating the Client-Side (JavaScript) Default Type

Next you need to add a JavaScript file that contains your default client type. You're not adding much in the way of client-side functionality with this control, so it's fairly simple. Right-click the `Client` folder and add new JavaScript file called `Xaml.debug.js`. Inside of that file, add the following script:

```
Type.registerNamespace('Wrox.Silverlight1_0.Controls');

Wrox.Silverlight1_0.Controls.Xaml = function
Wrox$Silverlight1_0$Controls$Xaml(domElement) {
    /// <param name="domElement" domElement="true"></param>
    var e = Function._validateParams(arguments, [
        {name: "domElement", domElement: true}
```

```
        ]);
        if (e) throw e;

        Wrox.Silverlight1_0.Controls.Xaml.initializeBase(this, [domElement]);

    }

    Wrox.Silverlight1_0.Controls.Xaml.registerClass("Wrox.Silverlight1_0.Controls.Xaml"
    , Sys.UI.Control);
```

Right now, you're not doing anything besides simply registering the client-side type as a `Sys.UI.Control`. This is a big departure from the Xaml control being baked into the ASP.NET framework. It wraps a lot of the Silverlight control functionality and adds some new features, like the `toggleFullScreen` method that takes care of switching to full screen mode through the Silverlight control's `FullScreen` property.

It's actually quite involved, and, given that a lot of it is simply wrapping the Silverlight control functionality, we're not going to focus on replicating all of that in our Xaml control because that's not the point here. Rather, we'll just have you add a couple of properties that correspond to properties on the server-side control to make them easily available on the client for the purposes of illustration. The two you'll add are `MinimumSilverlightVersion` and `ParentElementID`.

To do this, you first need to add the properties in the JavaScript as follows in Listing 5-4. Remember that because JavaScript doesn't have a concept of properties per se, what you actually end up using is a getter and setter method. Those familiar with Java, MSIL, and other languages that don't have properties will find this familiar. The convention for JavaScript is `get_<property name>` and `set_<property name>`.

Listing 5-4: Xaml Client-Side Control Properties

```
function Wrox$Silverlight1_0$Controls$Xaml$get_minimumSilverlightVersion() {
    /// <value type="String"></value>
    if (arguments.length !== 0) throw Error.parameterCount();
    return this._minimumVersion || "";
}
function Wrox$Silverlight1_0$Controls$Xaml$set_minimumSilverlightVersion(value) {
    var e = Function._validateParams(arguments, [{name: "value", type: String}]);
    if (e) throw e;

    if (!value.match(/^\d+\.\d+$/)) {
        throw Error.argument("minimumSilverlightVersion", "Not a valid Silverlight
        version number.");
    }
    this._minimumVersion = value;
}
function Wrox$Silverlight1_0$Controls$Xaml$get_parentElementID() {
    /// <value type="String"></value>
    if (arguments.length !== 0) throw Error.parameterCount();
    return this._parentElementID || "";
}
```

Listing 5-4: *(continued)*

```
function Wrox$Silverlight1_0$Controls$Xaml$set_parentElementID(value) {
    var e = Function._validateParams(arguments, [{name: "value", type: String}]);
    if (e) throw e;
    this._parentElementID = value;
}
function Wrox$Silverlight1_0$Controls$Xaml$initialize() {
    Wrox.Silverlight1_0.Controls.Xaml.callBaseMethod(this, "initialize");
}
function Wrox$Silverlight1_0$Controls$Xaml$dispose() {
    this._disposed = true;
    Wrox.Silverlight1_0.Controls.Xaml.callBaseMethod(this, "dispose");
}

Wrox.Silverlight1_0.Controls.Xaml.prototype = {
    get_minimumSilverlightVersion:
    Wrox$Silverlight1_0$Controls$Xaml$get_minimumSilverlightVersion,
    set_minimumSilverlightVersion:
    Wrox$Silverlight1_0$Controls$Xaml$set_minimumSilverlightVersion,
    get_parentElementID: Wrox$Silverlight1_0$Controls$Xaml$get_parentElementID,
    set_parentElementID: Wrox$Silverlight1_0$Controls$Xaml$set_parentElementID,
    initialize: Wrox$Silverlight1_0$Controls$Xaml$initialize,
    dispose: Wrox$Silverlight1_0$Controls$Xaml$dispose
}
```

First, you declare six functions, using your control full name + method name (replacing dots with `$`) to declare the actual functionality of the methods themselves. These will never be called directly and just give you an easy way to optimize the script so that the method declarations are processed only once. Then you set up the JavaScript prototype for this object to be an object with your methods. Note that you add the `initialize` and `dispose` methods just to be a good object citizen. You don't have anything particularly heavy to dispose of, and you're relying on `Silverlight.js` to do the heavy lifting of initializing the Silverlight control itself.

The net result of all this is that your client-side type now has six methods that correspond to your two properties and the `initialize` and `dispose` methods:

- `get_minimumSilverlightVersion`
- `set_minimumSilverlightVersion`
- `get_parentElementID`
- `set_parentElementID`
- `initialize`
- `dispose`

> *If you don't understand all of the goo but want to, we suggest reading Wrox's* Professional JavaScript for Web Developers *by Nicholas C. Zakas and/or* Professional ASP.NET 2.0 AJAX *by Matt Gibbs and Dan Wahlin because such coverage is beyond the scope of this book, and we won't be covering it here.*

Embedding and Registering the New Client-Side Type

The next steps are similar to what you did to set up the `Silverlight.js` script:

1. Mark the script as an embedded resource.
2. Add a new resource key to the `Client.Resources.Keys` class:

```
/// <summary>
/// XAML default client type.
/// </summary>
public const string XamlControl =
    "Wrox.Silverlight1_0.Controls.Client.Xaml.debug.js";
```

3. Add a `WebResourceAttribute` to the `AssemblyInfo` file like so:

```
[assembly: WebResource(Resources.Keys.XamlControl,
Resources.ContentTypes.Javascript)]
```

But you may have noticed that the script filename is `<name>.debug.js`. This is to illustrate how you can substitute a debug version of a script that will have the original source (including good spacing, indentation, and comments) with an optimized one using one of the many free JavaScript cruncher/optimizers that, while optimizing JavaScript for smallest download, renders the script illegible. So what you'll want to do is also create a `<name>.js` (without the `debug`) as you did with the `debug` version and, on your key from the preceding Step 2, add a conditional compilation statement like so:

```
#if DEBUG
    public const string XamlControl =
        "Wrox.Silverlight1_0.Controls.Client.Xaml.debug.js";
#else
    public const string XamlControl =
        "Wrox.Silverlight1_0.Controls.Client.Xaml.js";
#endif
```

What this does, based upon build configuration, is decide which version of the script is registered as the `XamlControl` resource. If it's the debug configuration, the debug script is used to facilitate debugging. If it's release, the optimized version is used. In addition to these steps, you'll want to set up a batch file and/or build step to crunch the debug version into the release version. (In other words, you only maintain/update the debug version — the release should always just be an optimized/crunched copy of it.)

Implementing AJAX Extension Methods

You're now ready to proceed to the implementation of the two abstract methods on `ScriptControl`, `GetScriptDescriptors`, and `GetScriptReferences` on the server-side `Xaml` control. First, the implementation of `GetScriptDescriptors`:

```
/// <summary>
/// Gets the script descriptors for this control.
/// </summary>
/// <returns>The script descriptors for this control.</returns>
protected override IEnumerable<ScriptDescriptor> GetScriptDescriptors()
{
```

```
        ScriptControlDescriptor xaml =
            new ScriptControlDescriptor(this.ClientType, this.ClientID);
        AddDescriptorProp(xaml, "minimumSilverlightVersion",
        this.MinimumSilverlightVersion);
        AddDescriptorProp(xaml, "parentElementID", this.ParentElementID);
        yield return xaml;
    }

    void AddDescriptorProp(ScriptControlDescriptor desc, string name, string value)
    {
        if (!string.IsNullOrEmpty(value))
            desc.AddProperty(name, value);
    }
```

Because the return type is `IEnumerable`, you can use the nifty yield enumerator language feature of C# 2.0+. You could, alternatively, have returned an array or some other type that implements `IEnumerable<ScriptDescriptor>`, but this current way seems cleaner and easier to read. The first step is to create the `ScriptControlDescriptor`, which tells AJAX Extensions about your client-side control type. You use the `ClientType` property to supply the client type name, and the second parameter is the client-side ID of this control, which is used to associate the client-side JavaScript type with the rendered control.

To this, you add the two properties that you set up in your client-side type, `minimumSilverlightVersion` and `parentElementID`. Now you see it is important to follow the property name convention because AJAX Extensions assumes these and uses them to set the value you supply.

The `AddDescriptorProp` method does a couple of things for you. First, it cuts out repetitive code, and second, it slightly optimizes it because the properties themselves access the view state bag and do some null checking; therefore, you don't want to call your getters more than necessary. By passing the property values into the method, .NET makes a copy of the value returned from your getters so that further operations on the values can use the local method parameter copy rather than going through the property getter each time.

Next, you implement `GetScriptReferences`:

```
    /// <summary>
    /// Gets the script references for this control.
    /// </summary>
    /// <returns>The script references for this control.</returns>
    protected override IEnumerable<ScriptReference> GetScriptReferences()
    {
        if (this._scripts != null) // then return all supplied scripts
            foreach (ScriptReference r in this._scripts)
                yield return r;
        yield return new ScriptReference(
            this.Page.ClientScript.GetWebResourceUrl(typeof(Client.Resources),
            Client.Resources.Keys.SilverlightLibrary));
        yield return new ScriptReference(
            this.Page.ClientScript.GetWebResourceUrl(typeof(Client.Resources),
            Client.Resources.Keys.XamlControl));
    }
```

First, you check to see if you have any scripts that have been supplied by the control consumer; if so, you enumerate through those and yield each one as a result of your own enumerator. Then you return a reference to your Silverlight library, and finally, you return a reference to the new client-side Xaml control type script file.

Now you may be thinking, "Hey, didn't I already add a reference to the Silverlight library in `OnPreRender`?" If so, congrats for being so astute. You did, and you need to remove that line of code because you're letting the ASP.NET AJAX `ScriptManager` manage that reference for you now. This is the line to remove from `OnPreRender`:

```
// ensure that the silverlight library is registered
Client.Resources.RegisterClientScriptResource(
    this.Page, Client.Resources.Keys.SilverlightLibrary);
```

Now maybe your `RegisterClientScriptResource` method isn't so useful, but that's okay. If you want to use it in some other control that maybe isn't "AJAXified," you can still use it there.

That's all you have to do to refactor the Xaml control into an ASP.NET AJAX denizen. In the final section of this chapter, we'll take all this to the next level and actually create a derivative of the Xaml control, adding some AJAX functionality to create a dynamic Silverlight control.

Creating Dynamic Silverlight User Interfaces with ASP.NET

To wrap up this chapter we're going to illustrate how you can put a custom AJAX control to work for you with Silverlight to build a dynamic user interface. In order to do this, you'll build a simple command-oriented control that uses some animation and a callback. You can call it `ButtonBar`, because as the name implies, it will be a toolbar (bar) of buttons.

Creating the Button Template

The first step in your new custom control is to create an XAML button template. We used Expression Blend 2 Preview (you can use Expression Blend 2 when it releases) to create the initial button template because it is easiest to draw and visualize using that tool — at this point in time, it is the best option for designing Silverlight. The button template consists of three rectangles and a textbox, grouped inside of a canvas. As you know by now, you are very limited in Silverlight 1.0 in terms of controls, but with a little effort, you can emulate a button. Listing 5-5 contains the resulting button template XAML.

Listing 5-5: Button Template XAML

```
<Canvas xmlns="http://schemas.microsoft.com/client/2007"
    xmlns:x="http://schemas.microsoft.com/winfx/2006/xaml"
    x:Name="buttonTemplate_{id}"
    Width="202" Height="52"
    Canvas.Left="8" Canvas.Top="{buttonTop}">
  <Rectangle x:Name="dropShadow_{id}"
```

Listing 5-5: *(continued)*

```
            Fill="#80000000"
            Width="200" Height="50"
            RadiusX="15" RadiusY="15"
            Canvas.Left="2" Canvas.Top="2"/>
      <Rectangle x:Name="boundingBox_{id}"
           Width="200" Height="50"
           RadiusX="15" RadiusY="15">
        <Rectangle.Fill>
          <LinearGradientBrush StartPoint="0,0" EndPoint="0,1">
            <GradientStop Offset="0" Color="#FF510303"/>
            <GradientStop Offset="1" Color="#FFFE4242"/>
          </LinearGradientBrush>
        </Rectangle.Fill>
      </Rectangle>
      <Rectangle x:Name="lighting_{id}"
           Width="198" Height="48"
           RadiusX="14" RadiusY="14"
           Canvas.Left="1" Canvas.Top="1">
        <Rectangle.Fill>
          <LinearGradientBrush StartPoint="0,0" EndPoint="0,1">
            <GradientStop Offset="0" Color="#FFFFFFFF"/>
            <GradientStop Offset="1" Color="#00FFFFFF"/>
          </LinearGradientBrush>
        </Rectangle.Fill>
      </Rectangle>
      <TextBlock x:Name="buttonText_{id}"
             Width="149" Height="17"
             Canvas.Left="28" Canvas.Top="18"
             FontFamily="Verdana" FontWeight="Bold"
             TextWrapping="Wrap" />
    </Canvas>
```

We had to do a little manual massaging of the markup, but Expression helped us get 90 percent of the way there. The first rectangle (Silverlight does z-order where first to last corresponds to back to front, a.k.a., the painter's algorithm) is the drop shadow behind the button, the second is the main rectangle, and the third provides a top-down lighting effect to give the "gel" kind of feel. The `TextBlock` provides you with a simple way to put text onto the button. The end result of a button using this template is shown in Figure 5-11.

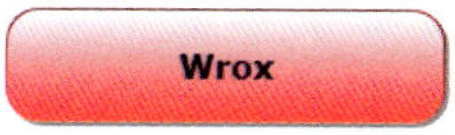

Figure 5-11

The other thing you may note in the XAML is the occasional `{something}`. These are arbitrary placeholders that will be used to customize the identifiers and provide the correct `Top` location so that the buttons do not overlap. Remember that in Silverlight 1.0, the only layout option is `Canvas`, which uses an absolute positioning scheme; so you have to manually lay out the buttons by specifying the `Top` position for each button. This `ButtonBar` will have only vertical layout for simplicity's sake. Similarly, we're constraining the width and height to a specific amount both for simplicity and consistency. Though the text block will wrap if the text is too long, you are advised to try to make it fit for aesthetic reasons.

Also, note that we put the two standard Silverlight/WPF namespaces on the root canvas; this is required, or at least the "x" namespace is required, in order to use the `x:Name` attribute on elements. Now, what you need to do is add a `ButtonTemplate.xaml` file to the `Client` directory in the controls project and just plop this XAML into it. If you try to view in a designer, it may not like the `{}` values, so you'll want to temporarily remove those to edit the template in a designer.

Once you add `ButtonTemplate.xaml`, you'll also want to follow the standard steps we set previously for embedding client resources:

1. Mark it embedded.
2. Add a key to the `Resources.Keys` class:

```
/// <summary>
/// XAML Button Template
/// </summary>
public const string ButtonTemplate =
    "Wrox.Silverlight1_0.Controls.Client.ButtonTemplate.xaml";
```

3. Add a `WebResource` attribute to `AssemblyInfo`:

```
[assembly: WebResource(Resources.Keys.ButtonTemplate,
Resources.ContentTypes.Xaml)]
```

4. You might note the new `Xaml` content type, which also needs to be added to the `Resources.ContentTypes` class:

```
/// <summary>
/// This XAML MIME content type.
/// </summary>
public const string Xaml =
    "text/xaml";
```

The next thing to do in preparation is to embed the XAML for the control's main/default scene. This one is super simple. You're merely creating a root canvas element with a few minimal properties that you can use to add buttons to later:

```
<Canvas
  xmlns="http://schemas.microsoft.com/client/2007"
  xmlns:x="http://schemas.microsoft.com/winfx/2006/xaml"
  Background="#00FFFFFF"
  x:Name="mainCanvas"
  >
</Canvas>
```

The only thing of note here is that you use transparent white as the background, so whatever you set as the Silverlight control background will be used (or maybe even the HTML page itself). We've embedded this as `ButtonBar.xaml` in the `Client` directory following the embedding scheme just outlined.

The last bit of XAML to do is to create some animations to add some interactivity to your control (that is, after all, the point of Silverlight, right?). This is easy to do (compared to doing something like this in, say, JavaScript). You're going to add a bit of springiness to your buttons. To do so, you just need two storyboards, one to expand out the button on hover and one to shrink it back down when leaving. Listing 5-6 shows the XAML for that.

Listing 5-6: Button Storyboard Template XAML

```
<Storyboard xmlns:x="http://schemas.microsoft.com/winfx/2006/xaml"
      x:Name="{name}">
  <DoubleAnimationUsingKeyFrames
       BeginTime="00:00:00"
       Storyboard.TargetName="dropShadow_{id}"
       Storyboard.TargetProperty="(FrameworkElement.Width)">
    <SplineDoubleKeyFrame KeyTime="00:00:00.1" Value="{commonWidth}"/>
  </DoubleAnimationUsingKeyFrames>
  <DoubleAnimationUsingKeyFrames
       BeginTime="00:00:00"
       Storyboard.TargetName="dropShadow_{id}"
       Storyboard.TargetProperty="(FrameworkElement.Height)">
    <SplineDoubleKeyFrame KeyTime="00:00:00.1" Value="{commonHeight}"/>
  </DoubleAnimationUsingKeyFrames>
  <DoubleAnimationUsingKeyFrames
       BeginTime="00:00:00"
       Storyboard.TargetName="boundingBox_{id}"
       Storyboard.TargetProperty="(FrameworkElement.Width)">
    <SplineDoubleKeyFrame KeyTime="00:00:00.1" Value="{commonWidth}"/>
  </DoubleAnimationUsingKeyFrames>
  <DoubleAnimationUsingKeyFrames
       BeginTime="00:00:00"
       Storyboard.TargetName="boundingBox_{id}"
       Storyboard.TargetProperty="(FrameworkElement.Height)">
    <SplineDoubleKeyFrame KeyTime="00:00:00.1" Value="{commonHeight}"/>
  </DoubleAnimationUsingKeyFrames>
  <DoubleAnimationUsingKeyFrames
       BeginTime="00:00:00"
       Storyboard.TargetName="lighting_{id}"
       Storyboard.TargetProperty="(FrameworkElement.Width)">
    <SplineDoubleKeyFrame KeyTime="00:00:00.1" Value="{lightingWidth}"/>
  </DoubleAnimationUsingKeyFrames>
  <DoubleAnimationUsingKeyFrames
       BeginTime="00:00:00"
       Storyboard.TargetName="lighting_{id}"
       Storyboard.TargetProperty="(FrameworkElement.Height)">
    <SplineDoubleKeyFrame KeyTime="00:00:00.1" Value="{lightingHeight}"/>
  </DoubleAnimationUsingKeyFrames>
  <DoubleAnimationUsingKeyFrames
       BeginTime="00:00:00"
       Storyboard.TargetName="buttonText_{id}"
       Storyboard.TargetProperty="(Canvas.Left)">
    <SplineDoubleKeyFrame KeyTime="00:00:00.1" Value="{textLeft}"/>
  </DoubleAnimationUsingKeyFrames>
```

(Continued)

Listing 5-6: *(continued)*

```
    <DoubleAnimationUsingKeyFrames
         BeginTime="00:00:00"
         Storyboard.TargetName="buttonText_{id}"
         Storyboard.TargetProperty="(Canvas.Top)">
      <SplineDoubleKeyFrame KeyTime="00:00:00.1" Value="{textTop}"/>
    </DoubleAnimationUsingKeyFrames>
  </Storyboard>
```

Note you're following the same approach as with the button template, using placeholders for values. There are a number of ways to dynamically generate XAML, and this is one of the easier ones, though obviously it may not be the most efficient. If you knew you'd need to create large numbers of items or needed more dynamism, you could, for example, load an XAML template into an XML document and modify node values using XPath. The issue there is you add more complexity and more code (and you have to know XPath).

Another approach is that of using ASP.NET and inline scripting to emit the XAML (much like ASP of yore). This is not the ideal solution. You'll end up with difficult-to-maintain spaghetti code just like you used to have in ASP.

Another option, which is probably the best if you've got any amount of complexity, is to use XSLT, but of course, there you have to know XSLT and XPath, and your data has to be in XML (or transformed to XML).

A final option we'll mention is using LINQ to XML, which will be released to market with .NET 3.5. The problem there is similar to the first solution, though using LINQ is a bit easier than working with the XML objects directly. VB's implementation in particular has nice support, but you end up having your code be somewhat spaghetti-like. Once we have a Silverlight-friendly version of XamlWriter, that might be the best option.

But we digress. Although it looks a tad verbose and intimidating, the preceding XAML is really quite simple. The first six animations are really three groups of two, one for each rectangle. For each one, you are going to increase the width and height to the specified value in one tenth of a second. You're using the `UsingKeyFrames` approach because that's what Blend does when you create a timeline animation. You could also use a plain `DoubleAnimation`. The last two animations are used to keep the text centered in the button as it expands and collapses.

Recall that the only layout option is absolute, which means you're responsible for simple things like centering. Welcome back to the good old days of typewriters, where you get to calculate the center for yourself! The last thing to note in this block is that this same set of animations will be used for both the expand and shrink animations. You'll see how all this gets put together soon.

Creating the ButtonBar Server-Side Code

Now you're ready to move on to the control itself. Thanks to your shiny new Xaml control, you can save yourself some time and just inherit from it. So following the steps for your Xaml control, add a

`ButtonBar.cs` using the Web Custom Control item template to the root of the project. Then delete most of the standard goo so that your class looks like so:

```
/// <summary>
/// Provides a vertical bar of buttons based on bound data.
/// </summary>
[ToolboxData("<{0}:ButtonBar runat=server></{0}:ButtonBar>")]
public sealed class ButtonBar : Xaml
{
}
```

We're sealing it (or marking it NotInheritable in VB) because we're not designing for extensibility here and sealing improves .NET runtime performance (by a tiny bit). More importantly, it communicates the intent of not extending this control. Designing for extensibility is surprisingly difficult, so only do it when you intend to.

The next step is to add some properties. First, override the `DefaultClientType` to be a new type you'll create for this control:

```
/// <summary>
/// Gets the default client/Javascript type for this control.
/// </summary>
protected override string DefaultClientType
{
    get
    {
        return "Wrox.Silverlight1_0.Controls.ButtonBar";
    }
}
```

In case you don't recall how this property is used, it is used in the ASP.NET AJAX control descriptor to tell the framework what the client type is. By overriding this, you can rely on the base class functionality to specify the type in the control descriptor, as you'll see later in the chapter.

```
/// <summary>
/// Gets or sets the button template source.
/// </summary>
/// <remarks>By default, this will use the embedded button template.</remarks>
[DefaultValue("")]
[Category("Appearance")]
[UrlProperty]
[Bindable(true)]
[Description("The button template source.")]
public string ButtonTemplateUrl
{
    get
    {
        return ((this.ViewState["ButtonTemplateUrl"] as string) ?? "");
    }
    set
    {
        this.ViewState["ButtonTemplateUrl"] = value;
    }
```

```
}

/// <summary>
/// Gets or sets the button storyboard template source.
/// </summary>
/// <remarks>By default, this will use the embedded button storyboard
template.</remarks>
[DefaultValue("")]
[Category("Appearance")]
[UrlProperty]
[Bindable(true)]
[Description("The button storyboard template source.")]
public string ButtonStoryBoardTemplateUrl
{
    get
    {
        return ((this.ViewState["ButtonStoryBoardTemplateUrl"] as string) ?? "");
    }
    set
    {
        this.ViewState["ButtonStoryBoardTemplateUrl"] = value;
    }
}
```

Both of these properties provide a level of customizability to your control. Although, by default, you use the templates you embedded in the previous section, users of the control can provide you with custom templates. This isn't the ideal way to provide XAML customization in a control, but it suffices and is relatively easy to understand and use with decent documentation.

```
/// <summary>
/// Gets or sets the client-side script method that supplies a
/// <see cref="MenuItemCollection"/>.
/// </summary>
/// <remarks>This is called from the client to build out the
/// list of items.  DataMethod signatures should include {callback}
/// which should be called with the results (an array of JavaScript
/// objects with properties matching those on the <see cref="MenuItem"/>
/// class) as the first parameter.</remarks>
[DefaultValue("")]
[Category("Behavior")]
[Bindable(true)]
[Description("The client-side script method that supplies a MenuItemCollection.")]
public string DataMethod
{
    get
    {
        return ((this.ViewState["DataMethod"] as string) ?? "");
    }
    set
    {
        this.ViewState["DataMethod"] = value;
    }
}
```

This method is interesting, maybe even odd, but we're using it to illustrate the collusion of ASP.NET AJAX and Silverlight. If you simply wanted to bind the data on the server, as with a standard ASP.NET control, you'd probably go with the more typical `DataSource` approach. Note the reference to the `MenuItemCollection` in the XML comment. What you're saying here is that you're expecting to be able to call the specified client-side method and have it return a collection (array in JavaScript) of `MenuItems`, which are defined as shown in Listing 5-7 in the `MenuItem.cs` class (which you should add to the root of the project with this code).

Listing 5-7: Menu Item and Collection Classes

```
using System;
using System.Collections.ObjectModel;

namespace Wrox.Silverlight1_0.Controls
{
    /// <summary>
    /// This class is used as a Data Transfer Object for menu items.
    /// </summary>
    [Serializable]
    public sealed class MenuItem
    {
        #region Constructors
        /// <summary>
        /// Creates an instance.
        /// </summary>
        public MenuItem() { }
        /// <summary>
        /// Creates an instance with the given values.
        /// </summary>
        /// <param name="text">Item text.</param>
        public MenuItem(string text) : this(text, null, null) { }
        /// <summary>
        /// Creates an instance with the given values.
        /// </summary>
        /// <param name="text">Item text.</param>
        /// <param name="navigateUrl">URL to navigate to for item.</param>
        public MenuItem(string text, string navigateUrl) : this(text, navigateUrl,
        null) { }
        /// <summary>
        /// Creates an instance with the given values.
        /// </summary>
        /// <param name="text">Item text.</param>
        /// <param name="navigateUrl">URL to navigate to for item.</param>
        /// <param name="onClick">A client-side click handler for item.</param>
        public MenuItem(string text, string navigateUrl, string onClick)
        {
            _Text = text;
            _NavigateUrl = navigateUrl;
            _OnClick = onClick;
        }
        #endregion

        #region Fields & Properties
```

(Continued)

Listing 5-7: *(continued)*

```
        string _NavigateUrl;
        /// <summary>
        /// Gets or sets the URL to navigate to when clicking.
        /// </summary>
        /// <remarks>If <see cref="OnClick"/> is set, this value is
        ignored.</remarks>
        public string NavigateUrl
        {
            get { return _NavigateUrl; }
            set { _NavigateUrl = value; }
        }

        string _OnClick;
        /// <summary>
        /// Gets or sets the name of a client-side event handler for the click
        event.
        /// </summary>
        /// <remarks>This overrides the <see cref="NavigateUrl"/>.</remarks>
        public string OnClick
        {
            get { return _OnClick; }
            set { _OnClick = value; }
        }

        string _Text;
        /// <summary>
        /// Gets or sets the text to display.
        /// </summary>
        public string Text
        {
            get { return _Text; }
            set { _Text = value; }
        }
        #endregion
    }

    /// <summary>
    /// A collection of menu items.
    /// </summary>
    public sealed class MenuItemCollection : Collection<MenuItem>
    { }
}
```

The server-side types are there to facilitate server-side code that wants to provide a set of menu items; on the client, as long as you supply an array of objects with the matching properties, that's all you need to do. We chose `MenuItem` as the type to be generic and to illustrate that you could use the approach we're taking here to build a full-fledged AJAX-based menu control (with hierarchy). Again, for simplicity, though, we're keeping it to a simple, one-level vertical list of buttons. You'll see how this is used when you get to the JavaScript.

The final property you want to add to the ButtonBar class is to override the XamlUrl:

```
/// <summary>
/// Gets the main scene XAML URL, which defaults to the embedded empty, transparent
canvas.
/// </summary>
public override string XamlUrl
{
    get
    {
        string s = base.XamlUrl;
        return s.Length == 0 ?
            this.Page.ClientScript.GetWebResourceUrl(
            typeof(Client.Resources), Client.Resources.Keys.ButtonBarXaml) : s;
    }
    set
    {
        base.XamlUrl = value;
    }
}
```

Although you still allow consumers of the control to supply their own main XAML scene, to which you'll add the buttons, the default is to use the embedded XAML from the previous section (the simple, transparent canvas).

Before you move on to wrap up the server-side ButtonBar class, you need to go ahead and add your client-side JavaScript resources for this control. As you did with Xaml, you'll add a ButtonBar.debug.js as well as a ButtonBar.js to the Client directory, embed them, add the key with the conditional compilation (for debug versus release), and add the WebResourceAttribute in the AssemblyInfo. In the ButtonBar.debug.js, to start with, you'll simply define your type:

```
Type.registerNamespace('Wrox.Silverlight1_0.Controls');

Wrox.Silverlight1_0.Controls.ButtonBar = function
Wrox$Silverlight1_0$Controls$ButtonBar(domElement) {
    /// <param name="domElement" domElement="true"></param>
    var e = Function._validateParams(arguments, [
        {name: "domElement", domElement: true}
    ]);
    if (e) throw e;

    this._host = domElement;

    Wrox.Silverlight1_0.Controls.ButtonBar.initializeBase(this, [domElement]);
}
Wrox.Silverlight1_0.Controls.ButtonBar.registerClass("Wrox.Silverlight1_0.Controls.
ButtonBar", Wrox.Silverlight1_0.Controls.Xaml);
```

To this, you can go ahead and add your "properties" (that is, getters and setters) for the new properties you defined:

```
function Wrox$Silverlight1_0$Controls$ButtonBar$get_buttonTemplateUrl() {
    /// <value type="String"></value>
```

```
        if (arguments.length !== 0) throw Error.parameterCount();
        return this._buttonTemplateUrl || "";
    }
    function Wrox$Silverlight1_0$Controls$ButtonBar$set_buttonTemplateUrl(value) {
        var e = Function._validateParams(arguments, [{name: "value", type: String}]);
        if (e) throw e;

        this._buttonTemplateUrl = value;
    }
    function Wrox$Silverlight1_0$Controls$ButtonBar$get_buttonStoryBoardTemplateUrl() {
        /// <value type="String"></value>
        if (arguments.length !== 0) throw Error.parameterCount();
        return this._buttonStoryBoardTemplateUrl || "";
    }
    function Wrox$Silverlight1_0$Controls$ButtonBar$set_
    buttonStoryBoardTemplateUrl(value) {
        var e = Function._validateParams(arguments, [{name: "value", type: String}]);
        if (e) throw e;

        this._buttonStoryBoardTemplateUrl = value;
    }
    function Wrox$Silverlight1_0$Controls$ButtonBar$get_dataMethod() {
        /// <value type="String"></value>
        if (arguments.length !== 0) throw Error.parameterCount();
        return this._dataMethod || "";
    }
    function Wrox$Silverlight1_0$Controls$ButtonBar$set_dataMethod(value) {
        var e = Function._validateParams(arguments, [{name: "value", type: String}]);
        if (e) throw e;

        this._dataMethod = value;
    }
```

Now you can go ahead and wrap up your server-side code. First, you override the `GetScriptReferences` method to add your new `ButtonBar` client-side type script:

```
    /// <summary>
    /// Gets the script references for this control.
    /// </summary>
    /// <returns>The script references for this control.</returns>
    protected override IEnumerable<ScriptReference> GetScriptReferences()
    {
        List<ScriptReference> refs = new
        List<ScriptReference>(base.GetScriptReferences());
        refs.Add(new ScriptReference(
            this.Page.ClientScript.GetWebResourceUrl(typeof(Client.Resources),
            Client.Resources.Keys.ButtonBarControl)));
        return refs;
    }
```

As you can see, you get a list of scripts from your base class (`Xaml`), which should include both the `Silverlight.js` library and the `Xaml` client-side type script. To this, you add your new script. As an aside, we found that C# warns you if you try to call a base method from within an iterator. Because using the yield keyword creates an iterator type (behind the scenes), you can't be sure that base will be what you expect. Therefore, you don't want to use another iterator here (using yield return), but you instead create a generic list and just return it. The same thing applies for your overriding getting descriptors.

The interesting thing with the `GetScriptDescriptor` method is that because you're deriving from the `Xaml` type, which uses the `DefaultClientType` to create a `ScriptControlDescriptor` and then registers its properties, you can refactor the `Xaml` class to provide a new method just specifically for setting up the control descriptor:

```
/// <summary>
/// Gets the control descriptor for this control.
/// </summary>
/// <remarks>Inheritors should override and add their own properties,
etc.</remarks>
/// <returns>The control descriptor for this control.</returns>
protected virtual ScriptControlDescriptor GetControlDescriptor()
{
    ScriptControlDescriptor xaml =
    new ScriptControlDescriptor(this.ClientType, this.ClientID);
    AddDescriptorProp(xaml, "minimumSilverlightVersion",
    this.MinimumSilverlightVersion);
    AddDescriptorProp(xaml, "parentElementID", this.ParentElementID);
    return xaml;
}
```

Then you update the `Xaml` class's implementation of `GetScriptDescriptors` to be the following:

```
/// <summary>
/// Gets the script descriptors for this control.
/// </summary>
/// <returns>The script descriptors for this control.</returns>
protected override IEnumerable<ScriptDescriptor> GetScriptDescriptors()
{
    yield return GetControlDescriptor();
}
```

The end result (for `Xaml`) is the same as it was previously, but now you can just override your new `GetControlDescriptor` method and let your base class declare the descriptor using the `ClientType` and add its properties; then all you have to do is add your new properties. The reason this is better than just overriding `GetScriptDescriptors` is that you'd have to either redeclare the stuff that your base class declared or, worse, assume that, for example, the first `ScriptDescriptor` in the enumeration is the `ScriptControlDescriptor`, call the base, get the first one, and cast it, which creates an extremely brittle coupling between the two classes. Using the preceding approach lets the base class explicitly declare its intent to create and add a `ScriptControlDescriptor` and lets inheritors either replace it or simply add to it, as you do with the `ButtonBar`.

```
/// <summary>
/// Gets the control descriptor for this control.
/// </summary>
/// <returns>The control descriptor for this control.</returns>
protected override ScriptControlDescriptor GetControlDescriptor()
{
```

```
        ScriptControlDescriptor desc = base.GetControlDescriptor();
        string url = this.ButtonTemplateUrl;
        AddDescriptorProp(desc, "buttonTemplateUrl", url.Length == 0 ?
            this.Page.ClientScript.GetWebResourceUrl(
            typeof(Client.Resources), Client.Resources.Keys.ButtonTemplate) : url);
        url = this.ButtonStoryBoardTemplateUrl;
        AddDescriptorProp(desc, "buttonStoryBoardTemplateUrl", url.Length == 0 ?
            this.Page.ClientScript.GetWebResourceUrl(
            typeof(Client.Resources), Client.Resources.Keys.ButtonStoryBoardTemplate) :
            url);
        AddDescriptorProp(desc, "dataMethod", this.DataMethod);
        return desc;
    }
```

You can see here you just get the base descriptor and add your new properties to it. As noted before, you're by default providing your embedded templates so that if consumers don't specify a button or button storyboard template, you'll supply the built-in ones. If you were building a more fully customizable control, you could, for example, embed several different templates to provide different looks and animations and let the user either select one of those with, for example, an enumeration or still supply a custom one as you're allowing here.

That's all you need to do on the server side for this control. The real work for it is in the client JavaScript.

Creating the ButtonBar Client-Side Code

You already have your basic type and a few property methods in place, but you're far from done on the client. Unlike the Xaml control, you're actually going to do a little bit of fancy scripting for this one to highlight one way that you can create dynamic Silverlight controls using ASP.NET AJAX. The first two methods you'll add to your script are some standard but important ones when creating ASP.NET AJAX client-side controls:

```
function Wrox$Silverlight1_0$Controls$ButtonBar$initialize() {

    var downloader = this.get_element().createObject("downloader");
    downloader.addEventListener("completed",
        Function.createDelegate(this, this._btnTemplateDownloaded));
    downloader.open("GET", this.get_buttonTemplateUrl());
    downloader.send();

    Wrox.Silverlight1_0.Controls.ButtonBar.callBaseMethod(this, "initialize");
}
function Wrox$Silverlight1_0$Controls$ButtonBar$dispose() {
    this._disposed = true;

    if (this._buttonTemplate)
        delete this._buttonTemplate;
    if (this._buttonStoryBoardTemplate)
        delete this._buttonStoryBoardTemplate;
    Wrox.Silverlight1_0.Controls.ButtonBar.callBaseMethod(this, "dispose");
}
```

Your `dispose` method is pretty normal. The only two resources you're explicitly disposing (because they could be large) are the cached button and storyboard templates. These are created as a result of downloading them from the server asynchronously, which you start in your initialize method.

In that method, you use the ASP.NET AJAX Library `get_element` method to get the DOM element for this control, which in this case is the Silverlight DOM control element. On this, you call the `createObject` method, which in Silverlight 1.0 only lets you create the Silverlight downloader, and that's precisely what you want. To this, you attach your completed event handler using the ASP.NET AJAX Library `createDelegate` method. (Using this lets you keep the "this" context to be the current instance; otherwise, it is replaced with a reference to the browser window.) And the last thing you do here is specify the HTTP verb (`GET`) and the URL, which is whatever you set on the server to be your button template URL. By default, if you recall, that's going to be a web resource URL to your embedded button template. And finally, you send the request.

The next method to consider is the completion handler:

```
function Wrox$Silverlight1_0$Controls$ButtonBar$btnTemplateDownloaded(sender, args)
{
    this._buttonTemplate = sender.ResponseText;

    var downloader = this.get_element().createObject("downloader");
    downloader.addEventListener("completed",
        Function.createDelegate(this, this._btnStoryTemplateDownloaded));
    downloader.open("GET", this.get_buttonStoryBoardTemplateUrl());
    downloader.send();
}
```

This is what is called when the downloader completes. If you're wondering about the method name difference, remember that when you set up the JavaScript type's prototype method, you provide friendly names for each of these methods. This method first gets the `ResponseText`, which will be an XAML button template, caches it in the `this._buttonTemplate` object variable, and then creates a downloader to download the button storyboard template in the same way, which leads you to that method.

```
function Wrox$Silverlight1_0$Controls$ButtonBar$btnStoryTemplateDownloaded(sender,
args)
{
    this._buttonStoryBoardTemplate = sender.ResponseText;

    this._topOffset = 8;
    this._buttonIndex = 0;

    var dataMethod = this.get_dataMethod();
    if (dataMethod && dataMethod.length > 0)
    {
        eval(dataMethod.replace(/{callback}/,
            'Function.createDelegate(this, ↵
            Wrox$Silverlight1_0$Controls$ButtonBar$dataDownloaded)'));
    }
    else
    {
        for (var i = 1; i < 5; i++)
        {
```

```
                this.addButton('Wrox Button ' + i, "http://www.wrox.com", null);
            }
        }
    }
```

First, this one caches the storyboard template, and then it is off to create the buttons. To do this, you set up a couple of counters:

- `this._topOffset` keeps track of the `Top` position for the next button.
- `this._buttonIndex` provides a simple way to reliably provide unique identifiers (`x:Name` in your templates) so that you can map animations to buttons as you'll see later in this chapter.

Then you check what was set for the `DataMethod` property (in the server-side class). If it was not set, you create a handful of default buttons, which can be fun, but usually you want to specify them. To do that, the method call should include a `{callback}` placeholder that you can replace with your callback and evaluate using the JavaScript `eval` method, which parses and executes the script given to it.

```
function Wrox$Silverlight1_0$Controls$ButtonBar$dataDownloaded(results)
{
    if (results && results.length > 0)
    {
        for (var i = 0; i < results.length; i++)
        {
            var b = results[i];
            this.addButton(b.Text, b.NavigateUrl, b.OnClick);
        }
    }
}
```

And finally, the last step of initialization is to create buttons based on the menu items supplied to your callback function:

```
function Wrox$Silverlight1_0$Controls$ButtonBar$addButton(text, navUrl, onClick)
{
    var sl = this.get_element();

    var id = this._buttonIndex;
    var xaml = this._buttonTemplate
        .replace(/{id}/g, id)
        .replace(/{buttonTop}/, this._topOffset);

    this._buttonIndex++;
    this._topOffset += 62;

    var button = sl.content.createFromXaml(xaml);

    button.addEventListener("MouseEnter",
        Function.createDelegate(this, this._onMouseEnter));
    button.addEventListener("MouseLeave",
        Function.createDelegate(this, this._onMouseLeave));

    if (onClick)
```

```
        {
            button.addEventListener("MouseLeftButtonUp", onClick);
            button.Cursor = "Hand";
        }
        else if (navUrl)
        {
            button.addEventListener("MouseLeftButtonUp",
                Function.createDelegate(this, function() { window.location.href =
                navUrl; }));
            button.Cursor = "Hand";
        }

        sl.content.root.children.add(button);

        var boundingBox = button.findName("boundingBox_" + id);
        var buttonText = button.findName("buttonText_" + id);
        buttonText.text = text;
        buttonText.setValue("Canvas.Top", ((boundingBox.Height -
        buttonText.ActualHeight) / 2));
        buttonText.setValue("Canvas.Left", ((boundingBox.Width -
        buttonText.ActualWidth) / 2));
    }
```

To create a button, you get your Silverlight DOM control element using `this.get_element`, get the current button index as the `id` value, replace all instances of `{id}` in the template with the current `id`, and replace the `{buttonTop}` XAML placeholder with the current top offset. This provides you with the XAML for this particular button.

After incrementing your button index and top offset, you go ahead and use the Silverlight `createFromXaml` method to create your new button. Then you add your `MouseEnter` and `MouseLeave` event handlers, which will be used to animate the buttons. If the menu item specified an `OnClick` handler, you go ahead and set the new button's `MouseLeftButtonUp` (the closest thing to `OnClick` in Silverlight) to use that handler; otherwise, if the menu item specified a `NavigateUrl`, you set up a handler to navigate to the URL when the button is clicked. In both of those cases, you set the `Cursor` to be `Hand` to let the user know that the button is clickable (a good, general usability principle).

Because dynamically created Silverlight objects won't render until they're added to the visible element tree, you add the button to the root's children collection. With the default template, this just adds the button to the empty, transparent main canvas. This is where, if you were building out, say, a hierarchy in a richer menu control, you'd want to add it to the current, particular canvas in the menu tree, but for simplicity, here you're just slapping it on the root.

Now that it is added to the visible tree, it will render, so you can set the text property and center it reliably. (If it isn't rendered, it won't know what its actual dimensions are.) So you get the bounding box rectangle, that is, the rectangle you want to center in; then you get the text block itself and set its text. The last step sets the `Canvas.Top` and `Canvas.Left` attached properties using the simple centering algorithm you learned (like we said) in typing class, that is, bounding dimension minus actual dimension divided by two.

That's it for the button! It's there, visible, and the text is centered. If supplied, it will call the appropriate click handler when clicked. So you're done, right? Not quite. You wanted to make this dynamic; otherwise, you're not adding much value using Silverlight for this. That's where the storyboards and animations come into play. Remember, you set up the MouseEnter and MouseLeave event handlers, so let's look at those now:

```
function Wrox$Silverlight1_0$Controls$ButtonBar$onMouseEnter(sender, args)
{
    this._startStoryBoard(this._getElementId(sender), true);
}
function Wrox$Silverlight1_0$Controls$ButtonBar$onMouseLeave(sender, args)
{
    this._startStoryBoard(this._getElementId(sender), false);
}
```

That's not really helpful, is it? The getElementId method (marked with an _ to follow JavaScript conventions for indicating it is private), simply extracts the ID from the sender's name property. Recall that your template appends _{id} to the various names to enable you to reliably find/target the various elements in the template.

```
function Wrox$Silverlight1_0$Controls$ButtonBar$getElementId(obj)
{
    var name = obj.name;
    return name.substring(name.indexOf('_')+1);
}
```

The _startStoryBoard method is where all the goodness happens for the animations:

```
function Wrox$Silverlight1_0$Controls$ButtonBar$startStoryBoard(id, expanding)
{
    var name = (expanding ? "buttonExpand_" : "buttonShrink_") + id;
    var sl = this.get_element();
    var storyBoard = sl.content.root.findName(name);
    if (!storyBoard)
    {
        // get text block for determining text target left/top for centering
        var buttonText = sl.content.root.findName("buttonText_" + id);

        var template = sl.content.root.findName("buttonTemplate_" + id);

        var targetWidth = expanding ? template.width+3 : template.width-2;
        var targetHeight = expanding ? template.height+3 : template.height-2;

        // replace the ID and the text left/top in the shrinker template
        var xaml = this._buttonStoryBoardTemplate
            .replace(/{name}/, name)
            .replace(/{id}/g, id)
            .replace(/{commonWidth}/g, targetWidth)
            .replace(/{commonHeight}/g, targetHeight)
            .replace(/{lightingWidth}/, targetWidth - 2)
            .replace(/{lightingHeight}/, targetHeight - 2)
            .replace(/{textLeft}/, ((targetWidth - buttonText.ActualWidth) / 2))
            .replace(/{textTop}/, ((targetHeight - buttonText.ActualHeight) / 2));
        storyBoard = sl.content.createFromXaml(xaml);
        template.resources.add(storyBoard);
    }
    storyBoard.begin();
}
```

Here's where you find or create the appropriate storyboard for the current action. The first step is to figure out the name, which if you're expanding, will be `buttonExpand_{id}` and if you're shrinking will be `buttonShrink_{id}`. You use this name to try to find the storyboard first. If you find it, simple enough, you just call the `begin` method to start it. However, of course, it won't be there the first time this is called for the button, so in that case, you have to create it from your template.

First you grab the text block that you'll use to provide target left and top positioning for the animation; then you grab the button template itself (the canvas that groups the various button elements together). To figure out the target width and height, you use an algorithm that is related to the template/canvas dimensions. You assume that the canvas will be 2 pixels larger than the visible elements themselves. So, if you're expanding, you set the target dimension to be canvas dimension plus 3, which equates to a plus 5 for the internal elements, and if you are shrinking, you set it to canvas dimension minus 2. This algorithm could be customized with some properties that let the user specify target values, or if the template itself wanted to hard code values, it could do that. In this case, you're just assuming the expand/contract approach.

Now that you have your data, you can go ahead and "instantiate" the template with your values, again using the centering algorithm for the text block to keep it centered during the resizing. With the "instance" XAML in hand, you call the `createFromXaml` method to actually instantiate the storyboard and animations, and the last step is to add the new storyboard to the button template's resource dictionary using `resources.add`. That's all you do here. After the first time in, the storyboard is in the resources and is found, so it won't be re-created.

The final step to complete the client-side script is to set up the prototype property with all the methods you've been defining:

```
Wrox.Silverlight1_0.Controls.ButtonBar.prototype = {
    get_buttonTemplateUrl:
    Wrox$Silverlight1_0$Controls$ButtonBar$get_buttonTemplateUrl,
    set_buttonTemplateUrl:
    Wrox$Silverlight1_0$Controls$ButtonBar$set_buttonTemplateUrl,
    get_buttonStoryBoardTemplateUrl:
    Wrox$Silverlight1_0$Controls$ButtonBar$get_buttonStoryBoardTemplateUrl,
    set_buttonStoryBoardTemplateUrl:
    Wrox$Silverlight1_0$Controls$ButtonBar$set_buttonStoryBoardTemplateUrl,
    get_dataMethod: Wrox$Silverlight1_0$Controls$ButtonBar$get_dataMethod,
    set_dataMethod: Wrox$Silverlight1_0$Controls$ButtonBar$set_dataMethod,
    addButton: Wrox$Silverlight1_0$Controls$ButtonBar$addButton,
    _btnTemplateDownloaded:
    Wrox$Silverlight1_0$Controls$ButtonBar$btnTemplateDownloaded,
    _btnStoryTemplateDownloaded:
    Wrox$Silverlight1_0$Controls$ButtonBar$btnStoryTemplateDownloaded,
    _getElementId: Wrox$Silverlight1_0$Controls$ButtonBar$getElementId,
    _startStoryBoard: Wrox$Silverlight1_0$Controls$ButtonBar$startStoryBoard,
    _onMouseEnter: Wrox$Silverlight1_0$Controls$ButtonBar$onMouseEnter,
    _onMouseLeave: Wrox$Silverlight1_0$Controls$ButtonBar$onMouseLeave,
    initialize: Wrox$Silverlight1_0$Controls$ButtonBar$initialize,
    dispose: Wrox$Silverlight1_0$Controls$ButtonBar$dispose
}
```

Using the ButtonBar Control

Now you have a custom button bar control ready to use. To use it, you create an ASP.NET AJAX-enabled web site by right-clicking the solution, as shown in Figure 5-12 (or using File ➪ New ➪ Web Site...).

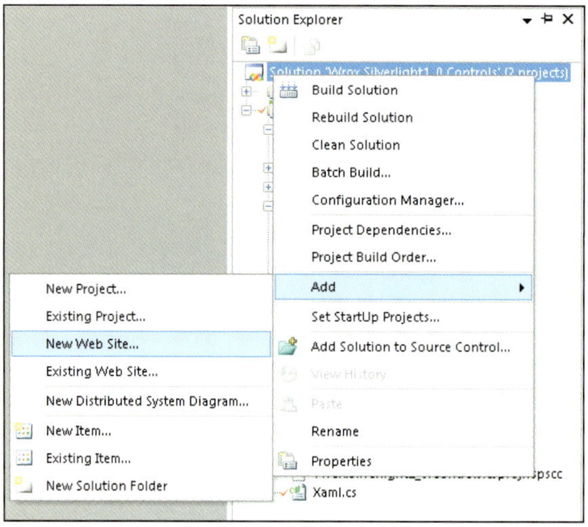

Figure 5-12

Choose the ASP.NET AJAX-Enabled Web Site template (see Figure 5-13). If you installed ASP.NET 2.0 AJAX Extensions, you should see this template.

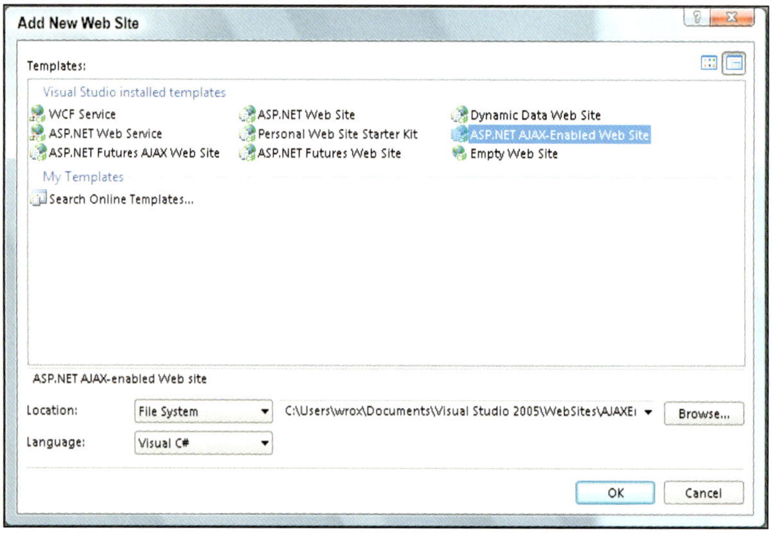

Figure 5-13

Now add a Project reference to the Wrox.Silverlight1_0.Controls and open the Default.aspx. To it, add this tag registration directive:

```
<%@ Register TagPrefix="wroxAg" Namespace="Wrox.Silverlight1_0.Controls"
Assembly="Wrox.Silverlight1_0.Controls" %>
```

Then declare the ButtonBar control like this:

```
<wroxAg:ButtonBar runat="server" DataMethod="PageMethods.GetButtons({callback})"
    ID="MyButtons" Width="300" Height="400" />
```

Note that we're using Page Methods, which, if used appropriately, are a nice productivity feature of ASP.NET. If you have a method that is specific to the page that you need to expose to client-side script, this is a nice alternative to creating a web service, referencing, and using it because it saves you a few steps. That said, if you have a service/remote client method that needs to be exposed to more than just this page, go ahead and create the web service. We're just demonstrating this here, so we're using Page Methods. To do this, add the following server-side script block to the page:

```
<script runat="server">
    [System.Web.Services.WebMethod]
    public static Wrox.Silverlight1_0.Controls.MenuItemCollection GetButtons()
    {
        Wrox.Silverlight1_0.Controls.MenuItemCollection items =
            new Wrox.Silverlight1_0.Controls.MenuItemCollection();
        items.Add(new Wrox.Silverlight1_0.Controls.MenuItem("Wrox",
        "http://www.wrox.com"));
        items.Add(new Wrox.Silverlight1_0.Controls.MenuItem("Google",
        "http://www.google.com"));
        items.Add(new Wrox.Silverlight1_0.Controls.MenuItem("Live.com",
        "http://www.live.com"));
        items.Add(new Wrox.Silverlight1_0.Controls.MenuItem("dotNetTemplar",
        "http://dotNetTemplar.net"));
        items.Add(new Wrox.Silverlight1_0.Controls.MenuItem("Say Hello!", null,
        "SayHello"));
        return items;
    }
</script>
```

To create a Page Method, just create a static method on the page (or its code behind) and mark it with the WebMethodAttribute. ASP.NET AJAX takes care of the rest for you (that is, creating a client-side proxy for the methods). It's this proxy that you supply as the DataMethod on your control, including the placeholder for the callback — ASP.NET AJAX's proxy automatically adds a success and an error callback to your method signature.

In your method, as you can see, you just create a `MenuItemCollection` and add a handful of items to it. All but one uses the `NavigateUrl`; the last one supplies an `OnClick` handler, which is defined in a client-side script block.

```
<head runat="server">
    <title>Demo Buttons</title>
    <script type="text/javascript">
    function SayHello()
    {
        alert('Hello!');
    }
    </script>
</head>
```

Finally, you just need to let ASP.NET AJAX know you're using Page Methods by setting the `EnablePageMethods` to true on the `ScriptManager` for the page:

```
<asp:ScriptManager ID="ScriptManager1" EnablePageMethods="true" runat="server" />
```

That's all there is to it. The end result looks like Figure 5-14.

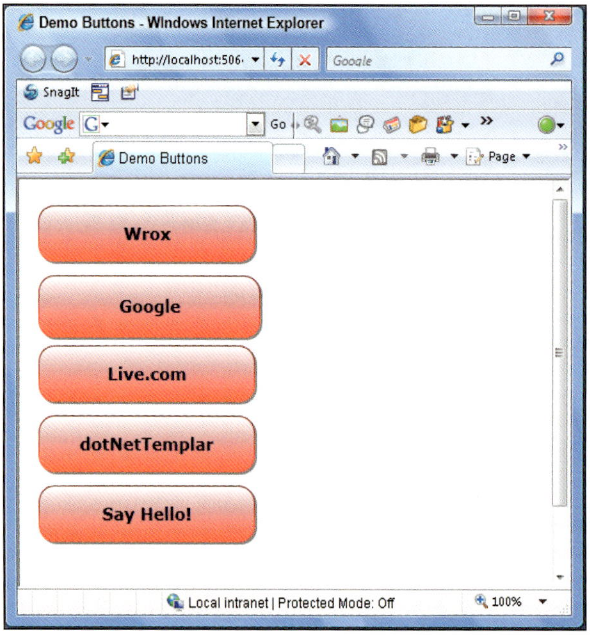

Figure 5-14

Final Thoughts/Recommendations

The purpose of this section was to show one way that you can create a dynamic Silverlight UI with custom ASP.NET AJAX controls. It's a tad more difficult to use than if you had done the data binding on the server side, and that's definitely a viable option for some controls. In fact, a menu or button bar control would probably be better implemented using server-side binding as the primary mechanism simply because it is a bit easier to use. (You don't have to force users to supply something like your `DataMethod`.)

There was also some tight coupling between your enter/leave event handlers in that they expected a certain ID/Name format and assumed that it was a shrink/expand animation going on. To enable more customization, you'd want to empower consumers to create different kinds of animations by, for example, letting them specify the `MouseEnter/Leave` handlers (as well as the animation templates, if they so desire). But as you can see, it's already pretty complex to create a custom, ASP.NET AJAX-driven Silverlight control, so we didn't want to muddy the waters any more than necessary to teach the elementary concepts and approaches.

Summary

This chapter took on the subject of using ASP.NET and Silverlight together. First, we discussed a number of common scenarios and when it is best to consider using Silverlight or just ASP.NET. After that, we covered what it would take to create a basic Silverlight-oriented web custom control for ASP.NET, which we then took a step further by making it an ASP.NET AJAX custom control, following the model that Microsoft is using in its upcoming release of its Xaml and Media controls. Finally, we explored how to create a dynamic Silverlight UI using a custom ASP.NET AJAX control for Silverlight. Using the scenario analysis and the in-depth exploration of creating custom, Silverlight-oriented controls, you now have the foundations necessary to go forth and create your own dynamic user interfaces with Silverlight 1.0 and ASP.NET.

6

Silverlight 1.1 and the CLR

Talk about buzz. Silverlight 1.1 has generated the most buzz of any technology in recent memory, and for good reason — it has the most promise of any recent technology to make our lives as business application developers easier. Finally we have the potential to create extremely rich user experiences using a reliable, cross-platform technology that has a familiar, well-designed framework, great tooling, and an awesome developer community. It's everything we've ever wanted!

Well, almost. Silverlight 1.1 certainly has a ton of promise, but some key elements are missing in the 1.1 iteration:

- **Text Support** — Both in terms of display and input, Silverlight is lacking severely in text support. Before it can become the next great technology, it needs to acquire, at a minimum, basic textual input features, and to make it really shine, it needs to develop document and markup features as compelling (or more so) than HTML and CSS. WPF is a good paradigm for this.
- **Control Model** — To empower control developers, particularly third parties, Silverlight needs to develop a robust control model.
- **Layout Options** — Right now, all we have is `Canvas`. We need more, familiar layout options such as flow/wrap, grid/table, and so on to make regular application development feasible.
- **Data Binding/Templating** — All business applications deal with data, and to make regular application development reasonable, we need a good template-based data binding mechanism. Again, WPF has the best implementation of this.
- **Styling** — CSS has shown the value of separating appearance from function, and WPF took it a step further to make controls "lookless," enabling complete redesign of a control's appearance. Also, the ability to reuse styling across controls and even applications is critical for maintainable applications and consistency.
- **Localization** — In this increasingly globalized world, a new web-based technology must have a strong internationalization story, and it needs to be easy to use in the UI layer.

The good news is that Microsoft is aware of all of this and is actively researching how best to build out Silverlight while making it feasible to run cross-platform and minimize download size and client requirements. It's a tough task, but developers will surely have a gem when all's said and done.

Now that we've added a breeze of reality and a dash of hope, we can talk about what we do know about Silverlight 1.1 today. As of this writing, we're in the 1.1 Alpha Refresh release, which is essentially (feature-wise) the same as the original alpha. The nice thing is that the feature set is pretty much on par with 1.0, so everything you learned about 1.0 is applicable. The primary difference is, of course, that 1.1 gives us the CLR on the client, whereas with 1.0, we're stuck with JavaScript in terms of automation.

We say that 1.0 and 1.1 are basically the same, as if having a CLR and parts of the .NET Framework is something to sneeze at. Of course, it is one of the more revolutionary advancements in distributed application development, not because the capabilities in themselves are revolutionary (after all, at the most basic level, it is essentially like a Java applet), but because it is as if we are finally going to be able to work with both arms — not having one tied behind our backs while trying to create rich, maintainable, cross-platform applications that are relatively easy to build, something we just don't have when depending on the mishmash of technologies (HTML, CSS, JavaScript, and so on) and varying interpretations of those by browsers.

To illustrate the difference between 1.0 (unmanaged, you could say) and 1.1 (managed) Silverlight, consider Figures 6-1 and 6-2. These illustrate the relationship between Silverlight and the related technologies. In the unmanaged/1.0 Silverlight illustration (Figure 6-1), you see that essentially we're just introducing a scriptable object — everything else about building a Rich Internet Application (RIA) today remains true. In the managed/1.1 (Figure 6-2), you see the introduction of the CLR and managed libraries that we'll delve into in this chapter.

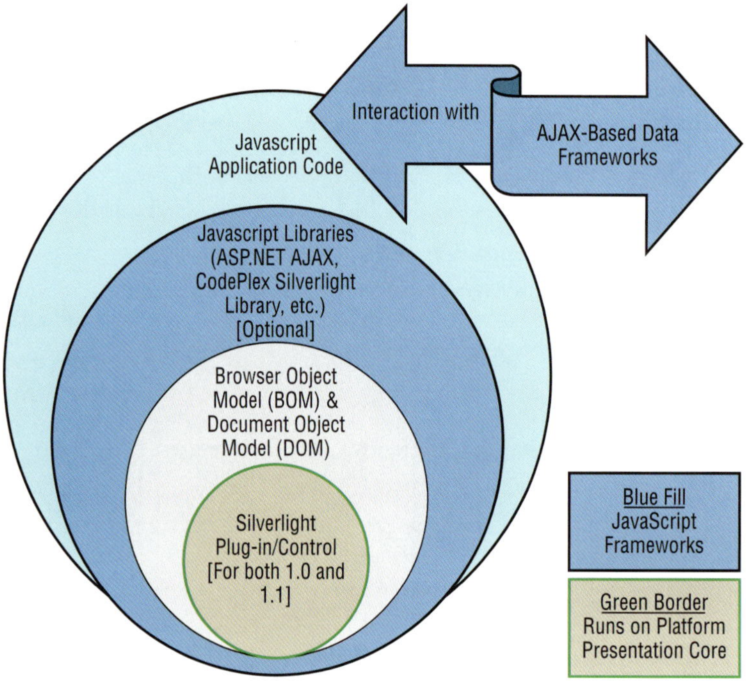

Figure 6-1

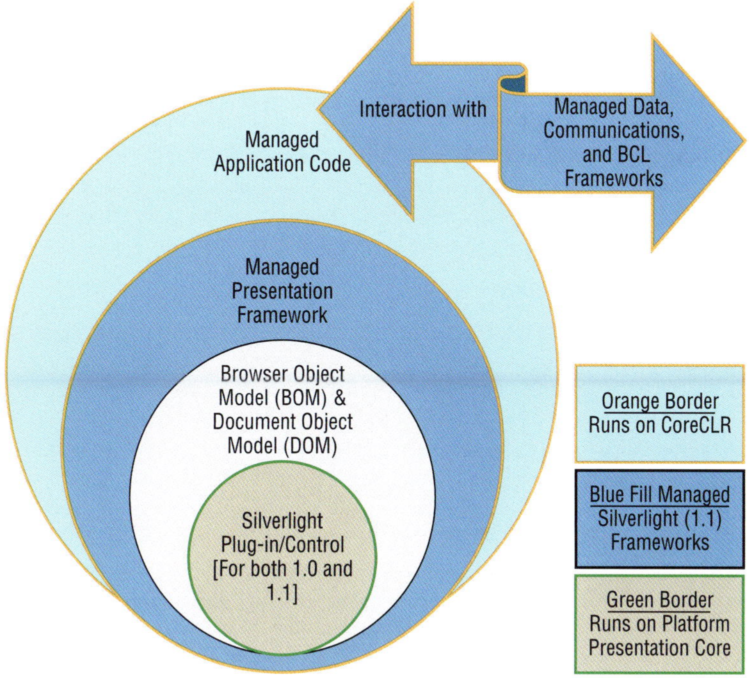

Figure 6-2

The purpose of this chapter is to introduce Silverlight 1.1 from a high level. We won't be delving into specifics or providing code examples here because 1.1 is still in Alpha and, as noted, has a lot to add and probably change. But there is still a fair bit to say about it because the target scenarios of rich Internet/distributed applications are pretty well known, and it is those that are driving the development of 1.1. Therefore, we already have a pretty good idea of the core functionality based on what's in the Alpha. Though the specific APIs can and will certainly change as managed Silverlight develops, the core functionality needed to support the target scenarios will not. So reading this chapter will give you a pretty good idea of the current capabilities and some idea of the APIs, giving you the foundation to explore further as the technology develops.

You should also check out our additional online chapter for this book that is devoted to 1.1 and has sample code that we intend to keep up to date as 1.1 develops. The online chapter is available along with the code download at `www.wrox.com`.

The CLR

First things first. The CLR for Silverlight is not the CLR that we .NET developers have come to know and love. It is its own thing, a scaled-down version that removes all that is perceived as unnecessary for enabling developers to create Rich Internet Applications (and presumably mobile applications at some point). One of the more foundational changes is that the thing that was touted as one of the great advances of .NET, Code Access Security (CAS), is a non-entity in Silverlight. This doesn't mean Silverlight code won't be secure — far from it! There are other security mechanisms that actually seem to make it more secure (or at least make security less complicated) that we'll get into later.

The key thing about the CLR — what most of the hubbub is about — is that it is cross-platform. Implementations are being written by Microsoft for both Windows (2000+) and Intel-based Macs, and there is already an implementation being provided by the folks who brought us Mono that runs on Linux. In short, the big news, for the few who haven't heard it, is that developers will be able to create applications using a version of the CLR that runs on all these major platforms, which means the final hurdle that is often the key motivation for building an HTML-based application — cross-platform reach — is being overcome.

That said, it is important to point out that in terms of important things like assembly, formats are the same in the new CLR, which has been termed by some the CoreCLR. The "core" terminology is a good one because it is a refactoring of the existing CLR that keeps only what is core to building these rich distributed, cross-platform applications. For instance, depending on what classes you are using from the.NET Framework, you could possibly simply just use your compiled assembly (without recompiling) in the CoreCLR. The most common cases for this will be for business class libraries, as you'll see later. It's all Just-in-Time (JIT) compiled from the Microsoft Intermediate Language (MSIL), just like it is in the familiar .NET CLR. It should be a given, then, that you keep your common type system.

Another feature of the CLR that is coming along is automatic memory management through garbage collection. You get to keep your nice managed exception handling, and though you don't get CAS, you actually get something that might be better (because CAS remains a mysterious art to many). Essentially, you're prevented from writing unsafe code thanks to the requirement that your code be "transparent," which means everything application developers write is 100 percent managed .NET, and you have to go through provided .NET libraries to access anything unmanaged. File system access is limited to isolated storage, network access is limited to HTTP, and there's no access to Windows-specific things like the registry or broad interop with unmanaged code — certainly no native P/Invoke stuff. So basically, the libraries you have prevent you from being insecure, thereby making any explicit security framework unnecessary, eliminating the need for CAS per se.

The Framework

Of course, mentioning that you might be able to reuse your libraries begs the question: Just what is and isn't in the Silverlight framework; that is, how do you know if you can just reuse your assemblies? The next sections outline at a high level what is currently known to be in 1.1 frameworks. Because it is in Alpha and there is still a lot of work to be done and decisions to be made by Microsoft (and because this is a 1.0 book), we're not going to delve into code samples. We're just going to talk about the key capabilities that you get and mention some of the familiar APIs we see in Silverlight 1.1. As we go over this, a clear reasoning will emerge that illustrates the driving principles behind what makes it into the Silverlight frameworks and what doesn't. Before we dive in, take a look at Figure 6-3, which illustrates the various frameworks we'll be looking at as well as their relationship to each other.

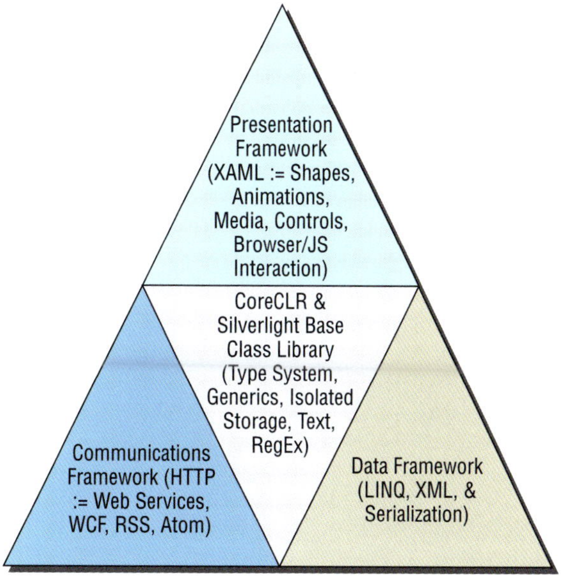

Figure 6-3

Base APIs

As mentioned, you keep your common type system, which means, by and large, you keep the System namespace and all the familiar base types that you often think of as primitives (Int32, Int64, Decimal, the beloved String, and all the rest). And there should be great rejoicing that you're getting System.Collections.Generic, a great boon that was added in .NET 2.0.

Here's a list of APIs in this area:

- **System**
- **System.Collections.Generic**
- **System.Globalization**
- **System.IO**
- **System.IO.IsolatedStorage**
- **System.Reflection**
- **System.Resources**
- **System.Text**
- **System.Text.RegularExpressions**

It's nice to know you get Reflection because once you get to know it, you often find it hard to do without to write truly generic code. Note the IsolatedStorage namespace; as mentioned, you don't get the full I/O API because you're running in a browser on any number of platforms. You need for disk access to be safe and reasonable to implement, so you get a nice little isolated playground.

The Globalization and Resources namespaces lay the foundation for internationalization (and of course embedding of other resources), though you will find a lacking for ease of use in the presentation framework right now. And given that so much of what you do is text-based, it's natural that you'd need the Text and RegularExpressions namespaces.

So that's about it for the base classes. As you can see, it's just refactored to what you need to develop rich distributed applications on multiple platforms.

Data APIs

It should come as no surprise, then, that there is sufficient support for XML in Silverlight. Although you won't get the full extent of everything that is in all the full frameworks, you'll get a sufficient subset to be able to read and write XML and even serialization. On top of that, because key scenarios are geared toward the web, you'll get the JavaScriptSerializer that'll give you an easy way to deal with the more compact JSON data exchange format in managed code.

Perhaps the most exciting thing in this area is that you'll get LINQ support, which is the new object-oriented query syntax (and supporting framework). Right now, it looks like you only get LINQ to XML (formerly known as XLINQ), but that makes sense given the communications channels you'll have, which we cover in the next section. Again, you see the guiding principle being supplying APIs that support rich distributed, cross-platform applications.

Here's a more complete list of APIs for data:

- **System.Xml**
    - XmlReader
    - XmlWriter
- **System.Xml.Serialization**
    - XmlSerializer
- **System.Browser.Windows.Serialization**
    - JavaScriptSerializer
- **System.Linq [Language Integrated Query]**
- **System.Xml.Linq [LINQ TO XML, a.k.a., XML Language Integrated Query]**
    - XAttribute
    - XDocument
    - XElement
    - XName
    - XNamespace
    - XNode
    - XText

Communications APIs

So with web-based applications as the focus, can you guess what communications protocols will be supported? If you guessed HTTP, you got it. For now, that appears to be the extent of it, and that explains why you only need XML LINQ libraries — you won't be linking directly to SQL! You'll have either XML or objects, both of which you get with LINQ and LINQ to XML.

- **System.ServiceModel (WCF)**
    - Web Services Client Support
- **System.Syndication**
    - Atom/RSS Support
- **System.Net**
    - HttpWebRequest
    - HttpWebResponse
- **System.Windows.Browser.Net (New in Silverlight)**
    - BrowserHttpWebRequest

In the Alpha, we're actually using the `XMLHTTPRequest` browser objects for our web requests and response, though we've been told they're refactoring it to use Silverlight-specific objects to enable key web scenarios (notably mashups — the ability to aggregate bits and pieces of other sites/applications into one). Due to the well-advised security-related restriction of only being able to call back to your "home" (server of origination), mashups currently have to use bridges (usually web services on the originating servers that simply wrap calls to other services on other sites), but they're looking into how to alleviate this burden in a secure way with Silverlight.

Also of note is the ServiceModel (WCF) support so that you'll be able to easily consume WCF-based services (probably just HTTP bindings), and as you'd expect, they'll be adding specific support for RSS and Atom, because those are also key scenarios in web applications.

Some Thoughts

That wraps it up for non-UI APIs. So now you should have a pretty good idea of whether or not that assembly you were thinking of will "just work" in Silverlight. If you have a pure business class library with just your business objects and logic, then yeah, it should work. If you're doing data access or using some sort of presentation layer interaction, you'll likely have to refactor.

In general, I'd be wary of "just using" existing application assemblies because I'll wager that they were designed to live in known environments (for example, Web, Win, or both). They may work, and as long as you do sufficient testing, it could be fine to just use them. I just wouldn't be overly optimistic on this front. And even if they do work (as, for example, you *could* just upgrade a VB app to VB.NET or an ASP app to ASP.NET), you may find that you want to refactor them to take advantage of scenarios that the Silverlight environment enables that you weren't using before (for instance, you may want to decorate them with serialization attributes).

Presentation APIs

Of course, what would Silverlight be without its presentation APIs? It is, after all, primarily a new presentation layer technology. Thankfully, Microsoft didn't re-reinvent the wheel here. They leveraged a lot of the great work and learning from Windows Presentation Foundation (WPF), and our hope is that they'll continue to do so as they build it out further. WPF is (was?) the next evolution in presentation technology; it takes the best from web-based technologies (particularly ASP.NET and CSS), the best in Windows, and the best in graphics and blends them together to create a very flexible and maintainable presentation technology.

Silverlight takes a subset of that and adds its own flair. We already know much about this by now because this area is where 1.0 and 1.1 are most similar (pretty much 100 percent similar in terms of capabilities and XAML); so we won't beat this point any longer. What's interesting and different in this area between 1.0 and 1.1 is in the automation (programming) of the presentation layer. What was just extremely loosely typed JavaScript becomes strongly typed .NET, and that, in itself, is a wondrous thing for any of you who've had to do much JavaScript development. (Those who haven't have likely gotten a taste in the preceding chapters!)

Even the most valiant efforts of Microsoft's most brilliant minds in the developer division have only marginally made JavaScript development easier. And that's not to badmouth them — they've done a *ton*. It's just that you can only do so much on such a shaky foundation as JavaScript, HTML, CSS, and the multifarious browsers.

Enter the Silverlight managed presentation framework. As you might imagine, all those nifty XAML elements you've been learning about (well, most) become classes of the same name and have the same properties. This is a major win for both WPF and Silverlight — XAML is essentially declarative (XML) objects with some extra grease to make things easier (to declare). So if you learn the XAML, you pretty much learn the object model and vice versa. The new stuff will mainly be in the methods, but even there, most of the methods are related to building out an object tree (like `Add`) or setting properties (like `SetValue<T>` for dependency properties). Then of course you have the control command methods (like `Begin`, `Start`, `Stop`, and so on to automate animations and media).

The following is a selection of these kinds of objects and where they live:

- **System.Windows.Media**
    - `ImageBrush`
    - `LinearGradientBrush`
    - `RadialGradientBrush`
    - `SolidColorBrush`
    - `VideoBrush`
    - `MatrixTransform`
    - `RotateTransform`
    - `ScaleTransform`
    - `SkewTransform`
    - `TranslateTransform`

- **System.Windows.Media.Animation**
    - `BeginStoryboard`
    - `ColorAnimation`
    - `ColorAnimationUsingKeyFrames`
    - `DoubleAnimation`
    - `DoubleAnimationUsingKeyFrames`
    - `PointAnimation`
    - `PointAnimationUsingKeyFrames`
    - `Storyboard`
- **System.Windows.Shapes**
    - `Line`
    - `Path`
- **System.Windows.Controls**
    - `Canvas`
    - `Control`
    - `Image`
    - `MediaElement`
    - `OpenFileDialog`
    - `TextBlock`
    - and more . . .
- **System.Windows.Documents**
    - `Glyphs`
    - `Inline`
    - `LineBreak`

Nothing in this list should come as a surprise if you've read other chapters in this book, so we won't go into depth on the capabilities of each here. About the only new/interesting one in this list is the `OpenFileDialog`. You use this to enable users to supply files to your application; it's the only way to access the file system outside of isolated storage. Once you have the results, you can load the files into memory, save them in isolated storage (assuming they're under the [current] 1MB limit per application), or upload them to a server via web services.

Another interesting point to note is that you can use the `Image` element to either download directly using a URI, or you can use the built-in `Downloader` object (which has pretty much the same API it does in JavaScript) and set the results to the source of the `Image`, which provides a little more flexibility and ease for getting images from servers programmatically.

Where it gets interesting is in these next APIs:

- **System.Windows**
  - `Application`
  - `BackgroundWorker`
  - `WebApplication`
  - `XamlReader`

It's safe to assume that the `Application` object will, like its WPF counterpart, provide application-level functionality like application lifetime-related functionality and help with resource management (such as its `LoadComponent` method). `WebApplication` is the basic hook into web-related application functionality, and the `XamlReader` assists with, you guessed it, reading XAML. Thankfully, they're going to make multithreading easier by adding the `BackgroundWorker`, though many of the operations that might otherwise be noticeably blocking are asynchronous by default (chiefly using the HTTP web request to get data and resources); so you may not find yourself using that so much.

- **System.Windows.Browser**
  - `BrowserInformation`
  - `HtmlDocument`
  - `HtmlElement`
  - `HtmlPage`
  - `HtmlTimer`
  - `HttpUtility`

Perhaps the most interesting part of all the managed presentation framework is the bit that interacts with the browser. This is chiefly useful for those applications that will remain a blend of standard web presentation technologies (HTML, JavaScript, CSS) and Silverlight. We think we'll see these mostly in web-based portals like SharePoint and in situations where folks just want to add some Silverlight goodness to existing applications. It seems to us that once we have a fully baked Silverlight CLR and Framework, good tooling in Blend and Visual Studio, and rich controls from vendors like Infragistics, there will be little reason to continue developing using currently standard web technologies. The benefits of the client-side CLR and Framework in Silverlight are just too great to continue building on the shaky web technologies in use today.

For those applications that have a need to have interaction between managed code, JavaScript, and the HTML DOM (and BOM, a lesser-known acronym for Browser Object Model), Silverlight supplies a number of ways to interoperate.

- First, by registering a class with the `WebApplication` and marking it and members using a `ScriptableAttribute`, you can expose managed events, methods, and properties to JavaScript — these scriptable objects and their members have JavaScript proxies provided that can be called (in the case of properties and methods) and subscribed to (in the case of events).

- Second, through the types in the System.Windows.Browser (listed earlier), managed code can do things like access properties and subscribe to events on HTML elements as well as get information about the current document/page and navigate to other locations, including opening new windows, though as of now, this last seems to be using JavaScript and is subject to pop-up blockers.

That pretty much wraps it up for the discussions of the Silverlight frameworks/APIs. The following sections cover some other items of interest for application developers related to Silverlight 1.1.

Debugging

This is a very important feature, given the difficulty in debugging JavaScript today (though Visual Studio 2008 makes that much better). As you might expect, given that it is managed code that is type safe, you get all the debugging features you've come to know and love in Visual Studio. There's not much more to say about it because the goal is to provide pretty much the same debugging experience you get using other managed code, including great visualizers like the new LINQ visualizer you can get for Visual Studio 2008.

Dynamic Language Support

A key feature for bringing more web developers into the Silverlight fold (and .NET in general) is the new support for dynamic languages. Silverlight currently supports IronPython and Managed JScript. Microsoft is working to provide the best possible development experience (including rich debugging support) for these (and ultimately other) dynamic languages. Apart from the languages, the key extra bit of knowledge is that in addition to the standard Silverlight assemblies, the Dynamic Language Runtime (DLR) will be downloaded to the clients to compile and execute the dynamic languages at runtime.

A Quick Silverlight 1.1 Example

In addition to the additional online chapter for this book that we mentioned at the beginning of this chapter, there are lots of other resources and examples you can find online that demonstrate what you can do with Silverlight 1.1. For example, Infragistics has an alpha prototype at `labs.infragistics.com/silverlight` that shows and talks about what they're doing with Silverlight. One key, early example of a control that should prove useful to many is their Silverlight chart, which is a scaled back version of their WPF chart. You can see it in action on the `labs.infragistics.com` site, and Figure 6-4 is a screenshot to give you a taste.

Don't forget to check out the resources in Appendix C to find other ways to learn about Silverlight.

Figure 6-4

Summary

As noted, the purpose of this chapter was to provide an architectural overview of Silverlight 1.1 Alpha. We covered the core value proposition for managed Silverlight, areas where it needs further development, and the core functionality that is currently in Silverlight 1.1 as of this writing. We hope you agree that managed Silverlight shows great promise for web application development in the future. It's one of the most exciting technologies that Microsoft has produced, and we're sure we'll all be watching closely to see how it develops.

Again, don't forget about the online bonus chapter, available at `www.wrox.com`. It has an actual sample 1.1 application that you can download, play with, and learn from, and we'll be doing our best to keep it up to date as Silverlight 1.1 develops and matures.

7

Video Player: Silverlight 1.0 Case Example

One of the challenges of learning a new technology is that often you never get the opportunity to see the topics covered by a book applied in an actual application. To help see how you can use Silverlight to create a realistic, real-world application, we are including a case study on a Silverlight-based application called Lumos. Lumos is a video player that demonstrates how you can create rich, interactive Silverlight-based applications using Blend, ASP.NET AJAX, JavaScript, and XAML. You can view the Lumos application online by visiting `http://labs.infragistics.com/wrox/silverlight1_0/chapter7`.

Also note that the source code for the Lumos application is included along with the other code from the book and is available for download from `www.wrox.com`. *However, to keep the file size of the download manageable, the code for the Lumos application available for download includes only a couple of the video clips from the full application.*

Specifically, this chapter focuses on:

- Setting up the architecture and interface for the Lumos application
- Preparing the media for the application
- Coding the application

By the end of the chapter you'll have a good understanding of how to create your own Silverlight-based applications.

Getting Started

To get started creating Lumos, you first need to assemble all of the development tools needed to build a Silverlight application. The tools for building Silverlight applications have been discussed in detail in previous chapters in this book. The tools needed for building Lumos are:

- Visual Studio 2005
- Silverlight 1.0 and 1.0 SDK
- Expression Blend 2 August 2007 Preview
- Expression Encoder
- ASP.NET AJAX Extensions 1.0

Once you have all of the tools in place, you are ready to start building the application.

Designing the Application Architecture

Lumos is designed using a traditional three-tier application architecture, which allows it to clearly define the User Interface layer (UI), Client Logic, and Data layer components that make up the application. The three primary components of the application are shown in Figure 7-1.

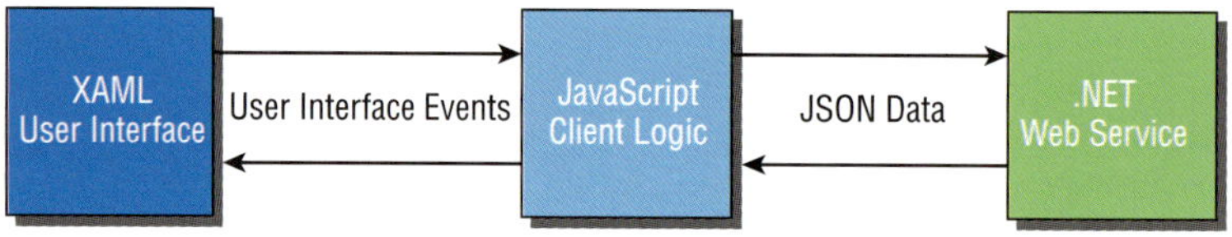

Figure 7-1

As in a traditional three-tier application, the UI component is responsible for defining the user interface that the end user interacts with. The Client Logic component contains all of the client-side logic needed by the application and serves as the broker between the UI component and the Web Services component. The Web Services component simply serves data to the Client Logic component.

To help you understand exactly how each of the three major components was created, the rest of the chapter walks you through each area in detail.

Designing the User Interface

The basic design of the Lumos player's user interface is fairly simple and is designed to make it as easy as possible for the end user to navigate the available video selections, to interact with a playing video, and to view contextual information as the video is playing. As shown in the basic diagram in Figure 7-2, the Lumos interface includes four major content areas: the Header, Navigation, Video Player, and Supplemental Information areas. Each of these areas performs a distinct function in the UI.

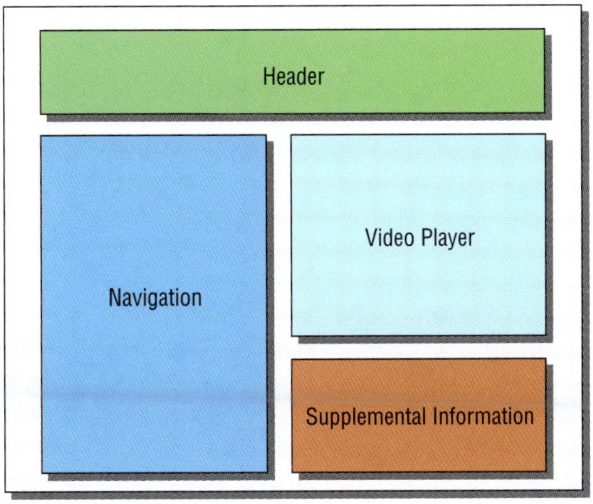

Figure 7-2

These base areas provide the end user with application navigation, information about the current state of the application, and information about the currently running video. When combined, the content areas form a simple, yet effective user interface. Figure 7-3 shows the completed application when running in the browser.

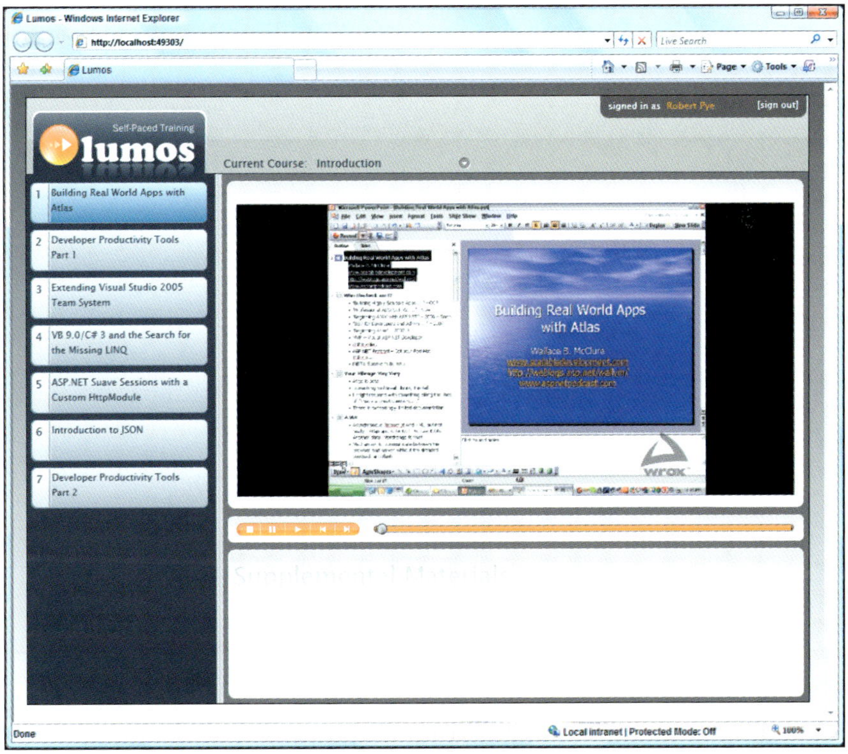

Figure 7-3

Once you or your designer has defined the basic layout of your application's user interface, you should start to think about how you can structure the XAML to allow you to compartmentalize portions of the UI into distinct blocks of logic. Isolating portions of the UI into separate XAML files allows you to logically organize your project into smaller, more manageable chunks of XAML and script rather than one giant XAML file. It can also allow you to identify areas of the UI that can be converted to reusable components.

Remember that the XAML files used to define your application's UI must be downloaded to the client, so the more you can reduce the initial size of the UI, the less your application has to download initially. You can then use application logic to determine how much additional UI will be needed and use a Load on Demand architecture to dynamically inject additional UI elements into the application at runtime.

In Lumos, two areas were identified as portions of the UI that could be isolated:

- The buttons used in the Navigation content area
- The video player–related UI

Each of these is isolated into its own XAML files, which gives the application a smaller main UI definition file and allows more efficient organization of the application. What results are three XAML files that form the Lumos UI:

- The `Scene.xaml` file contains the bulk of the UI and defines the basic structure of the application.
- The `Button.xaml` file contains the raw button definition used to create the Navigation area's buttons.
- And finally, the `VideoArea.xaml` file includes the UI for displaying and controlling the video playing in the application.

Figure 7-4 shows what `Scene.xaml` looks like when loaded in Expression Blend.

You can see the buttons and video area are not displayed because they are located in two other XAML files. Their contents are instantiated and injected into this main UI at runtime.

Managing the Developer/Designer Workflow

Considering how you can break down your user interface is an important part of the application design process. If you are working with an interface designer to design the application's user interface, it is important that you communicate with that person during the design process so that the application interface can be factored in such a way that it allows you to easily add the application logic. Thankfully, Microsoft has put considerable effort into enabling a smooth workflow between developers and designers.

Because Silverlight uses XAML as its UI definition language, it is very easy for developers and designers to work together to create stunning application user interfaces. Both Expression Blend, the tool typically used by designers, and Visual Studio 2005, the tool used by developers, understand the XAML language. This means that UI assets can be easily shared between developers and designers with little or no worries about the designer having to dig into code, or the developer having to interpret the designer's wishes from a static image. Instead, XAML and the development tools allow the developer and designer to work virtually simultaneously.

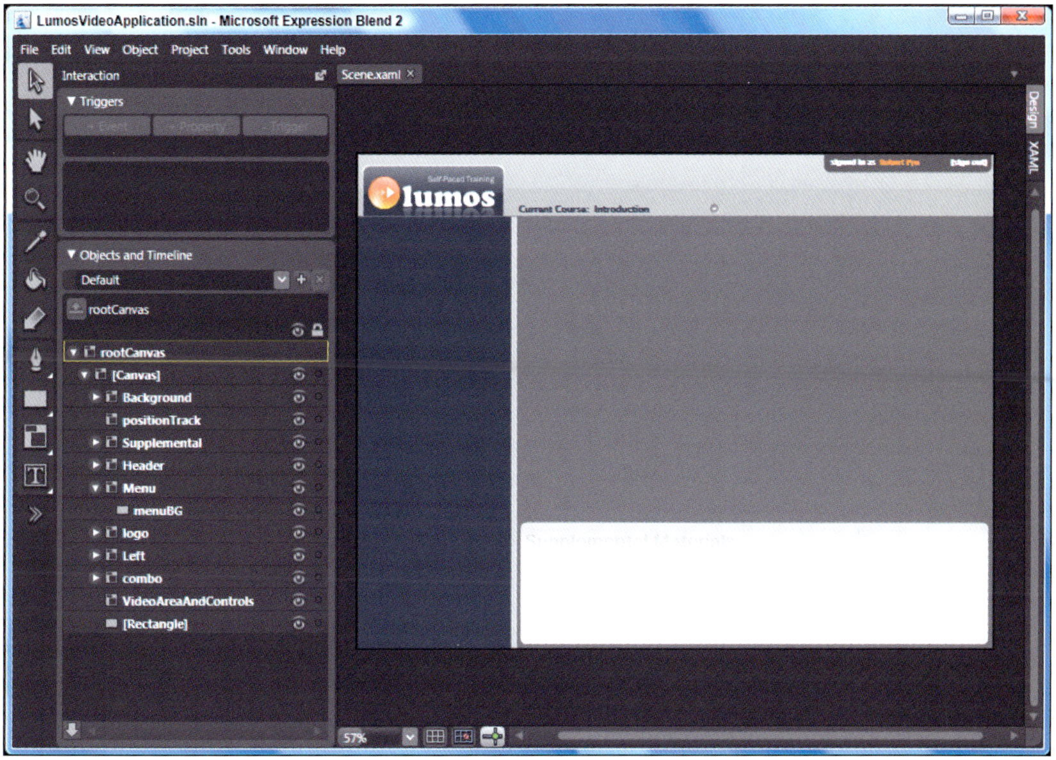

Figure 7-4

Preparing the Media for the Application

To prepare each video available in the Lumos player, Expression Encoder was used to convert each raw video file to a Silverlight-friendly format. The videos were converted to a VC-1 Broadband format, which provides a quality streaming video experience to the end user, but does result in a fairly large file size. Depending on your audience, you may choose to encode the media in a lower or higher quality media format.

Additionally, all of the media files included in the Lumos application include embedded markers. The markers denote chapters in the videos and are also used to generate the combo box items in the application. Markers are a great way to allow the user to jump immediately to different sections of the video, or you can use markers and the `MediaElement`'s events to trigger your application to display different data when a marker is encountered in the stream. The markers used in Lumos were added during the encoding process using Expression Encoder.

Markers and Expression Encoder are discussed more detail in Chapter 2 and Chapter 4.

Creating the Data Layer

The Data layer used by Lumos is actually quite simple. It consists of a single .NET web service that is exposed using the ASP.NET AJAX Extensions `ScriptService` attribute. The web service creates a generic `List` of `Video` objects, which is returned as JavaScript Object Notation (JSON) to the application. The code for the web service is shown in Listing 7-1.

Listing 7-1: The Lumos Web Service

```
[WebService(Namespace = "http://tempuri.org/")]
[WebServiceBinding(ConformsTo = WsiProfiles.BasicProfile1_1)]
[ScriptService]
[GenerateScriptType(typeof(Video))]
[ToolboxItem(false)]
public class LumosVideoService : System.Web.Services.WebService
{

    [WebMethod]
    [ScriptMethod(ResponseFormat = ResponseFormat.Json)]
    public Video[] GetVideos()
    {

        List<Video> videos = new List<Video>();
        videos.Add(
          new Video("Building Real World Apps with Atlas",
            "Wally McClure", "",
            "mcclure-atlanta-codecamp-atlas.wmv"));
        videos.Add(
          new Video("Developer Productivity Tools Part 1",
            "Scott Hanselman", "",
            "hanselman-productivity-tools-part1-beantown.net.wmv"));
        videos.Add(
          new Video("Extending Visual Studio 2005 Team System",
            "Jean-Luc David", "",
            "david-VS-Team-System-Atlanta-Code-Camp.wmv"));
        videos.Add(
          new Video("VB 9.0/C# 3 and the Search for the Missing LINQ",
            "Jim Wooley", "",
            "wooley-linq-atlanta-code-camp.wmv"));
        videos.Add(
          new Video("ASP.NET Suave Sessions with a Custom HttpModule",
            "J. Ambrose Little", "",
            "ambrose-suave.wmv"));
        videos.Add(
          new Video("Introduction to JSON",
            "Wally McClure", "",
            "wally-json.wmv"));
        videos.Add(
          new Video("Developer Productivity Tools Part 2",
            "Scott Hanselman", "",
            "hanselman-productivity-tools-part2-beantown.net.wmv"));
        return videos.ToArray();
    }
}
```

There are two items to note in this listing:

- First, the `WebService` class is marked with the `ScriptService` attribute. This allows you to access the web service through the ASP.NET AJAX `ScriptManager`'s `Services` tag. Doing this makes accessing the web service simple through JavaScript and means that you will only have to write a single line of code to get the data from the service.
- The second line to note is the `ScriptMethod` attribute that is applied to the `GetVideos` method. This attribute allows you to configure the format of the web service response. By default, the Lumos web service returns its data in a JSON serialized format. This makes using the service results in JavaScript simple. You could also choose to return the results as raw XML and use the browser's XML parser to manipulate the data.

Of course the actual work done by the Lumos web service probably does not represent a real-world web service. More likely you would be accessing a database and perhaps allowing the services to accept search parameters or user credentials as part of a rich Service-Oriented Architecture, and you certainly could easily modify Lumos to use a more complex service. The point to take away from the Lumos application is how you can easily use a web service, regardless of its complexity, to provide dynamic, runtime data to your Silverlight application.

Creating the Host Web Page

Finally, before you dig into the application code, it's important to look at the ASP.NET web page that will host the application. The page is very simple, consisting only of the ASP.NET AJAX `ScriptManager` control and a `<div>` to host the Silverlight player. Listing 7-2 shows the web page markup.

Listing 7-2: The Lumos Host ASP.NET Web Page

```
<!DOCTYPE HTML PUBLIC "-//W3C//DTD HTML 4.01 Transitional//EN"
"http://www.w3c.org/TR/1999/REC-html401-19991224/loose.dtd">

<html xmlns="http://www.w3.org/1999/xhtml">
<head>
    <title>Lumos</title>
</head>

<body>
    <form runat="server">

        <asp:ScriptManager ID="ScriptManager1" runat="server">
            <Scripts>
                <asp:ScriptReference Path="Silverlight.js" />
                <asp:ScriptReference Path="Default.html.js" />
                <asp:ScriptReference Path="Scene.xaml.js" />
                <asp:ScriptReference Path="Button.xaml.js" />
                <asp:ScriptReference Path="VideoArea.xaml.js" />
            </Scripts>
            <Services>
                <asp:ServiceReference Path="~/LumosVideoService.asmx" />
```

(Continued)

Listing 7-2: *(continued)*

```
                </Services>
            </asp:ScriptManager>

            <div id="SilverlightPlugInHost">
                <script type="text/javascript">
                    createSilverlight();
                    document.getElementById('SilverlightPlugInHost').focus();
                </script>
            </div>
        </form>
    </body>
    </html>
```

If you are not familiar with the `ScriptManager` control, it is a simple control included with the ASP.NET AJAX Extensions whose purpose is to ensure that scripts are loaded in the proper order and to help support features like partial page postbacks and, as Lumos uses, web service calls. Lumos uses the `ScriptManager` control to add references to all of the JavaScript files that will be used by the application. It is also used to reference the data web service, allowing you to easily call the service using JavaScript.

The last feature of the host web page is the `<div>` element that is used to host the Silverlight plug-in. Given the ID `SilverlightlightPlugInHost`, the element also contains the script block that calls the `createSilverlight` function to add the player to the element.

Coding Lumos

Now that you have seen the basic user interface design, and the back end data service of Lumos, you can start to examine the middle layer of the application, the Client logic. With the exception of the data service, Lumos is written entirely in JavaScript.

The entry point for the application is the `createSilverlight` function located in the `default.aspx.js` file. This function is the first script function called, and it is responsible for two functions: creating the `Scene` object, which is discussed in detail in the next section, and calling Silverlight's `createObjectEx` function, which adds the Silverlight player to the web page. Listing 7-3 shows the `createSilverlight` function.

Listing 7-3: Creating the Lumos Silverlight Player

```
function createSilverlight()
{
    //create an instance of the Scene class,
    //contained in Scene.xaml.js
    scene = new LumosVideoClient.Scene();

    //Create the Silverlight player object
```

Listing 7-3: *(continued)*

```
        Silverlight.createObjectEx({
            source: 'Scene.xaml',
            parentElement: document.getElementById('SilverlightPlugInHost'),
            id: 'SilverlightPlugIn',
            properties: {
                width: '1024',
                height: '768',
                background:'#ffffffff',
                isWindowless: 'false',
                version: '0.8'
            },
            events: {
                onError: OnErrorEventHandler,
                onLoad: Silverlight.createDelegate(scene, scene.handleLoad)
            },
            context: null
        });
    }
```

As explained in Chapter 4, the `createObjectEx` function allows you to specify event handler functions to attach to the player's `onError` and `onLoad` events as part of its parameters. In Lumos, the `onLoad` handler is attached by using Silverlight's `createDelegate` function. This function allows as its parameters an object instance and the function within that instance to use as the event handler. In this case, Lumos attaches the `handleLoad` function defined by the `scene` object.

The `handleLoad` function is used to perform a significant number of initialization functions, so it is key to the operation of the application.

Though the `createSilverlight` function serves as the entry point into the Lumos application, the primary application logic is divided into three separate JavaScript classes: `Scene`, `Button`, and `VideoArea`. The `Scene` class contains the primary application logic and manages the creation of the `VideoArea` and `Button` classes. Each class is discussed in detail in the following sections.

Scene Class

The `Scene` class serves as the primary control class for the Lumos application. It contains the Silverlight player's `onLoad` event handler, as well as functions to download the additional necessary UI assets and logic to create the Markers combo box UI element.

onLoad Handler

The Silverlight player `onLoad` event handler `handleLoad` function is the first function called by Silverlight once its initial XAML has been successfully loaded. It is responsible for initiating the download of the `VideoArea` user interface, retrieving the application's menu items, and creating the basic elements of the Markers combo box. Listing 7-4 shows the contents of the `handleLoad` function.

Listing 7-4: Handling the Silverlight Player's onLoad Event in Lumos

```
handleLoad: function(plugIn, userContext, rootElement)
{
    //Create a downloader to download the
    //VideoArea XAML from the server
    var videoareadownloader = plugIn.createObject("downloader");
    videoareadownloader.addEventListener("completed",
        Silverlight.createDelegate(
            this, this.handleVideoAreaDownloaderCompleted));
    videoareadownloader.addEventListener("downloadfailed",
        Silverlight.createDelegate(this, this.handleDownloadFailed));
    videoareadownloader.Open("GET","VideoArea.xaml");
    videoareadownloader.Send();

    //Fetch the video data from the web service
    LumosVideoApplication.LumosVideoService.GetVideos(
        Function.createDelegate(this, this.fetchMenuItemsSucceeded));

    //Set up the basics of the combobox
    plugIn.content.findName('combo').addEventListener(
        "MouseLeftButtonDown",
        Silverlight.createDelegate(
            this, this.handleComboMouseLeftButtonDown));
    plugIn.content.findName('combo').addEventListener(
        "MouseLeftButtonUp",
        Silverlight.createDelegate(
            this, this.handleComboMouseLeftButtonUp));

    //Locate the base combo canvas and set its ZIndex
    var combo = plugIn.content.findName('combo');
    combo.setValue("Canvas.ZIndex",10001);

    //Create the base combobox body canvas and set its properties
    combobody = plugIn.content.CreateFromXaml(
        "<Canvas Width='200' Canvas.Top='0' Visibility='Collapsed' " +
        "Canvas.Left='0' Height='200' x:Name='comboBody' " +
        "xmlns:x='http://schemas.microsoft.com/winfx/2006/xaml' " +
        "Canvas.ZIndex='2001'></Canvas>");

    combobody.setValue("Canvas.Top", combo.Height);
    combobody.setValue("Canvas.Left", -300 + combo.Width);
    combobody.addEventListener("MouseLeftButtonUp",
        Silverlight.createDelegate(
            this, this.handleComboBodyMouseLeftButtonUp));

    //Add the base combobox body to the combo canvas
    combo.children.add(combobody);
}
```

The first task of the `handleLoad` function is to create a new `downloader` object. This object is used to retrieve the `VideoArea.xaml` file from the server. The `VideoArea` XAML contains all of the video player and control user interface elements. The `downloader` object attaches its `Completed` event, which it uses to process the downloaded XAML and insert it into the main application's element tree. You will see this later in the chapter.

The next task of the `handleLoad` function is to retrieve the video data from the Lumos web service. This is done using a single line of JavaScript code that calls the `GetVideos` function, which accepts a `Completed` callback function as a parameter. You will see later in the chapter how the `Completed` callback is used to generate navigation buttons for the application.

The final task of the `handleLoad` function is to begin to create the base parts of the Markers combo box. This simulated combo box allows the end user to view and select a marker from the currently playing video and change the video's position to that marker. The `handleLoad` function instantiates a new XAML `Canvas` element that hosts the individual combo box items. Once instantiated, the function sets the basic positioning properties and then adds the `Canvas` to the combo `Canvas` element.

Inserting the VideoArea User Interface

As described in the previous section, the `handleLoad` function creates a `downloader` object that downloads the `VideoArea` user interface XAML. The `downloader` attaches an event handler that is raised once the download is completed. The event handler code is shown in Listing 7-5.

Listing 7-5: Creating the VideoArea XAML Content

```
handleVideoAreaDownloaderCompleted: function(sender, eventArgs)
{
    if(sender.status!=200)
    {
        //handle the error condition
        alert("An application resource failed " +
            "to download.\r\n\r\nUri: '" + sender.Uri + "'");
        return;
    }

    this.plugIn = sender.getHost();
    var videoareahost =
        this.plugIn.content.FindName("VideoAreaAndControls");

    videoarea = new LumosVideoClient.VideoArea(sender.ResponseText);
    videoareahost.children.add(videoarea.instance());
}
```

The completed event simply extracts the `ResponseText` from the `downloader` and instantiates a new `VideoArea` JavaScript object. The XAML element tree exposed by the instantiated `VideoArea` object is inserted as a child object into the application's main element tree. The `VideoArea` object, which includes all of the video playback and control-related functionality, is discussed in detail later in the chapter.

Instantiating Video Navigation

Another initialization routine kicked off by the `handleLoad` event handler is the retrieval of the video data from the Lumos video web service. As shown at the beginning of this section, the `handleLoad` event handler calls the web service's `GetVideo` function and provides the callback `fetchMenuItemsSucceeded` function as a function parameter.

When the `fetchMenuItemsSucceeded` function is raised, the application has successfully retrieved the video data. The data is provided to the handler as the result function parameter, and because each video returned from the web service corresponds to a menu item in the application's Navigation content area, the event handler stores the result data in the `menuItems` array.

Now that the menu item data has been retrieved, the application can create navigation buttons for each menu item. To do this, it first needs to retrieve the XAML that defines the navigation menu buttons. The application instantiates a new `downloader` object to download the `Button.xaml` file, which defines the button UI. The application performs this logic as part of the `fetchMenuItemsSucceeded` function, which is shown in Listing 7-6.

Listing 7-6: Creating and Inserting Navigation Buttons

```
fetchMenuItemsSucceeded: function(result)
{
    //place the web service calls in a variable
    menuItems = result;

    this.plugIn = $get("SilverlightPlugIn");

    // Create a Downloader object.
    var downloader = this.plugIn.createObject("downloader");

    downloader.addEventListener("downloadfailed",
        Silverlight.createDelegate(this, this.handleDownloadFailed));
    downloader.addEventListener("completed",
        Silverlight.createDelegate(
            this, this.handleButtonDownloadCompleted));

    // Initialize the Downloader request.
    downloader.Open("GET", "Button.xaml");

    // Execute the Downloader request.
    downloader.send();
},

handleButtonDownloadCompleted: function(sender, eventArgs)
{
    this.plugIn = sender.getHost();
    var top = DEFAULTTOP;

    var menu = this.plugIn.content.FindName("Menu");

    //create a button object for each menu item
    for (var item in menuItems)
    {
        var button = new LumosVideoClient.Button(
            sender.ResponseText.replaceAll("_0", item));
        button.instance().setValue("Canvas.Top", top);

        var index = String(parseInt(item)+1);
        button.instance().FindName("txtButtonIndex").Text = index;
        button.instance().FindName("txtButtonTitle").Text =
            menuItems[item].Title;
```

Listing 7-6: *(continued)*

```
            if (menu) {
                menu.children.add(button.instance());
            }

            top += 60;
        }
    }
```

The button `downloader` object also defines its own completed event handler, also shown in Listing 7-6. This handler takes the XAML from the button `downloader` object and, for each menu item, creates a new `Button` class. The `Button` class defines all of the basic logic included with the button and is discussed in detail later in the chapter. The basic properties of the newly instantiated `Button` class are set, and then the button is added as a child element to the application's existing `menu Canvas` element.

Combo Box Functions

The final task of the `Scene` class is to instantiate and control the Markers combo box elements. As stated earlier in the chapter, the Markers combo box simulates the basic behavior of a standard Windows combo box. Although it is fairly rudimentary compared to the Windows combo box control you may be used to, it does allow you to add some basic but familiar UI functionality to your application. The combo box element is shown expanded in Figure 7-5.

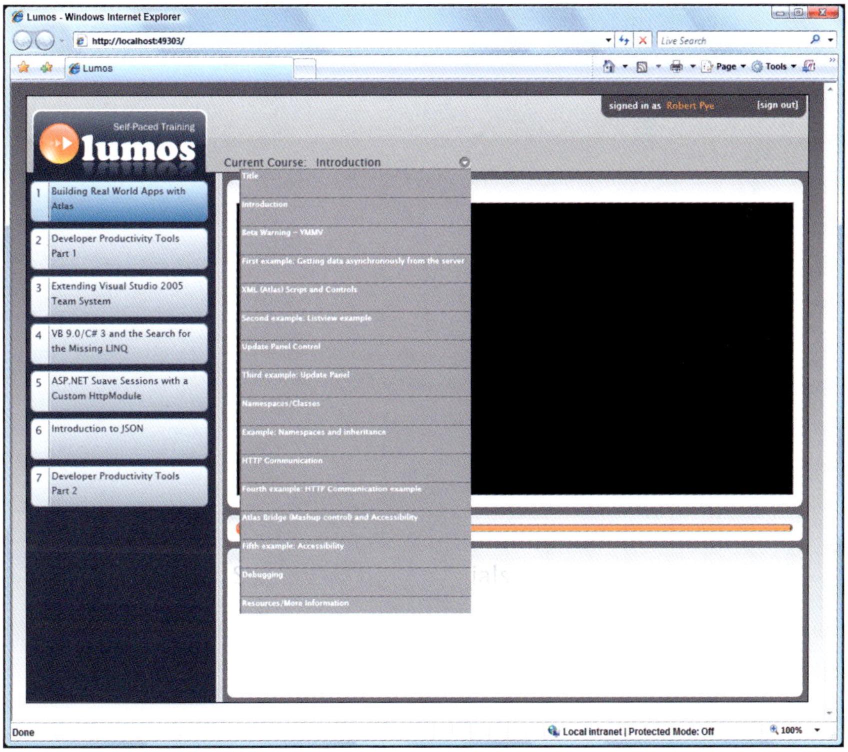

Figure 7-5

The Scene class includes event handlers that show and hide the comboBody Canvas element, which is the main element used to show the combo box contents. Listing 7-7 shows the event handlers attached to the combo box elements.

Listing 7-7: Defining Mouse Events for the Markers Combo Box

```
handleComboMouseLeftButtonDown: function(sender, mouseEventArgs)
{
    var combobody = sender.getHost().content.findName('comboBody')
    combobody.Visibility="Visible";
},

handleComboMouseLeftButtonUp: function(sender, mouseEventArgs)
{
    var combobody = sender.getHost().content.findName('comboBody')
    combobody.Visibility="Collapsed";
},

handleComboBodyMouseLeftButtonUp: function(sender, mouseEventArgs)
{
    var combobody = sender.getHost().content.findName('comboBody')
    combobody.Visibility="Collapsed";
},

handleComboItemMouseLeftButtonUp: function(sender, mouseEventArgs)
{
    var combobody = sender.getHost().content.findName('comboBody')
    combobody.Visibility="Collapsed";

    var player = sender.getHost().content.findName('thePlayer');
    var position = player.position;

    var tag = parseInt(sender.tag);


    //translate the media seconds into an actual time
    var markerseconds = player.Markers.getItem(tag).Time.Seconds;
    var position = player.position;
    position.seconds = markerseconds;
    player.position = position;
}
```

The majority of the event handlers simply control the visibility of the ComboBody canvas in the application. For example, when the end user clicks the combo canvas, causing the MouseLeftButtonDown event to fire, the application is directed to make the ComboBody element visible. When the user releases the left mouse button, one of several elements' MouseLeftButtonUp events may be raised, directing the application to collapse the ComboBody canvas.

One exception to the MouseLeftButtonUp is if the event is raised by an individual combo box item. In this case, not only does the canvas collapse, but the position of the video currently playing in the MediaElement is changed based on the specific item that was clicked.

The `Scene` class is also responsible for populating the combo box items into the combo box. The `loadComboBox` function is responsible for creating new combo box items based on the markers in the currently loaded video and inserting them into the `ComboBody` canvas. Listing 7-8 shows the `loadComboBox` function.

Listing 7-8: Loading Combo Box Items into the Combo Box

```
loadComboBox: function(list)
{
    this.plugIn = $get('SilverlightPlugIn');

    var combo = this.plugIn.content.findName('combo');

    combobody.children.Clear();
    combobody.height=(list.Count * 35) + 2;
    comboitemtop=1;

    var comboback = this.plugIn.content.CreateFromXaml(
        "<Rectangle Fill='#FF7A7A7A' Width='300' Height='" +
        combobody.height + "' />");
    combobody.children.add(comboback);

    for (var i=0;i<list.Count;i++)
    {
        var comboitemname = "ComboMenuItem_0".replaceAll("_0",i);
        var comboitem = this.plugIn.content.CreateFromXaml(
          "<Canvas Width='298' Height='35' x:Name='" +
          comboitemname + "' " +
          "xmlns:x='http://schemas.microsoft.com/winfx/2006/xaml' " +
          "Width='298' x:Name='" + comboitemname + "' Height='35' " +
          "Canvas.ZIndex='10002' Canvas.Left='1'>" +
          "<Rectangle Fill='#66FFFFFF' Height='35' Width='298' " +
          "Canvas.Left='1' /><TextBlock Foreground='#FFFFFF' " +
          "Canvas.Left='2' FontSize='10' " +
          "TextWrapping='Wrap' Width='296'>" +
          list.getItem(i).Text + "</TextBlock></Canvas>",true);

        comboitem.tag = i.toString();
        comboitem.setValue("Canvas.Top", comboitemtop );
        comboitemtop = comboitemtop + comboitem.Height + 1;

        comboitem.addEventListener("MouseLeftButtonUp",
            Silverlight.createDelegate(
                this, this.handleComboItemMouseLeftButtonUp));

        combobody.children.add(comboitem);
    }
}
```

This function, normally called when a new media file is loaded, accepts a list of markers as its sole parameter. The existing `ComboBody` elements are cleared, and then new combo box items are created for each marker in the list. Once the combo box item is created, its properties are set and event handlers are added, and then it is added as a child element to the `ComboBody` canvas element tree.

Button Class

As described earlier in this chapter, the simple `Button` class contains all of the logic required for the navigation buttons in the application and is contained in the `Button.xaml.js` file. The `Button` class constructor instantiates the button's element tree using Silverlight's `CreateFromXaml` function and assigns event handlers to the key events such as `MouseEnter`, `MouseLeave`, and `MouseLeftButtonUp`. The event handlers for these events are also contained in the class and are shown in Listing 7-9.

Listing 7-9: Defining the Button's Mouse Events

```
handleButtonMouseEnter: function(sender, eventArgs)
{
    if (currentindex ==
        (parseInt(sender.FindName('txtButtonIndex').Text)-1))
    {
        return;
    }

    this.setHoverStyle(sender);
},

handleButtonMouseLeftButtonUp: function(sender, eventArgs)
{
    if (currentindex != null) {
        this.setNormalStyle(
            sender.getHost().content.findName('Menu').children.GetItem(
                parseInt(currentindex)+1) );
    }

    currentindex = sender.FindName('txtButtonIndex').Text-1;

    this.setSelectedStyle(sender);

    videoarea.playMedia();
},

handleButtonMouseLeave: function(sender, eventArgs)
{
    if (currentindex ==
        (parseInt(sender.FindName('txtButtonIndex').Text)-1))
    {
        return;
    }

    this.setNormalStyle(sender);
}
```

The three events are responsible for managing the styles applied to the button given its current state. If end users move their mouse over a button, the event handler needs to change the button's style to the selected style. If the users actually click the button to select the video, the handler needs to assign the `Selected` style to the button. Three functions, `setNormalStyle`, `setSelectedStyle`, and `setHoverStyle`, are included in the class and contain the three different brushes used to change the button styles. These functions are called by the appropriate event handler function to change the button style.

VideoArea Class

The `VideoArea` class encapsulates all of the logic needed to control the video elements of the application into the single `VideoArea.xaml.js` file. This class includes logic to control the VCR buttons (Play, Pause, Stop), logic for the Next and Previous buttons, and logic for the trackbar elements.

When the `VideoArea` class is instantiated, event handlers are attached to all of the elements so that stylistic features such as mouse hover changes can occur, as well as behavior events such as mouse clicks and drag and drops.

The `MediaElement` is controlled primarily by the three VCR buttons, which are attached to three event handlers to provide mouse hover and click handling. The events are shown in Listing 7-10.

Listing 7-10: Defining VCR Button Mouse Events

```
handleVcrButtonMouseEnter: function(sender, mouseEventArgs)
{
    sender.findName('btn' + sender.Name + 'Fill').Fill="#ff000000";
},

handleVcrButtonMouseLeave: function(sender, mouseEventArgs)
{
    sender.findName('btn' + sender.Name + 'Fill').Fill="#ffffffff";
},

handleVcrButtonMouseLeftButtonUp: function(sender, mouseEventArgs)
{
    if (sender.getHost().content.
        findName('thePlayer').CurrentState!="Closed") {
        eval("sender.getHost().content.findName('thePlayer')." +
            sender.Name + "()");
    }
}
```

As you can see from the listing, two event handlers control the mouse hover changes for all three buttons by simply substituting the element name in the `findName` parameter.

The click actions are controlled by a single function that uses the JavaScript `eval` function and the button's name to dynamically execute a specific `MediaElement` command.

The class also includes event handlers that allow the end user to drag and drop the trackbar handle to change the position of the `MediaElement`'s video. Drag and drop in Silverlight is actually fairly simple, as was shown in Chapter 4, although if your application needs to restrict the drag-and-drop behavior, it can get a bit more complex. The Lumos application restricts the movement of the drag-and-drop operation to only a horizontal movement. Additionally, the drag-and-drop logic needs to restrict the user from dragging the handle beyond the bounds of the trackbar.

The drag action begins when the end user left-clicks the trackbar's handle. This causes the handle's `MouseButtonLeftDown` event to be raised, which gathers some basic position data and calls the Silverlight player's `CaptureMouse` function. Calling this function tells Silverlight to route all mouse events through the trackbar handle until the capture is released. The event handler function is shown in Listing 7-11.

Listing 7-11: Beginning the Drag Operation in the MouseLeftButtonDown Event

```
handlePositionHandleMouseLeftButtonDown: function(sender, mouseEventArgs)
{
    //figure out the offsets based on where the
    //mouse actually picked up the handle
    mousepositionleftoffset =
        mouseEventArgs.getPosition(null).x -
            sender.getValue("Canvas.Left");
    mousepositionrightoffset = sender.Width - mousepositionleftoffset;

    startinghandleposition = sender.getValue("Canvas.Left");
    startingmouseposition = mouseEventArgs.getPosition(null).x;

    //start the mouse capture
    sender.captureMouse();
},
```

Once the user begins to drag the mouse, the handle's `MouseMove` event is raised. This is where most of the logic for the drag action occurs. In this event handler, the application must determine how much the mouse has moved in the drag action, and map that to the distance that the handle must be moved on the trackbar. This becomes a challenge because the mouse events return coordinates that map to the entire Silverlight player, whereas the trackbar size is relative to its parent XAML element. Listing 7-12 shows the logic in the handle's `MouseMove` event.

Listing 7-12: Dragging the Position Handle in the MouseMove Event

```
handlePositionHandleMouseMove: function(sender, mouseEventArgs)
{
    //if we have mouse capture then
    if (sender.captureMouse())
    {

        //Get the basic track and handle values needed
        //to calculate the current handle position
        var track = sender.getHost().content.FindName('track');
        var trackleft = track.getValue('Canvas.Left');
        var handleleft = sender.getValue('Canvas.Left');
        var position = mouseEventArgs.getPosition(null).x;

        //Determine the difference between the starting
        //mouse position and its current position
        var positiondiff = position - startingmouseposition;

        //Translate the diff value onto the track and handle
        var handleposition = startinghandleposition + positiondiff;

        //check to see if the left edge of the handle has moved
        //past the left edge of the track
        if ( handleposition < trackleft ) {
            sender.setValue("Canvas.Left", trackleft );
            return;
```

Listing 7-12: *(continued)*

```
            }

            //check to see if the right edge of the handle has moved
            //past the right edge of the track
            if ( handleposition > (trackleft+track.Width) ) {
                sender.setValue("Canvas.Left",
                    (trackleft + track.Width) - (sender.width) );
                return;
            }

            //the position is OK.
            if ( !isNaN( handleposition ) ) {
                sender.setValue("Canvas.Left",  handleposition);
            }
        }
    }
```

Finally, the user releases the left mouse button and causes the `MouseLeftButtonUp` event to be raised. This event releases the mouse capture and then attempts to map the new position of the trackbar handle to a new position in the `MediaElement`. The logic for this is actually quite simple. By determining the distance between the handle and the left side of the track as a percentage, you can determine the percentage of time the `MediaElement` should assume has been played. Listing 7-13 shows the `MouseLeftButtonUp` event handler.

Listing 7-13: Ending the Drag Operation in the MouseLeftButtonUp Event

```
    handlePositionHandleMouseLeftButtonUp: function(sender, eventArgs)
    {
        //stop the mouse capture
        sender.releaseMouseCapture();

        //set the media position based on the handle position
        var track = sender.getHost().content.findName('track');
        var player = sender.getHost().content.findName('thePlayer');

        //where is the handle on the track?
        var trackwidth = track.Width;
        var trackleft = track.getValue("Canvas.Left");

        var handleposition =
            sender.getValue('Canvas.Left') + (sender.Width/2);

        var trackpercent = (handleposition-trackleft) / trackwidth;

        //translate the track percentage into the media position
        var duration = player.naturalDuration.Seconds;
        var mediaseconds = duration * trackpercent;

        //translate the media seconds into an actual time
        var position = player.position;
        position.seconds = mediaseconds;
        player.position = position;
    },
```

Summary

In this chapter, you were introduced to the Lumos sample application. This application attempts to show you a real-world example of a Siverlight 1.0–based application. You looked at the overall architecture of the application, as well as its basic user interface design and steps to prepare the videos that will be played by the application. The chapter also explored the web service used to provide data to the application.

Finally, the chapter walked you through the client logic of the application. Written entirely in JavaScript, the application logic dynamically downloads and instantiates portions of the user interface. JavaScript classes are used to control core application features like the `VideoArea` and its VCR control buttons and trackbar, as well as the dynamic addition of navigation buttons to the application.

Lumos demonstrates the concepts you will need to learn in order to fully leverage Silverlight as an application development platform.

A

Silverlight Object Reference

This appendix is designed to be a quick reference on the objects (classes) that can be instantiated via XAML or JavaScript to render the user interface you are creating in Silverlight. It lists in alphabetical order the non-abstract classes that deal with layout, shapes, geometries, animations, transformations, and text.

ArcSegment

Represents an elliptical arc between two points.

Properties	IsLargeArc, Name, Point, RotationAngle, Size, SweepDirection
Methods	GetValue, SetValue
Events	None

BeginStoryboard

A trigger action that begins a Storyboard and distributes its animations to their targeted objects and **Properties**.

Properties	Name, Storyboard
Methods	GetValue, SetValue
Events	None

BezierSegment

Represents a cubic Bezier curve drawn between two points.

Properties	Name, Point1 , Point2, Point3
Methods	GetValue, SetValue
Events	None

Canvas

Defines an area within which you can explicitly position child elements by using coordinates relative to the `Canvas` area.

Properties	Background, Canvas.Left, Canvas.Top, Canvas.ZIndex, Children, Clip, Cursor, Height, IsHitTestVisible, Name, Opacity, OpacityMask, RenderTransform, RenderTransformOrigin, Resources, Triggers, Visibility, Width
Methods	AddEventListener, CaptureMouse, FindName, GetHost, GetParent, GetValue, ReleaseMouseCapture, RemoveEventListener, SetValue
Events	GotFocus, KeyDown, KeyUp, Loaded, LostFocus, MouseEnter, MouseLeave, MouseLeftButtonDown, MouseLeftButtonUp, MouseMove

ColorAnimation

Animates the value of a `Color` property between two target values using linear interpolation over a specified `Duration`.

Properties	AutoReverse, BeginTime, By, Duration, FillBehavior, From, Name, RepeatBehavior, SpeedRatio, StoryBoard.TargetName, StoryBoard.TargetProperty, To
Methods	GetValue, SetValue
Events	None

ColorAnimationUsingKeyFrames

Animates the value of a `Color` property along a set of `KeyFrames` over a specified `Duration`. There are three types of `ColorKeyFrame` classes, one for each supported interpolation method: `LinearColorKeyFrame`, `DiscreteColorKeyFrame`, and `SplineColorKeyFrame`.

Properties	AutoReverse, BeginTime , Duration, FillBehavior, KeyFrames, Name, RepeatBehavior, SpeedRatio, StoryBoard.TargetName, StoryBoard.TargetProperty
Methods	GetValue, SetValue
Events	None

ColorKeyFrame

Defines an animation segment with its own target value and interpolation method for a `ColorAnimationUsingKeyFrames`.

Properties	KeyTime, Name, Value
Methods	GetValue, SetValue
Events	None

ColorKeyFrameCollection

Represents a collection of `ColorKeyFrame` objects that can be individually accessed by index.

Properties	Count, Name
Methods	Add, Clear, GetItem, GetValue, Insert, Remove, RemoveAt, SetValue
Events	None

DiscreteColorKeyFrame

Animates from the `Color` value of the previous key frame to its own `Value` using discrete interpolation.

Properties	KeyTime, Name, Value
Methods	GetValue, SetValue
Events	None

DiscreteDoubleKeyFrame

Animates from the `Double` value of the previous key frame to its own `Value` using discrete interpolation.

Properties	KeyTime, Name, Value
Methods	GetValue, SetValue
Events	None

DiscretePointKeyFrame

Animates from the `Point` value of the previous key frame to its own `Value` using discrete interpolation.

Properties	KeyTime, Name, Value
Methods	GetValue, SetValue
Events	None

DoubleAnimation

Animates the value of a `Double` property between two target values using linear interpolation over a specified `Duration`.

Properties	AutoReverse, BeginTime, By, Duration, FillBehavior, From, Name, RepeatBehavior, SpeedRatio, StoryBoard.TargetName, StoryBoard.TargetProperty, To
Methods	GetValue, SetValue
Events	None

DoubleAnimationUsingKeyFrames

Animates the value of a `Double` property along a set of `KeyFrames`.

Properties	AutoReverse, BeginTime, Duration, FillBehavior, KeyFrames, Name, RepeatBehavior, SpeedRatio, StoryBoard.TargetName, StoryBoard.TargetProperty
Methods	GetValue, SetValue
Events	None

DoubleCollection

Represents a collection of `Double` structures that can be individually accessed by index.

Properties	Count, Name
Methods	GetValue, SetValue
Events	None

DoubleKeyFrame

Defines an animation segment with its own target value and interpolation method for a `DoubleAnimationUsingKeyFrames`.

Properties	KeyTime, Name, Value
Methods	GetValue, SetValue
Events	None

DoubleKeyFrameCollection

Represents a collection of `DoubleKeyFrame` objects that can be individually accessed by index.

Properties	Count, Name
Methods	Add, Clear, GetItem, GetValue, Insert, Remove, RemoveAt, SetValue
Events	None

Downloader

Represents the set of download functionality for a Silverlight control. The **Properties** and **Methods** of the `Downloader` object are modeled after the XMLHttpRequest (XHR) set of APIs. XMLHttpRequest provides JavaScript and other web browser scripting languages the ability to transfer and manipulate XML data to and from a web server using HTTP.

Properties	DownloadProgress, Status, StatusText, URI
Methods	Abort, GetResponseText, Open, Send
Events	Completed, DownloadProgressChanged

DrawingAttributes

Represents the appearance of a Stroke.

Properties	Color, Height, Name, OutlineColor, Width
Methods	GetValue, SetValue
Events	None

Duration

Represents the duration of time that a timeline is active.

Properties	Name
Methods	GetValue, SetValue
Events	None

Ellipse

Draws an ellipse.

Properties	Canvas.Left, Canvas.Top, Canvas.ZIndex, Clip, Cursor, Fill , Height, Name, Opacity, OpacityMask, RenderTransform, RenderTransformOrigin, Resources, Stretch, Stroke, StrokeDashArray, StrokeDashCap, StrokeDashOffset, StrokeEndLineCap, StrokeLineJoin, StrokeMiterLimit, StrokeStartLineCap, StrokeThickness, Triggers, Width
Methods	AddEventListener, CaptureMouse, FindName, GetHost, GetParent, GetValue, ReleaseMouseCapture, RemoveEventListener, SetValue
Events	Loaded, MouseEnter, MouseLeave, MouseLeftButtonDown, MouseLeftButtonUp, MouseMove

EllipseGeometry

Represents the geometry of a circle or ellipse.

Properties	Center, Name, RadiusX, RadiusY, Transform
Methods	GetValue, SetValue
Events	None

FontFamily

Represents a family of related fonts.

Properties	Name
Methods	GetValue, SetValue
Events	None

GeometryCollection

Represents a collection of `Geometry` objects.

Properties	Count, Name
Methods	Add, GetItem, GetValue, Insert, Remove, RemoveAt, SetValue
Events	None

GeometryGroup

Represents a composite geometry, composed of other `Geometry` objects.

Properties	Children, Name, Transform
Methods	GetValue, SetValue
Events	None

Glyphs

Represents the set of glyphs that are used for rendering fixed text.

Properties	Canvas.Left, Canvas.Top, Canvas.ZIndex, Clip, Cursor, Fill , FontRenderingEmSize, FontUri, Height, Indices, Name, Opacity, OpacityMask, OriginX, OriginY, RenderTransform, RenderTransformOrigin, Resources, StyleSimulations, Triggers, UnicodeString, Width
Methods	AddEventListener, CaptureMouse, FindName, GetHost, GetParent, GetValue, ReleaseMouseCapture, RemoveEventListener, SetValue
Events	Loaded, MouseEnter, MouseLeave, MouseLeftButtonDown, MouseLeftButtonUp, MouseMove

GradientStop

Describes the location and color of a transition point in a gradient.

Properties	Color, Name, Offset
Methods	GetValue, SetValue
Events	None

GradientStopCollection

Represents a collection of `GradientStop` objects that can be individually accessed by index.

Properties	Count, Name
Methods	Add, Clear, GetItem, GetValue, Insert, Remove, RemoveAt, SetValue
Events	None

Image

Represents an image that is displayed. The `Source` property can be used to display an image, such as GIF, JPG, and PNG format files.

Properties	Canvas.Left, Canvas.Top, Canvas.ZIndex, Clip, Cursor, Height, Opacity, OpacityMask, RenderTransform, RenderTransformOrigin, Resources, Source, Stretch, Triggers, Width
Methods	AddEventListener, CaptureMouse, FindName, GetHost, GetParent, GetValue, ReleaseMouseCapture, RemoveEventListener, SetValue **Events** Loaded, MouseEnter, MouseLeave, MouseLeftButtonDown, MouseLeftButtonUp, MouseMove
Events	None

ImageBrush

Paints an area with an image.

Properties	AlignmentX, AlignmentY, ImageSource, Name, Opacity, RelativeTransform, Stretch, Transform
Methods	GetValue, SetValue
Events	None

InkPresenter

Element that displays ink and can be a child, sibling, or parent of other elements.

Properties	Background, Canvas.Left, Canvas.Top, Canvas.ZIndex, Children, Clip, Height, Name, Opacity, OpacityMask, RenderTransform, RenderTransformOrigin, Resources, Strokes, Triggers, Width
Methods	AddEventListener, CaptureMouse, FindName, GetHost, GetParent, GetValue, ReleaseMouseCapture, RemoveEventListener, SetValue
Events	GotFocus, KeyDown, KeyUp, Loaded, LostFocus, MouseEnter, MouseLeave, MouseLeftButtonDown, MouseLeftButtonUp, MouseMove

KeyboardEventArgs

Provides data for the `KeyUp` and `KeyDown` **Events**.

Properties	Ctrl, Key, PlatformKeyCode, Shift
Methods	None
Events	None

KeySpline

This object is used by a spline key frame to define animation progress.

Properties	KeyTime, Name, Value
Methods	GetValue, SetValue
Events	None

KeyTime

During the relative course of an animation, a `KeyTime` instance specifies the precise timing when a particular key frame should take place.

Properties	Name
Methods	GetValue, SetValue
Events	None

Line

Draws a straight line between two points.

Properties	Canvas.Left, Canvas.Top, Canvas.ZIndex, Clip, Cursor, Fill , Height, Name, Opacity, OpacityMask, RenderTransform, RenderTransformOrigin, Resources, Stretch, Stroke, StrokeDashArray, StrokeDashCap, StrokeDashOffset, StrokeEndLineCap, StrokeLineJoin, StrokeMiterLimit, StrokeStartLineCap, StrokeThickness, Triggers, Width, X1, X2, Y1, Y2
Methods	AddEventListener, CaptureMouse, FindName, GetHost, GetParent, GetValue, ReleaseMouseCapture, RemoveEventListener, SetValue
Events	Loaded, MouseEnter, MouseLeave, MouseLeftButtonDown, MouseLeftButtonUp, MouseMove

LinearColorKeyFrame

Animates from the `Color` value of the previous key frame to its own `Value` using linear interpolation.

Properties	KeyTime, Name, Value
Methods	GetValue, SetValue
Events	None

LinearDoubleKeyFrame

Animates from the `Double` value of the previous key frame to its own `Value` using linear interpolation.

Properties	KeyTime, Name, Value
Methods	GetValue, SetValue
Events	None

LinearGradientBrush

Paints an area with a linear gradient.

Properties	ColorInterpolationMode, EndPoint, GradientStops, MappingMode, Name, Opacity, RelativeTransform, SpreadMethod, StartPoint, Transform
Methods	GetValue, SetValue
Events	None

LinearPointKeyFrame

Animates from the `Point` value of the previous key frame to its own `Value` using linear interpolation.

Properties	KeyTime, Name, Value
Methods	GetValue, SetValue
Events	None

LineBreak

Represents an explicit new line in a `TextBlock`.

Properties	FontFamily, FontSize, FontStretch, FontStyle, FontWeight, Foreground, Name, TextDecorations
Methods	FindName, GetHost, GetValue, SetValue
Events	None

LineGeometry

Represents the geometry of a line.

Properties	EndPoint, Name, StartPoint, Transform
Methods	GetValue, SetValue
Events	None

LineSegment

Represents a line drawn between two points.

Properties	Name, Point
Methods	GetValue, SetValue
Events	None

MatrixTransform

Creates an arbitrary affine matrix transformation that is used to manipulate objects or coordinate systems in a 2-D plane.

Properties	Matrix, Name
Methods	GetValue, SetValue
Events	None

MediaAttributeCollection

Represents a collection of `MediaAttribute` objects.

Properties	Count
Methods	GetItem, GetItemByName
Events	None

MediaElement

Represents an object that contains audio, video, or both.

Properties	Attributes, AutoPlay, Balance, BufferingProgress, BufferingTime, Canvas.Left, Canvas.Top, Canvas.ZIndex, Children, Clip, CurrentState, Cursor, DownloadProgress, Height, IsMuted, Markers, NaturalDuration, NaturalVideoHeight, NaturalVideoWidth, Opacity, OpacityMask, Position, RenderTransform, RenderTransformOrigin, Resources, Source, Stretch, Triggers, Volume, Width
Methods	AddEventListener, CaptureMouse, FindName, GetHost, GetParent, GetValue, Pause, Play, ReleaseMouseCapture, RemoveEventListener, SetValue, Stop
Events	BufferingProgressChanged, CurrentStateChanged, DownloadProgressChanged, Loaded, MarkerReached, MediaEnded, MediaFailed, MediaOpened, MouseEnter, MouseLeave, MouseLeftButtonDown, MouseLeftButtonUp, MouseMove

MouseEventArgs

Provides data for mouse-related **Events**.

Properties	None
Methods	GetPosition, GetStylusInfo, GetStylusPoints
Events	None

ParserErrorEventArgs

Provides data for XAML parser error **Events**.

Properties	CharPosition, ErrorCode, ErrorMessage, ErrorType, LineNumber, XamlFile, XmlAttribute, XmlElement
Methods	None
Events	None

Path

Draws a series of connected lines and curves.

Properties	Canvas.Left, Canvas.Top, Canvas.ZIndex, Clip, Cursor, Data, Fill, Height, Name, Opacity, OpacityMask, RenderTransform, RenderTransformOrigin, Resources, Stretch, Stroke, StrokeDashArray, StrokeDashCap, StrokeDashOffset, StrokeEndLineCap, StrokeLineJoin, StrokeMiterLimit, StrokeStartLineCap, StrokeThickness, Triggers, Width
Methods	AddEventListener, CaptureMouse, FindName, GetHost, GetParent, GetValue, ReleaseMouseCapture, RemoveEventListener, SetValue
Events	Loaded, MouseEnter, MouseLeave, MouseLeftButtonDown, MouseLeftButtonUp, MouseMove

PathFigure

Represents a subsection of a geometry, a single connected series of two-dimensional geometric segments.

Properties	IsClosed, IsFilled, Name, Segments, StartPoint
Methods	GetValue, SetValue
Events	None

PathFigureCollection

Represents a collection of `PathFigure` objects that collectively make up the geometry of a `PathGeometry`.

Properties	Count, Name
Methods	Add, Clear, GetItem, GetValue, Insert, Remove, RemoveAt, SetValue
Events	None

PathSegmentCollection

Represents a collection of `PathSegment` objects that can be individually accessed by index.

Properties	Count, Name
Methods	Add, Clear, GetItem, GetValue, Insert, Remove, RemoveAt, SetValue
Events	None

PointAnimation

Animates the value of a `Point` property between two target values using linear interpolation over a specified `Duration`.

Properties	AutoReverse, BeginTime, By, Duration, FillBehavior, From, Name, RepeatBehavior, SpeedRatio, StoryBoard.TargetName, StoryBoard.TargetProperty, To
Methods	GetValue, SetValue
Events	None

PointAnimationUsingKeyFrames

Animates the value of a `Point` property along a set of `KeyFrames`. A key frame animation's target values are defined by its `KeyFrames` property, which contains a collection of `DoubleKeyFrame` objects. Each `DoubleKeyFrame` defines a segment of the animation with its own target `Value` and `KeyTime`. When the animation runs, it progresses from one key value to the next at the specified key times.

There are three types of `DoubleKeyFrame` classes, one for each supported interpolation method: `LinearDoubleKeyFrame`, `DiscreteDoubleKeyFrame`, and `SplineDoubleKeyFrame`.

Properties	AutoReverse, BeginTime, Duration, FillBehavior, KeyFrames, Name, RepeatBehavior, SpeedRatio, StoryBoard.TargetName, StoryBoard.TargetProperty
Methods	GetValue, SetValue
Events	None

PointCollection

Represents a collection of `Point` objects.

Properties	Count, Name
Methods	Add, Clear, GetItem, GetValue, Insert, Remove, RemoveAt, SetValue
Events	None

PointKeyFrame

Defines an animation segment with its own target value and interpolation method for a `PointAnimationUsingKeyFrames`.

Properties	KeyTime, Name, Value
Methods	GetValue, SetValue
Events	None

PointKeyFrameCollection

Represents a collection of `PointKeyFrame` objects that can be individually accessed by index.

Properties	Count, Name
Methods	Add, Clear, GetItem, GetValue, Insert, Remove, RemoveAt, SetValue
Events	None

PolyBezierSegment

Represents one or more cubic Bezier curves.

Properties	Name, Points
Methods	GetValue, SetValue
Events	None

Polygon

Draws a polygon, which is a connected series of lines that form a closed shape.

Properties	Canvas.Left, Canvas.Top, Canvas.ZIndex, Clip, Cursor, Fill, FillRule, Height, Name, Opacity, OpacityMask, Points, RenderTransform, RenderTransformOrigin, Resources, Stretch, Stroke, StrokeDashArray, StrokeDashCap, StrokeDashOffset, StrokeEndLineCap, StrokeLineJoin, StrokeMiterLimit, StrokeStartLineCap, StrokeThickness, Triggers, Width
Methods	AddEventListener, CaptureMouse, FindName, GetHost, GetParent, GetValue, ReleaseMouseCapture, RemoveEventListener, SetValue
Events	Loaded, MouseEnter, MouseLeave, MouseLeftButtonDown, MouseLeftButtonUp, MouseMove

Polyline

Draws a series of connected straight lines.

Properties	Canvas.Left, Canvas.Top, Canvas.ZIndex, Clip, Cursor, Fill, FillRule, Height, Name, Opacity, OpacityMask, Points, RenderTransform, RenderTransformOrigin, Resources, Stretch, Stroke, StrokeDashArray, StrokeDashCap, StrokeDashOffset, StrokeEndLineCap, StrokeLineJoin, StrokeMiterLimit, StrokeStartLineCap, StrokeThickness, Triggers, Width
Methods	FindName, GetValue, SetValue
Events	Loaded, MouseEnter, MouseLeave, MouseLeftButtonDown, MouseLeftButtonUp, MouseMove

PolyLineSegment

Represents a set of line segments defined by a `PointCollection` with each `Point` specifying the end point of a line segment.

Properties	Name, Points
Methods	GetValue, SetValue
Events	None

PolyQuadraticBezierSegment

Represents a set of quadratic Bezier segments.

Properties	Name, Points
Methods	GetValue, SetValue
Events	None

QuadraticBezierSegment

Creates a quadratic Bezier curve between two points in a `PathFigure`.

Properties	Name, Point1 , Point2
Methods	GetValue, SetValue
Events	None

RadialGradientBrush

Paints an area with a radial gradient.

Properties	Center, ColorInterpolationMode, GradientOrigin, GradientStops, MappingMode, Name, Opacity, RadiusX, RadiusY, RelativeTransform, SpreadMethod, Transform
Methods	GetValue, SetValue
Events	None

Rectangle

Draws a rectangle.

Properties	Canvas.Left, Canvas.Top, Canvas.ZIndex, Clip, Cursor, Fill , Height, Name, Opacity, OpacityMask, RadiusX, RadiusY, RenderTransform, RenderTransformOrigin, Resources, Stretch, Stroke, StrokeDashArray, StrokeDashCap, StrokeDashOffset, StrokeEndLineCap, StrokeLineJoin, StrokeMiterLimit, StrokeStartLineCap, StrokeThickness, Triggers, Width
Methods	AddEventListener, CaptureMouse, FindName, GetHost, GetParent, GetValue, ReleaseMouseCapture, RemoveEventListener, SetValue
Events	Loaded, MouseEnter, MouseLeave, MouseLeftButtonDown, MouseLeftButtonUp, MouseMove

RectangleGeometry

Describes a two-dimensional rectangle.

Properties	Name, RadiusX, RadiusY, Rect, Transform
Methods	GetValue, SetValue
Events	None

RepeatBehavior

Describes how a timeline repeats its simple duration.

Properties	Name
Methods	GetValue, SetValue
Events	None

ResourceCollection

Represents a collection of `Resource` objects.

Properties	Count
Methods	Add, Clear, GetItem, GetValue, Insert, Remove, RemoveAt, SetValue
Events	None

RotateTransform

Rotates an object clockwise about a specified point in a 2-D x-y coordinate system.

Properties	Angle, CenterX, CenterY, Name
Methods	GetValue, SetValue
Events	None

Run

Represents a discrete section of formatted or unformatted text.

Properties	FontFamily, FontSize, FontStretch, FontStyle, FontWeight, Foreground, Name, Text, TextDecorations
Methods	FindName, GetHost, GetValue, SetValue
Events	None

RuntimeErrorEventArgs

Provides data for runtime error **Events**.

Properties	CharPosition, ErrorCode, ErrorMessage, ErrorType, LineNumber, MethodName
Methods	None
Events	None

ScaleTransform

Scales an object in the 2-D x-y coordinate system.

Properties	CenterX, CenterY, Name, ScaleX, ScaleY
Methods	GetValue, SetValue
Events	None

Silverlight Control

Represents the Silverlight control hosted in the browser.

Properties	ActualHeight, ActualWidth, Background, EnableFramerateCounter, EnableHtmlAccess, EnableRedrawRegions, FullScreen, InitParams, IsLoaded, MaxFrameRate, Source, Version, Windowless
Methods	CreateFromXaml, CreateFromXamlDownloader, CreateObject, FindName
Events	OnError, OnFullScreenChange, OnLoad, OnResize

SkewTransform

Represents a 2-D skew.

Properties	AngleX, AngleY, CenterX, CenterY, Name
Methods	GetValue, SetValue
Events	None

SolidColorBrush

Paints an area with a solid color.

Properties	Color, Name, Opacity, RelativeTransform, Transform
Methods	GetValue, SetValue
Events	None

SplineColorKeyFrame

Animates from the `Color` value of the previous key frame to its own `Value` using splined interpolation.

Properties	KeySpline, KeyTime, Name, Value
Methods	GetValue, SetValue
Events	None

SplineDoubleKeyFrame

Animates from the `Double` value of the previous key frame to its own `Value` using splined interpolation.

Properties	KeySpline, KeyTime, Name, Value
Methods	GetValue, SetValue
Events	None

SplinePointKeyFrame

Animates from the `Point` value of the previous key frame to its own `Value` using splined interpolation.

Properties	KeySpline, KeyTime, Name, Value
Methods	GetValue, SetValue
Events	None

Storyboard

Controls and provides object and property targeting information for its child animations.

Properties	AutoReverse, BeginTime, Children, Duration, FillBehavior, RepeatBehavior, SpeedRatio, StoryBoard.TargetName, StoryBoard.TargetProperty
Methods	Begin, Pause, Resume, Stop
Events	Completed

Stroke

Represents a collection of points that correspond to a stylus-down, move, and stylus-up sequence.

Properties	DrawingAttributes, Name, StylusPoints
Methods	GetBounds, GetValue, HitTest, SetValue
Events	None

StylusInfo

Represents information about the state of the stylus.

Properties	IsInverted, Name, DeviceType
Methods	GetValue, SetValue
Events	None

StylusPoint

Represents a single point collected while the user is inking with the stylus or mouse.

Properties	Name, PressureFactor, X, Y
Methods	GetValue, SetValue
Events	None

StylusPointCollection

Represents a set of related `StylusPoint` objects.

Properties	Count
Methods	Add, AddStylusPoints, GetValue, SetValue
Events	None

TextBlock

Represents a lightweight object for displaying single line and multiline, multiformatted text.

Properties	ActualHeight, ActualWidth, Canvas.Left, Canvas.Top, Canvas.ZIndex, Clip, Cursor, FontFamily, FontSize, FontStretch, FontStyle, FontWeight, Foreground, Height, Name, Opacity, OpacityMask, RenderTransform, RenderTransformOrigin, Resources, Text, TextDecorations, TextWrapping, Triggers, Visibility, Width
Methods	AddEventListener, CaptureMouse, FindName, GetHost, GetParent, GetValue, ReleaseMouseCapture, RemoveEventListener, SetFontSource , SetValue
Events	None

Timeline

Defines a segment of time. Unlike the other classes in this appendix, this is an abstract class.

Properties	AutoReverse, BeginTime, Duration, FillBehavior, Name, RepeatBehavior, SpeedRatio, StoryBoard.TargetName, StoryBoard.TargetProperty
Methods	GetValue, SetValue
Events	None

TimelineCollection

Represents a collection of `Timeline` objects.

Properties	Count
Methods	Add, Clear, GetItem, GetValue, Insert, Remove, RemoveAt, SetValue
Events	None

TimelineGroup

Represents a timeline that may contain a collection of child `Timeline` objects.

Properties	Children, Name
Methods	GetValue, SetValue
Events	None

TimelineMarker

Represents metadata associated with a specific point in a media file.

Properties	Text, Time, Type
Methods	None
Events	None

TimelineMarkerCollection

Represents a collection of `TimelineMarker` objects.

Properties	Count, Name
Methods	Add, Clear, GetItem, GetValue, Insert, Remove, RemoveAt, SetValue
Events	None

TimelineMarkerEventArgs

Contains arguments for the `MediaElement`, `MarkerReached` event.

Properties	Marker
Methods	None
Events	None

TimeSpan

Represents a time interval.

Properties	Name
Methods	GetValue, SetValue
Events	None

TransformCollection

Represents a collection of `Transform` objects that can be individually accessed by index.

Properties	Count, Name
Methods	Add, GetItem, GetValue, Insert, Remove, RemoveAt, SetValue
Events	None

TransformGroup

Represents a composite Transform composed of other `Transform` objects.

Properties	Children, Name
Methods	GetValue, SetValue
Events	None

TranslateTransform

Translates, or moves, an object in the 2-D x-y coordinate system.

Properties	Name, X, Y
Methods	GetValue, SetValue
Events	None

TriggerAction

Describes an action to perform for a trigger.

Properties	Count, Name
Methods	GetValue, SetValue
Events	None

TriggerActionCollection

Represents a collection of `TriggerAction` objects that can be individually accessed by index.

Properties	Count, Name
Methods	Add, Clear, GetItem, GetValue, Insert, Remove, RemoveAt, SetValue
Events	None

TriggerCollection

Represents a collection of `Trigger` objects.

Properties	Count, Name
Methods	Add, Clear, GetItem, GetValue, Insert, Remove, RemoveAt, SetValue
Events	None

UIElementCollection

Represents a collection of `UIElement` objects.

Properties	Count, Name
Methods	Add, Clear, GetItem, GetValue, Insert, Remove, RemoveAt, SetValue
Events	None

VideoBrush

Paints an area with video.

Properties	Name, Opacity, RelativeTransform, SourceName, Stretch, Transform
Methods	GetValue, SetValue
Events	None

B

XAML Reference

If you have already read the entire book, you have a pretty good idea of what XAML is and how it works. This appendix serves as a reference point for some of the details of XAML that may not have been covered in the book. Though this appendix is not a complete reference on XAML, it gives you the pertinent details that will answer the questions you have to be successful with Silverlight.

For a complete reference on XAML, you should visit the XAML reference on MSDN at `http://msdn2.microsoft.com/en-us/library/ms747122.aspx`*, which includes XAML characteristics for WPF as well.*

Introducing XAML

As we indicated in Chapter 1, from the beginning, back in 1997 when we had Visual InterDev, one of the promises of visual development with Microsoft tools was code and design separation, in other words freeing the developer to write code, while the designer works solely on the design and layout aspects of an application. Mostly because a developer and a designer are always using different tools and different languages, this promise has never been fulfilled. XAML finally provides a unified markup that can not only describe what a control is and how it fits into a page, but also how layout, and more importantly, the overall look and feel of the controls on a page are defined. A designer can use XAML to create a mock-up of a page or an application, and a developer can take that XAML markup and use it directly in his project files. Because partial classes and code behind files in the latest versions of Visual Studio allow you to separate the code logic from the layout and control definitions, using XAML gives the opportunity to have this separation of the design from the code.

To give you an idea of how XAML works, look at the code in Listing B-1, which is the same listing we showed you in Chapter 1 as Listing 1-9 and is an XAML snippet from a Silverlight application that shows `Hello World` in a `TextBlock`.

Listing B-1: Basic XAML to Display Hello World in a Silverlight Player

```
<Canvas x:Name="parentCanvas"
        xmlns="http://schemas.microsoft.com/client/2007"
        xmlns:x="http://schemas.microsoft.com/winfx/2006/xaml"
        Width="640"
        Height="480"
        Background="White"
        >
    <Block>Hello World</Block>
</Canvas>
```

Listing B-2 (which repeats Listing 1-10 from Chapter 1) shows how the XAML can get more complex, demonstrating adding various animations to the text block control. In this example, four different transforms are occurring:

- `ScaleTransform` — Stretches or shrinks an object horizontally or vertically.
- `SkewTransform` — Creates the illusion of three-dimensional depth in a two-dimensional object.
- `RotateTransform` — Rotates an object by a specified angle around the CenterX and CenterY of an object.
- `TranslateTransform` — Translates, or moves, an object in the two-dimensional x-y coordinate system.

You can refer back to Chapter 2 to get more details on these transforms.

Listing B-2: XAML Showing a Custom Transform on a TextBlock Element

```
<Canvas
    xmlns="http://schemas.microsoft.com/client/2007"
    xmlns:x="http://schemas.microsoft.com/winfx/2006/xaml"
    Width="640" Height="480"
    Background="White">
        <Canvas.Triggers>
            <EventTrigger RoutedEvent="Canvas.Loaded">
                <BeginStoryboard>
                    <Storyboard x:Name="Timeline1"/>
                </BeginStoryboard>
            </EventTrigger>
        </Canvas.Triggers>
        <Block Width="349" Height="67"
            Canvas.Left="150"
            Canvas.Top="140" Text="Hello World"
            Wrapping="Wrap"
            RenderTransformOrigin="0.5,0.5"
            x:Name="Block">
            <Block.RenderTransform>
                <TransformGroup>
                    <ScaleTransform ScaleX="1" ScaleY="1"/>
                    <SkewTransform AngleX="0" AngleY="0"/>
```

Listing B-2: *(continued)*

```
                        <RotateTransform Angle="0"/>
                        <TranslateTransform X="0" Y="0"/>
                    </TransformGroup>
                </Block.RenderTransform>
            </Block>
    </Canvas>
```

The XAML in Listing B-2 is obviously more complex, and may seem daunting. Learning XAML is like learning HTML; there are a lot of details, but for most of your applications, you are using tools to build the XAML and not hand-coding it yourself. The reason why it is important to understand XAML is the same reason why it is important to know HTML if you are a web developer. There are times when you need to look at the pure HTML to understand or debug a page, just as there will be times when you are looking at XAML and you need to understand why something is happening in your Silverlight application.

Tools like Microsoft Expression Blend 2.0, Visual Studio 2005 with the Silverlight project support, and Visual Studio 2008 are all Rapid Application Development (RAD) tools that you can use to create the XAML in your Silverlight applications. However, right now Microsoft Expression Blend 2.0, which is explained in detail in Chapter 3, is really the only tool that gives you a nice design-time experience, where you can drag and drop controls onto the design surface and switch between the designer view and the XAML view. No doubt, as Silverlight matures and goes into a release stage, and as Visual Studio 2008 nears release, the appropriate tools will be released that will let you design applications in a RAD fashion.

Before we delve deeper into XAML, an important issue using XAML in Silverlight versus using XAML in WPF is that not all things are created equal. Because Silverlight is optimized for speed and fast delivery of rich, interactive applications to the browser, the XAML available to Silverlight applications is a subset of the XAML that can be used in a full desktop-based WPF application. In WPF, each XAML element maps directly to a corresponding class in the .NET Framework. In Silverlight, the XAML parser is part of the Silverlight player, so there is no dependency on the .NET Framework for it to run. To you this means that if you are working in WPF now, and you are wondering why certain things are not working in Silverlight, you need to reference Appendix A which lists all of the objects that are available to you in Silverlight. The list is much shorter than what a WPF developer expects. Tradeoffs needed to be made in order to keep a smaller runtime, so the XAML available is not as complete. In Silverlight 1.1, the options available to you are more complete, but the runtime is larger. So you lose the flexibility of a very small runtime versus the convenience of a richer object model.

Silverlight XAML Basics

XAML is a case-sensitive declarative language, based on XML, that lets you create the user interface of a Silverlight application in a descriptive markup. Similar to the way ASP.NET or Windows Forms work with the concept of a code behind file, you can specify code files that contain JavaScript that respond to events and manipulate the objects created in the XAML file. XAML is so important for the evolution of how you create the user interface because the user interface is separate from the code files. This means that a designer using tools like Expression Blend can create a UI using XAML, and that same XAML can be used in Visual Studio 2005 and integrated into a larger project. As a matter of fact, Expression Blend and Visual Studio 2005 share the same project structure, so the `.csproj` files can be opened by either tool. The ability for a designer to express a user interface and have it directly used without alteration in an application is something that has never been possible with Microsoft tools. There has always been a large amount of throw-away art work, because developers would get a mock-up and try to duplicate it.

XAML files have an `.xaml` extension, and at first glance might be confused with an XML data file. This makes sense, because XML (eXtensible Markup Language) is the basis for XAML (eXtensible Application Markup Language). Listing B-3 shows a typical Silverlight XAML file, which is also broken down in Table B-1.

Listing B-3: A Typical XAML File

```
<Canvas
  xmlns="http://schemas.microsoft.com/client/2007"
  xmlns:x="http://schemas.microsoft.com/winfx/2006/xaml">
      <Rectangle
         Width="200"
         Height="200"
         Fill="Blue" />
</Canvas>
```

Table B-1: Breakdown of a Typical XAML File

XAML	Description
`<Canvas`	Opening object element of the root element.
`xmlns="http://schemas.microsoft.com/client/2007"`	The default Silverlight namespace.
`xmlns:x="http://schemas.microsoft.com/winfx/2006/xaml">`	The XAML namespace.
`<Rectangle Width="200" Height="200" Fill="Blue" />`	XAML declaration of a `Rectangle` object with the `Width`, `Height`, and `Fill` attributes set.
`</Canvas>`	End of object element for the root, closed because there are no other child elements in this XAML file.

Later in this appendix, we talk more about the root element described in Table B-1.

Declaring Objects in XAML

You can use either the object element syntax or the attribute syntax to declare objects in XAML:

- **Object element syntax** — Uses opening and closing tags to declare an object as an XML element. You can use this syntax to declare root objects or set complex property values.
- **Attribute syntax** — Uses an inline value to declare an object, in the same way you would set attributes on an XML element, to set property values.

Object or Content Element Syntax

Most elements are created using the object (or content) element syntax, which is used in Listing B-1 to create the `TextBlock` object:

```
<TextBlock>Hello World</TextBlock>
```

This syntax maps to:

```
<ObjectName>. . .</ObjectName>
```

where `ObjectName` is the name of the object that you are trying to instantiate. The following example uses object element syntax to declare a `Canvas`:

```
<Canvas>
</Canvas>
```

Some objects, such as `Canvas`, can contain other objects, like `Rectangle` or `TextBlock`:

```
<Canvas>
    <TextBlock>
    </TextBlock>
</Canvas>
```

If an object does not contain other objects, you can optionally declare it using one tag instead of two:

```
<Canvas>
    <Rectangle />
</Canvas>
```

When you are creating objects, there really is no bad or good way. The hierarchy of the XAML documents, which is covered later in this appendix, does not change.

Attribute Element Syntax

XAML also supports the less verbose attribute syntax for setting properties. The following markup creates a green rectangle with a height and width of 100 pixels.

```
<Rectangle Fill="Green" Height="100" Width="100" />
```

Property Element Syntax

Attribute syntax is not possible on certain object properties because the object or information necessary to provide the property value cannot be adequately expressed as a simple string. For these cases, the property element syntax can be used. Property element syntax sets the referenced property of the containing element with a new instance of the type that the property takes as its value, for example:

```
<objectName>
    <objectName.property>
        <object propertyValue = "" />
    </objectName.property>
</objectName>
```

Listing B-4 uses property element syntax to add a `Stroke` with a `LinearGradientBrush` to a `Rectangle` element.

Listing B-4: Using the Property Element Syntax

```
<Rectangle Width="485" Height="60"
           Canvas.Left="99" Canvas.Top="55">
    <Rectangle.Stroke>
        <LinearGradientBrush EndPoint="1,0.5" StartPoint="0,0.5">
            <GradientStop Color="#FF483333" Offset="0.308"/>
            <GradientStop Color="#FF514C4C" Offset="0.1070303"/>
        </LinearGradientBrush>
    </Rectangle.Stroke>
    <Rectangle.Fill>
        <LinearGradientBrush EndPoint="1,0.5" StartPoint="0,0.5">
            <GradientStop Color="#FF000000" Offset="0"/>
            <GradientStop Color="#FFFFFFFF" Offset="1"/>
        </LinearGradientBrush>
    </Rectangle.Fill>
</Rectangle>
```

Setting a Property Using Implicit Collection Syntax

When a property takes a collection, you can omit the collection element and simply specify its contents instead. This is known as *implicit collection syntax*. Listing B-5, demonstrated in Figure B-1, shows how you can omit the `GradientStopCollection` for a `LinearGradientBrush` and simply specify its `GradientStop` objects. The `GradientStopCollection` is included in the first `LinearGradientBrush`, but omitted from the second.

Listing B-5: Using the Implicit Collection Syntax to Assign Properties in XAML

```
<Rectangle Width="100" Height="100"
  Canvas.Left="0" Canvas.Top="30">
    <Rectangle.Fill>
        <LinearGradientBrush>
            <LinearGradientBrush.GradientStops>

                <!-- Here the GradientStopCollection tag is used. -->
```

Listing B-5: *(continued)*

```
                    <GradientStopCollection>
                        <GradientStop Offset="0.0" Color="Red" />
                        <GradientStop Offset="1.0" Color="Blue" />
                    </GradientStopCollection>
                </LinearGradientBrush.GradientStops>
            </LinearGradientBrush>
        </Rectangle.Fill>
    </Rectangle>


    <Rectangle Width="100" Height="100"
      Canvas.Left="100" Canvas.Top="30">
        <Rectangle.Fill>
            <LinearGradientBrush>
                <LinearGradientBrush.GradientStops>

                    <!-- Notice that the GradientStopCollection tag
                 is omitted. -->
                    <GradientStop Offset="0.0" Color="Red" />
                    <GradientStop Offset="1.0" Color="Blue" />
                </LinearGradientBrush.GradientStops>
            </LinearGradientBrush>
        </Rectangle.Fill>
    </Rectangle>
```

There are times when you can omit both the collection element and the property element tags, as Listing B-6 demonstrates.

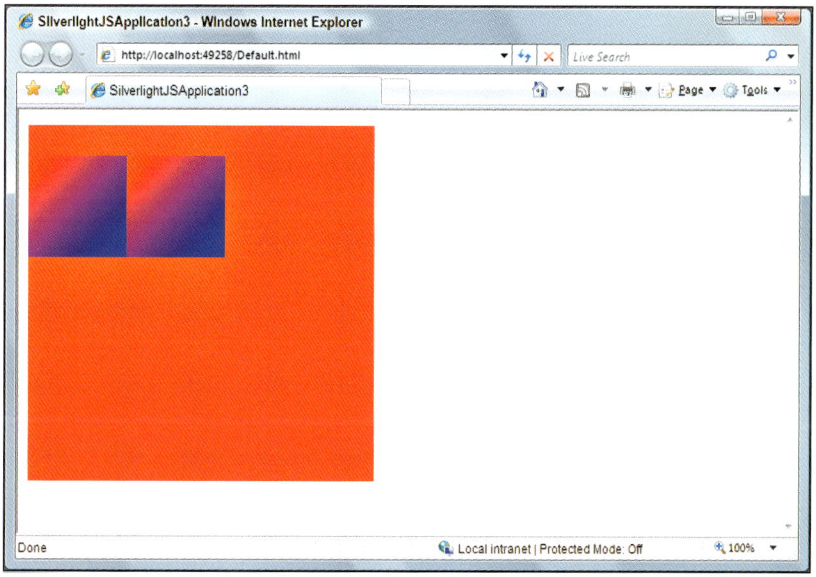

Figure B-1

Listing B-6: Implicit Collection Syntax Omitting Both the Collection Element and the Property Elements

```
<Rectangle Width="100" Height="100"
  Canvas.Left="200" Canvas.Top="30">
    <Rectangle.Fill>
        <LinearGradientBrush>
            <GradientStop Offset="0.0" Color="Red" />
            <GradientStop Offset="1.0" Color="Blue" />
        </LinearGradientBrush>
    </Rectangle.Fill>
</Rectangle>
```

Deciding When to Use Attribute or Property Element Syntax to Set a Property

As you learned earlier in the appendix, all properties support either the attribute or property element syntax. Some properties support only specific scenarios, which is dependent on the type of object property it accepts.

Primitive types, such as a `Double` and `Integer`, support only the attribute element syntax. The following example uses attribute element syntax to set the width of a rectangle. The `Width` property supports attribute syntax because the property value is a `Double`.

```
<Rectangle Width="100" />
```

Whether or not you can use attribute syntax to set a property depends on whether the object you use to set that property supports attribute syntax. The following example uses attribute syntax to set the fill of a rectangle. The `Fill` property supports attribute syntax when you use a `SolidColorBrush` to set it, because `SolidColorBrush` supports attribute syntax.

```
<Rectangle Fill="Blue" />
```

Whether or not you can use property element syntax to set a property depends on whether the object you use to set that property supports object element syntax. If the object supports object element syntax, the property supports property element syntax. The following example uses property element syntax to set the fill of a rectangle. The `Fill` property supports attribute syntax when you use a `SolidColorBrush` to set it, because `SolidColorBrush` supports attribute syntax.

```
<Rectangle>
    <Rectangle.Fill>
        <SolidColorBrush />
    </Rectangle.Fill>
</Rectangle>
```

XAML Hierarchy

When you add XAML objects to the Silverlight control, you are defining a hierarchical tree structure with a root object. All XAML files have a root element. In Silverlight, the root element is always a `Canvas` object; it is the only object that can contain other Silverlight objects. In Listing B-7, the XAML example creates an object hierarchy containing a parent `Canvas` object and a child `TextBlock` and `Canvas` object. In this case, the first `Canvas` object defined is the root object for the tree structure.

Listing B-7: Example of an XAML Hierarchy with Two Canvas Objects with Various Child Elements

```
<!-- The top-most object in the XAML hierarchy is -->
<!-- referred to as the root object. -->
<Canvas
  xmlns="http://schemas.microsoft.com/client/2007"
  Loaded="onLoaded">

    <!-- Canvas objects can be a child of another Canvas object. -->
    <Canvas
      Canvas.Left="20" Canvas.Top="20">
        <Rectangle
          Width="200" Height="35"
          Fill="Red" />
        <Block
          Canvas.Left="25" Canvas.Top="5"
          Foreground="White" FontFamily="Verdana"
          FontSize="18" FontWeight="Bold"
          ="Child Canvas Block" />
    </Canvas>

    <Block
      Canvas.Left="40" Canvas.Top="60"
      Foreground="Black" FontFamily="Verdana"
      FontSize="18" FontWeight="Bold"
      Text="Hello Silverlight" />
</Canvas>
```

When the Silverlight player attempts to render the XAML content, it is converted into a hierarchical tree structure with a root object. Figure B-2 demonstrates the tree structure for the code in Listing B-7.

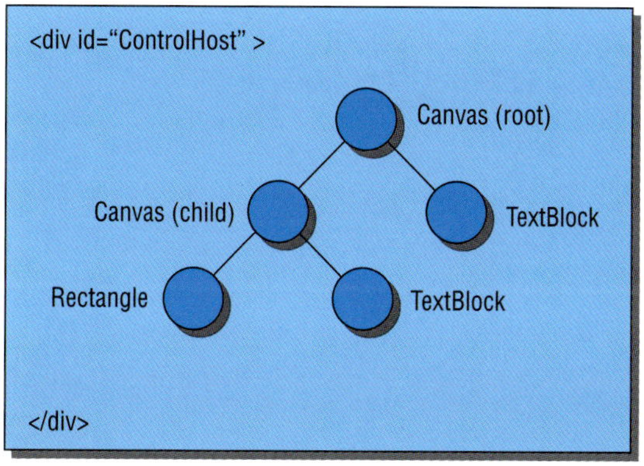

Figure B-2

The tree structure determines the rendering order of Silverlight objects. The order of traversal starts with the root object, which is the top-most node in the tree structure. The root object's children are then traversed, left to right. If an object has children, its children are traversed before the object's siblings. This means the content of a child object is rendered in front of the object's own content. Figure B-3 shows the rendered output from the previous XAML example, showing the rendering order sequence.

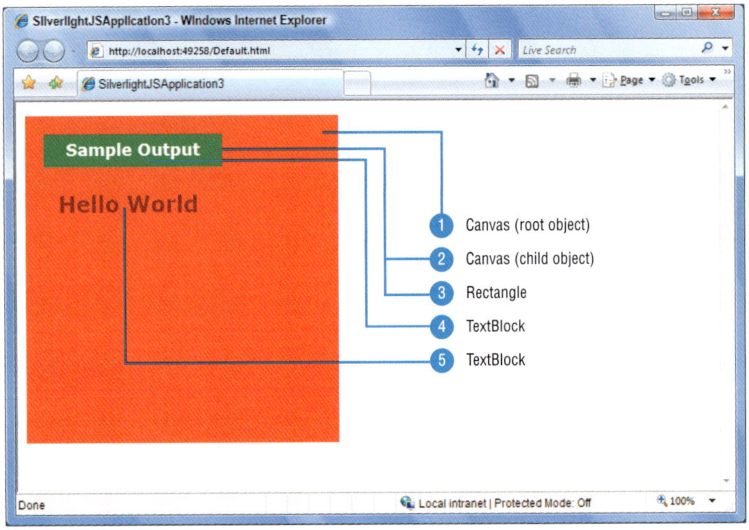

Figure B-3

Adding XAML Objects to the Silverlight Object Hierarchy

When you create content for a Silverlight control, you set the `source` property of the control to reference XAML content, as Listing B-8 highlights.

Listing B-8: Setting the source Property to Assign an XAML File to the Silverlight Player

```
<object
  type="application/ag-plugin"
  id="silverlight1"
  width="350"
  height="350">
  <param name="source" value="Scene.xaml" />
  <param name="background" value="Red" />
</object>
```

When the Silverlight player gets the XAML file, its content is parsed and converted into the root-tree structure and the content is rendered. Setting the `source` property is typically done indirectly through the use of JavaScript helper files. Listing B-9 demonstrates the use of the `createSilverlight` function, which is contained in the `default.html.js` file referenced in the head section of the HTML document.

Listing B-9: Setting the XAML Property Indirectly Through JavaScript

```
<!DOCTYPE HTML PUBLIC "-//W3C//DTD HTML 4.01
Transitional//EN" "http://www.w3c.org/TR/1999/REC-html401-19991224/loose.dtd">
<html xmlns="http://www.w3.org/1999/xhtml">
    <head>
        <title>HelloSilverlight</title>
        <script type="/javascript" src="Silverlight.js"></script>
        <script type="/javascript" src="Default.html.js"></script>
        <script type="/javascript" src="Scene.xaml.js"></script>
    </head>

    <body>
        <div id="SilverlightControlHost">
            <script type="/javascript">
                createSilverlight();
            </script>
        </div>
    </body>
</html>
```

Another way to add XAML to the hierarchy of what the Silverlight player has rendered is by using JavaScript and the `createFromXaml` function. Listing B-10 demonstrates using JavaScript to append a `TextBlock` to an existing `Canvas` object.

Listing B-10: Using createFromXaml to Append XAML to an Existing Structure

```
// MouseLeftButtonUp event handler for the Canvas object.
function onMouseLeftButtonUp(sender, mouseEventArgs)
{
    // Retrieve a reference to the control.
    var control = sender.getHost();

    // Create a Block using a literal XAML string.
    var block = control.content.createFromXaml
        ('<Block Canvas.Top="50">This is new </Block>');

    // Append the Block to the sender, or Canvas, object.
    sender.children.add(block);
}
```

Later in this appendix you learn more about referencing the Silverlight object using the `getHost` function and the `getElementById` function.

Events and the Silverlight Control

As Chapter 1 discusses, the Silverlight object model defines a set of objects that allow you to create a Silverlight application. The Silverlight object model is exposed through the Silverlight control, which is created in your HTML page as the host to the XAML you want to render. Figure B-4 demonstrates this relationship.

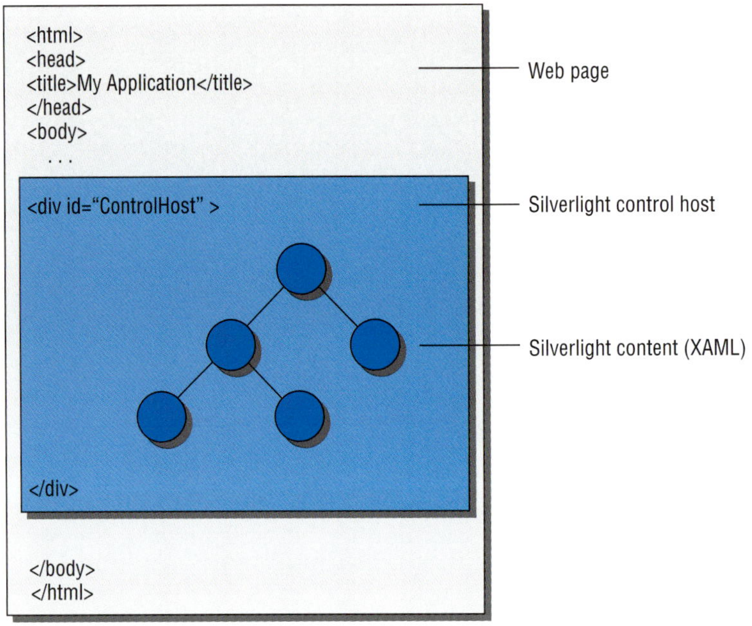

Figure B-4

This section discusses the Silverlight objects, how you reference them, and how you handle, add, and remove events on those objects. Because you cannot create fully interactive applications in XAML alone, it is important to understand how all of the elements — the objects in XAML, the HTML, and the JavaScript — work together to deliver the richness that Silverlight offers.

Code Behind and x:Name

In XAML, the `x:Name` attribute is used as a unique identifier to the elements you define. No different than HTML, where the `id` attribute denotes the uniqueness of an element, Silverlight needs a way to isolate and reference elements in XAML so they can be acted upon in the code behind files. Technically, in Silverlight 1.0 there are no code behind files because all coding is handled via JavaScript. But by using `<script>` tags in your HTML pages, you can define the code files that have access to DOM for the page in which you are running the Silverlight control.

When the `x:Name` attribute is used, the named elements are treated as regular object instances via JavaScript, so you have all of the runtime accessibility that you would expect. Listing B-11 demonstrates an XAML file where most of the elements are uniquely named for reference in a JavaScript file.

Listing B-11: XAML Using the x:Name Attribute

```
<Canvas
xmlns="http://schemas.microsoft.com/client/2007"
xmlns:x="http://schemas.microsoft.com/winfx/2006/xaml">
    <Canvas>
        <Canvas x:Name="Canvas"
                Canvas.Left="0" Canvas.Top="65">
            <MediaElement x:Name="Media1"
                          Source="video1.wmv"
                          Width="300" Height="300" >
            </MediaElement>

            <Canvas.RenderTransform>
                <TransformGroup>
                    <SkewTransform AngleY="-19"
                                   AngleX="0"
                                   CenterX="0"
                                   CenterY="0"/>
                    <ScaleTransform ScaleY="1"
                                    ScaleX = "1"
                                    CenterX="0"
                                    CenterY="0"/>
                </TransformGroup>
            </Canvas.RenderTransform>
        </Canvas>

        <Canvas x:Name="RefImageCanvas"
                Canvas.Left="227" Canvas.Top="587">

            <MediaElement x:Name="RefImage"
                          Source="video1.wmv"
                          Width="300"
                          Height="300" Volume="0">
            </MediaElement>

            <Canvas.RenderTransform>
                <TransformGroup>
                    <SkewTransform
                        x:Name="RefSkewTransform"
                        AngleY="19" AngleX="-41"
                        CenterX="0" CenterY="0" />
                    <ScaleTransform
                        x:Name="RefScaleTransform"
                        ScaleY="-1" ScaleX="1"
                        CenterX="0" CenterY="0" />
                </TransformGroup>
            </Canvas.RenderTransform>

            <Canvas.OpacityMask>
                <LinearGradientBrush
                        StartPoint="0.5,0.0"
                        EndPoint="0.5,1.0">
```

(Continued)

Listing B-11: *(continued)*

```
                    <GradientStop
                        Offset="0.345"
                        Color="#00000000"
                        x:Name="RefgdStop1" />
                    <GradientStop
                        Offset="1.0"
                        Color="#CC000000"
                        x:Name="RefgdStop2" />
                </LinearGradientBrush>
            </Canvas.OpacityMask>
        </Canvas>
    </Canvas>
</Canvas>
```

The next sections demonstrate how to act on the elements defined with the `x:Name` attribute.

Silverlight Player Events

The Silverlight player exposes a number of events you can define in XAML that allow you to interact with XAML elements, determine the state change of elements, and handle errors on the Silverlight player. Table B-2 lists the events that are available to the XAML elements running in the Silverlight player. Listing B-12 demonstrates the usage of some of the listed events. Note that the `MouseMove` event is specified on the `Canvas` object, as well as the `Rectangle` objects defined in the `Canvas`. This highlights that you can have the same event fire on different objects, which we cover next.

Table B-2: Silverlight Player Events

`OnError`	`LostFocus`	`MediaEnded`
`OnFullScreenChange`	`KeyUp`	`MediaFailed`
`OnLoad`	`BufferingProgressChanged` (Media)	`MediaOpened`
`OnResize`	`KeyDown`	`MouseEnter`
`Completed` (Downloader)	`Completed` (Storyboard)	`MouseLeave`
`DownloadProgressChanged` (Downloader)	`CurrentStateChanged`	`MouseLeftButtonDown`
`GotFocus`	`DownloadProgressChanged` (MediaElement)	`MouseLeftButtonUp`
`Loaded`	`MarkerReached`	`MouseMove`

Listing B-12: Using Events in XAML

```
<Canvas
  xmlns="http://schemas.microsoft.com/client/2007"
  xmlns:x="http://schemas.microsoft.com/winfx/2006/xaml"

  MouseMove="rootCanvasMouseMove">

    <Rectangle
      MouseMove="rect1MouseMove"
      Width="100" Height="100"
      Fill="PowderBlue" />

    <Rectangle
      MouseMove="rect2MouseMove"
      Canvas.Top="50" Canvas.Left="50"
      Width="100" Height="100"
      Fill="Gold" Opacity="0.5" />

    <Block
      x:Name="statusBlock"
      Canvas.Top="180" />

</Canvas>
```

Like events in WPF and JavaScript, Silverlight supports *event bubbling*, specifically for input events, like `MouseMove`. A bubbled event is an event that is passed from a child object and is forwarded upward to each of its ancestors in the object hierarchy.

Event bubbling means that if multiple `MouseMove` events, for example, are defined for an object and its ancestors, the event is received by each object in the ancestor hierarchy, starting with the object that directly receives the event. The way events bubble up to the parent is important because you may want ensure that a specific action takes place on a specific object and not depend on its parent to handle the action.

Listing B-13 demonstrates this in a clearer fashion. Because both `Rectangle` elements have a `MouseMove` event defined, and the `Canvas` element has a `MouseMove` event defined, if the mouse is moved over either `Rectangle`, the `onRectMouseMove` event is fired. And because the `Canvas` is looking for a `MouseMove` event, the mouse move over the `Rectangles` is bubbled up through the object hierarchy to the `Canvas` element.

Listing B-13: Event Bubbling and XAML

```
<Canvas
  xmlns="http://schemas.microsoft.com/client/2007"
  xmlns:x="http://schemas.microsoft.com/winfx/2006/xaml"
  MouseMove="onCanvasMouseMove"
  Loaded="onLoaded">

    <Rectangle
      x:Name="RectA"
```

(Continued)

Listing B-13: *(continued)*

```
        MouseMove="onRectMouseMove"
        Width="100" Height="100" Fill="Red" />

      <Rectangle
        x:Name="RectB"
        MouseMove="onRectMouseMove"
        Width="100" Height="100" Fill="Blue"
        Canvas.Top="25" Canvas.Left="25" Opacity="0.5" />

    </Canvas>
```

Defining Event Handlers

Similar to the way events are handled in ASP.NET or Windows Forms, the event handlers in Silverlight have two parameters:

- `sender` — Identifies the Silverlight object that generated the event. You can retrieve the type value of the object by calling the `toString` method on the parameter value.
- `eventArgs` — Identifies the set of argument values for the specific event. An event, such as the `Loaded` event, does not define any event arguments, so the value of `eventArgs` is null.

If the Silverlight event handler function does not reference the `sender` and `eventArgs` parameters, which is the case for many of the examples that I have demonstrated, you do not have to define them as part of the function declaration.

Table B-3 is an example of the event parameters for the `KeyDown` event of the Silverlight player. This example is typical of how you will see events described in the Silverlight 1.0 SDK.

Table B-3: Event Parameters for the KeyDown Event

Event Parameter	Description
`sender`	Object Identifies the object that invoked the event.
`keyEventArgs`	Object
`keyEventArgs.key`	Integer that indicates that a key is pressed. This value is not operating system-specific.
`keyEventArgs.platformKeyCode`	Integer that indicates that a key is pressed. This value is operating system-specific.
`keyEventArgs.shift`	Boolean value that indicates whether the Shift key is down.
`keyEventArgs.ctrl`	Boolean value that indicates whether the Ctrl key is down.

As an example of the KeyDown event, Listing B-14 demonstrates how you would define the event on the Canvas element in XAML.

Listing B-14: Defining the KeyDown Event in XAML

```
<Canvas
  xmlns="http://schemas.microsoft.com/client/2007"
  xmlns:x="http://schemas.microsoft.com/winfx/2006/xaml"
  KeyDown="onKeyDown">

    <Block
         x:Name="Block1"
         Text=" KeyDown Event Arguments" />

</Canvas>
```

After you have defined the event and added other visual elements to your XAML, you use JavaScript to handle the events. Listing B-15 demonstrates the JavaScript that is used to handle the KeyDown event on the TextBlock element.

Listing B-15: Handling the KeyDown Event in JavaScript

```
function onKeyDown(sender, keyEventArgs)
{
    var Block = sender.findName("Block1");

    var msg  = "key: " + keyEventArgs.key;
        msg += " platformKeycode: " + keyEventArgs.platformKeyCode;
        msg += " shift: " + keyEventArgs.shift;
        msg += " ctrl: " + keyEventArgs.ctrl;

    Block. = msg;
}
```

Notice the use of findName on the sender argument passed to the function. By determining which object is passed to the function, you can decide whether or not you want to do anything with the event.

For a generic example of determining the sender, consider the JavaScript in Listing B-16, which gives an alert message of the sender object back to the caller. You might use something like this when troubleshooting your code.

Listing B-16: Simple Example of Determining the sender Object

```
function onKeyDown(sender, eventArgs)
{
    alert("Sender = " + sender.toString());
}
```

Listing B-17 shows how to use the `FindName` method to search the Silverlight object tree for a specific named object. Notice that the `eventArgs` parameter is omitted because it is not referenced by the function.

Listing B-17: Function Declaration with the eventArgs Omitted

```
function onLoaded(sender)
{
    sender.findName("Block1"). = Date();
}
```

Defining Events in JavaScript

If you are adding or removing event handlers via JavaScript, you will use the `addEventListener` and `removeEventListener` methods on the elements on which you want to add or remove events. You use the following syntax:

Element.addEventListener(`"EventName"`, `"EventHandler"`);

For example, Listing B-18 demonstrates adding the `onMouseEnter` and `onMouseLeave` event handlers to the `TextBlock` element named `Status`.

Listing B-18: Adding Event Listeners to XAML Elements

```
function onLoaded(sender, eventArgs)
{
    Block = sender.findName("Status");
    Block.addEventListener("MouseEnter", "onMouseEnter");
    Block.addEventListener("MouseLeave", "onMouseLeave");
}
```

To remove an existing event handler function, use the `RemoveEventListener` method, as demonstrated in Listing B-19.

Listing B-19: Removing Event Listeners on XAML Elements

```
function removeEvents()
{
    Block.removeEventListener("MouseEnter", "onMouseEnter");
    Block.removeEventListener("MouseLeave", "onMouseLeave");
}
```

Referencing the Silverlight Control

By using the `getHost` function on any object passed to a JavaScript function that is handling a Silverlight named event, you can get a reference to the Silverlight control element. Listing B-20 demonstrates using the `getHost` function.

Listing B-20: Using getHost to Retrieve a Reference of the Silverlight Control

```
function onKeyUp(sender, keyEventArgs)
{
    if ((keyEventArgs.key == 51) && (keyEventArgs.ctrl == true))
    {
        var control = sender.getHost();
        alert("Silverlight version: " + control.settings.version);
    }
}
```

The `getHost` function does not return an addressable instance of the DOM that the player is running. For that, you need to use the `findName` method.

Finding an XAML Object Using findName

You can find any object in the Silverlight object hierarchy by using the `findName` method and referencing the object's `x:Name` attribute value. The `findName` function will search the entire object hierarchy of the DOM running in the Silverlight control, so the location of an element in the hierarchy does not matter. If the element passed to the `findName` function cannot be found, a null value is returned. Listing B-21 demonstrates using the `findName` function as well as how to properly check if the object being sought exists.

Listing B-21: Using the findName Function to Search the DOM

```
function onLoaded(sender, eventArgs)
{
    // Retrieve the object corresponding to the x:Name attribute value.
    var canvas = sender.findName("rootCanvas");

    // Determine whether the object was found.
    if (canvas != null)
    {
        alert(canvas.toString());
    }
    else
    {
        alert("Object not found");
    }
}
```

Referencing an XAML Object in a Collection

You can retrieve a specific child of a parent object by referencing the index of the collection of the parent object with the `getItem` function. Listing B-22 demonstrates how to retrieve a child of a parent `Canvas` object by using the `getItem` method.

Listing B-22: Using the getItem Function to Return Collection Objects

```
function getObject(parent, index)
{
    // Determine if the index is valid.
    if (index < parent.children.count)
    {
        // Retrieve the child object at
        //the specified index in the collection.
        var object = parent.children.getItem(index);
    }

    return object;
}
```

Enumerating Child Objects

You can enumerate the child of a parent object by accessing the children collection of the parent object. Listing B-23 demonstrates how to enumerate the children of a parent `Canvas` object.

Listing B-23: Enumerating Child Objects in a Collection

```
function getChildren(parent)
{

    var i;
    // Enumerate the children of the Canvas object.
    for (i = 0; i < parent.children.count; i++)
    {
        var child = parent.children.getItem(i);

        // Display the index and type of the child object.
        alert(i + ": " + child.toString());
    }
}
```

Referencing Object Properties

You can reference object properties at runtime by using the `getValue` and `setValue` methods, each of which is discussed in the short sections that follow.

Using the getValue Method

You can use the getValue method to get the value of a property. You can also use the abridged "." (dot) notation as an equivalent syntax of the getValue method. Listing B-24 shows how to get a property value by using both the getValue method and abridged "." notation.

Listing B-24: Using getValue to Access an Object's Property

```
function onMouseLeftButtonUp(sender, index)
{
    // Get the property value using the getValue method.
    var opacity = sender.getValue("opacity");

    // Get the property value using the equivalent "." notation.
    var opacity = sender.opacity;
}
```

Using the setValue Method

You can use the setValue method to set the value of a property. You can also use the abridged "." (dot) notation as an equivalent syntax of the SetValue method. Listing B-25 shows how to set a property value by using both the setValue method and abridged "." notation.

Listing B-25: Using the setValue Method to Change an Element's Property Value

```
function onMouseEnter(sender, index)
{
    // Set the property value using the setValue method.
    sender.setValue("opacity", 0.5);

    // Set the property value using the equivalent "." notation.
    sender.opacity = 0.5;
}
```

For properties that are attached properties, such as Canvas.Top, you must use the abridged "." notation syntax in a slightly different way. Listing B-26 demonstrates how this syntax would look.

Listing B-26: Special Use of "." Notation on Elements with Attached Properties

```
// Set the property value using the SetValue method.
sender.setValue("Canvas.Top", 40);

// Set the property value using the equivalent "." notation.
sender["Canvas.Top"] = 40;
```

Summary

This appendix gave you a good foundation for the various aspects of using XAML in your Silverlight 1.0 applications. There are a few takeaways about Silverlight XAML that you need to remember:

- Silverlight XAML is a subset of WPF XAML, so theoretically an application in Silverlight can move up to WPF. However, because of the differences in XAML, moving an application from WPF to Silverlight will most likely not work.
- The Silverlight player is a browser plug-in, so the XAML you are using is built into the player; it is not based on .NET Framework objects.
- XAML alone cannot build Silverlight applications. You need HTML to host the Silverlight player, which in turn hosts the XAML, and you need JavaScript to write code that responds to event handlers defined in XAML.
- XAML opens the doors for designers and developers to work closely, because the same language (XAML) that is used to style applications is also used to define the user interface.
- The X in XAML is for extensible — so as Silverlight matures and the capabilities of the player are such that you can add your own extensions, your applications will become more powerful.

C

Silverlight Online Resources

As is the case when you are dealing with any new technology, it always helps to have some resources to draw on for more information. This appendix lists some online resources you can consult to learn more about Silverlight and about using it to create your applications.

Author Blogs

Devin Rader: `www.geekswithblogs.com/devin`

J. Ambrose Little: `www.dotnettemplar.net`

Jason Beres: `www.geekswithblogs.com/jberes`

Silverlight Influential Blogs

Scott Guthrie: `http://weblogs.asp.net/scottgu/`

Tim Sneath: `http://blogs.msdn.com/tims/`

Joe Stegman: `http://blogs.msdn.com/jstegman`

Mike Harsh: `http://blogs.msdn.com/mharsh/`

Nick Kramer: `http://blogs.msdn.com/nickkramer`

Michael Schwarz: http://weblogs.asp.net/mschwarz

Silverlight SDK Blog: http://blogs.msdn.com/silverlight_sdk

Lee Brimelow: http://www.thewpfblog.com

Resource Web Sites

Silverlight.net: http://www.silverlight.net

MSDN Silverlight Dev Center: http://msdn.microsoft.com/silverlight

Infragistics Silverlight 1.1 Sample Application: http://labs.infragistics.com

Silverlight 1.0 Intellisense add-in: http://www.codeplex.com/intellisense

Microsoft Expression: http://www.microsoft.com/expression

ASP.NET AJAX Site: http://ajax.asp.net

Silverlight Nibbles: http://www.nibbletutorials.net/

Microsoft ASP.NET Futures: http://www.asp.net/downloads/futures/

Index

A

actualHeight property, resizing Silverlight control, 22
AddDescriptorProp method, 165
addEventListener method, 117–118, 268
Adobe Fireworks to WPF/XAML Exporter, 87
Adobe Illustrator to WPF/XAML Export Plug-in, 87
Advanced Stream Redirector (ASX) playlist file format, 46–47
AJAX Extensions. *see* ASP.NET 2.0 AJAX Extensions
Alpha Refresh Release. *see* Silverlight 1.1 Alpha Refresh Release
animations
adding to button template, 169–170
controlling in Storyboards using mouse events, 127–128
creating basic, 56–58
creating timelines for, 80–83
working with Storyboards, 80
APIs, Silverlight 1.1
Base, 193–194
Communication, 195
Data, 194
Presentation, 196–199
architecture, designing application, 202
ArcSegment object, 221
artwork, created outside of Blend, 84–88
ASP.NET
Silverlight technology vs., 2
using Silverlight 1.0 with, 139–142
ASP.NET, creating custom controls, 142–158
adding Silverlight JavaScript library, 146–150
adding Xaml control properties, 150–154
overview of, 142
rendering Xaml control, 154–158
setting up project, 142–146
ASP.NET, creating Silverlight user interface, 166–187
creating button template, 166–170
creating ButtonBar client-side code, 178–183
creating ButtonBar server-side code, 170–178
using ButtonBar control, 184–187
ASP.NET 2.0 AJAX Extensions, 158–166
accessing Silverlight player, 104
adding class-oriented properties, 160–161
creating client-side ButtonBar class, 178–183
creating client-side (JavaScript) default type, 161–163
embedding and registering new client-side type, 164
implementing methods, 164–166
refractor into ScriptControl, 158–159
Silverlight technology vs., 2
ASP.NET AJAX-Enabled Web Site template, 184–187
ASP.NET Futures, 142
Asset Library, Blend, 77
Asset tools, Blend Toolbox, 64
ASX (Advanced Stream Redirector) playlist file format, 46–47
attribute syntax, 255, 258
attributes, Silverlight control, 150–154
attributes, Silverlight object, 18–20

audio
adding with MediaElements, 46, 78–79
adding with MediaElements and JavaScript, 134–138
supported formats for, 46–47
AutoReverse property, animations, 57

B

Base APIs, Silverlight 1.1, 193–194
BeginStoryboard object, 221
BezierSegment object, 222
Bindable attribute, Xaml control, 150–154
bitmaps, including in project, 84–86
Blend (Microsoft Expression Blend 2.0), 59–89
Create New Project dialog, 60–61
creating timelines in, 80–83
Design Workspace overview, 62
getting latest Blend 2 Preview, 60
Interaction panel, 63–66
layout and design in, 74–79
panels, overview, 62–63
Project panel, 66–68
Properties panel, 68–74
as Rapid Application Development tool, 26, 253–254
starter template, 61–62
storyboards and, 80
Toolbox, 63
working with artwork created outside of, 84–88
blogs, resources for, 273–274
brackets [ ], in Blend, 65
browsers
Silverlight vs. ASP.NET, 141
support for Silverlight, 3–4
Brush editor
applying brush value, 71
Gradient Brushes, 71–73
overview of, 70
SolidColorBrush, 71
Brush tools, Blend Toolbox
defined, 64
painting video onto objects using, 52–53
painting with, 41–45
supported for TextBlock objects, 41
BufferingProgressChanged event, 136–137
business class libraries, in CoreCLR, 192
Button class
application navigation buttons and, 213
example application, 216
VideoArea class, 217–219
ButtonBar control, ASP.NET Silverlight user interface
creating client-side code, 178–183
creating server-side code, 170–178
creating XAML button template, 166–170
using, 184–187
ButtonBar.debug.js, 175
ButtonBar.js, 175

C

Canvas object
properties, methods and events of, 222
as root element of XAML file, 258–260
Canvas objects
nesting canvas objects within, 32–33
positioning elements within, 31–32
size of actual Silverlight control and, 34
captureMouse function, 123–125
CAS (Code Access Security), 191–192
case-sensitivity, of XAML, 253
categories, animation, 57
child objects, enumerating in collection, 270
Class item template, JavaScript library, 147–148
class library, custom controls, 142–143
Client Logic component, example application
Button class, 216
combo box functions, 213–215
createSilverlight function, 208–209
designing architecture, 202
inserting VideoArea user interface, 211
instantiating video navigation, 211–213
onLoad event handler, 209–211
Scene class, 209
VideoArea class, 217–219

client-side scripting, 4
ClientType property, adding to Xaml control, 160–161
CLR (Common Language Runtime). ***see*** **Silverlight 1.1 Alpha Refresh Release**
Code Access Security (CAS), 191–192
code behind files, XAML and, 262
collections
enumerating child objects in, 270
referencing XAML objects in, 270
ColorAnimation object, 222
ColorAnimationUsingKeyFrames object, 223
ColorKeyFrame object, 223
ColorKeyFrameCollection object, 223
Combine tools, 77
Common Language Runtime. ***see*** **Silverlight 1.1 Alpha Refresh Release**
Communication APIs, Silverlight 1.1, 195
Completed event, Downloader, 130
control model, Silverlight, 189
controls. ***see*** **ASP.NET, creating custom controls**
CoreCLR, defined, 192
Create New Project dialog, in Blend, 60–61
createDelegate function, 179, 209
CreateFromXaml function
adding XAML file to Silverlight player with JavaScript, 261
creating client-side ButtonBar class, 181
downloading image and media content in packages, 133
downloading XAML content in packages, 132
instantiating and inserting XAML elements, 108–111
createFromXamlDownloader ( ) function, 132
createMySilverlightControl function, 94, 95
createObject method
creating client-side ButtonBar class, 179
Downloader using, 128
function of, 95
instantiating Silverlight player using, 94
overview of, 95
parameters of, 95
player initialization events of, 101–102
player initialization properties of, 100–101
player initParams of, 102–103
using element and parent IDs, 99
XAML source parameter of, 97–99
createObjectEx function
building Silverlight applications, 16–17
createSilverlight function showing, 20–21
creating Silverlight player using, 18
example application with, 209
overview of, 95
rendering Xaml control with, 154–158
specifying Silverlight XAML content in, 97–98
createSilverlight function
adding XAML file to Silverlight player, 260–261
building Silverlight applications, 16
example application, 208–209
parameterized, 21
showing createObjectEx method call, 20–21
cross-platform, CLR as, 192
.csproj files, opening, 254
CSS, 34, 189
Cursor property, TextBlock, 44

D

Data APIs, Silverlight 1.1, 194
data binding, and Silverlight 1.1, 141, 189
Data layer, creating, 206–207
data visualization, Silverlight vs. ASP.NET, 141
DataMethod property, 180
debugging, Silverlight 1.1, 199
default files, in Silverlight projects, 14
DefaultClientType property, 171
Default.html file
building Silverlight applications, 15–16
defined, 14
Silverlight project starter template, 61
working with, 11
Default.html.js file, 14, 61

Description attribute, Xaml control, 150–154
design surface, in Blend, 74–75
Design Workspace
- adding MediaElements, 78–79
- Interaction panel, 63–66
- layout and design in, 74–78
- organized into panels, 62–63
- overview of, 62
- Project panel, 66–68
- Properties panel, 68–74
- Toolbox, 63–64

designers
- installing tools, 10
- workflow management, 204–205

developers
- installing tools, 10
- workflow management, 204–205

DiscreteColorKeyFrame object, 224
DiscreteDoubleKeyFrame object, 224
DiscretePointKeyFrame object, 224
dispose method, 179
<div> tag, 20
DLR (Dynamic Language Runtime), 199
DOM (document object model)
- accessing Silverlight player from, 104
- searching using findName, 269
- Silverlight and, 3–4

DoubleAnimation object, 170, 224
DoubleAnimationUsingKeyFrames object, 225
DoubleCollection object, 225
DoubleKeyFrame object, 225
DoubleKeyFrameCollection object, 225
Downloader object
- downloading fonts using, 133–134
- downloading packages using, 131–133
- example application using, 210–213
- overview of, 128–131
- properties, methods and events of, 226

DownloadFailed event, 130
DownloadProgressChanged event, 130, 136–137
drag and drop, implementing, 123–125
drag operations, mouse events, 218–219
drawing
- with text, 41–45
- using Blend path tools, 76–77
- using Blend shape tools, 75–76

DrawingAttributes object, 226
Duration object, 226
Dynamic Language Runtime (DLR), 199
dynamic language support, 199

E

easing, applied to key frames, 83
editors
- Brush, 70–73
- property, 69–70
- transform, 73–74

element IDs, 99
Ellipse object, 227
Ellipse tool, Blend Toolbox, 75
EllipseGeometry object, 227
embed tag, HTML, 18
embedding, new client-side type, 164
encoding
- adding markers to video files, 49–52
- audio and video formats, 47

errorEventArgs, onError event, 113–114
Esc key, 24
Event Bubbling, XAML and, 122–123, 265–266
event handlers
- adding or removing, 268
- declaring XAML, 115–118
- defining, 266–268

eventArgs parameter, event handlers, 266–268
events
- createObject function player initialization, 101–102
- Downloader, 130
- player initialization, 101–102
- of UIElement class objects, 30

exporting
- to bitmaps, 85
- to XAML in other tools, 86–88

Expression Media Encoder
adding markers to video files, 49–52
encoding audio and video formats, 47
preparing media for application, 205
eXtensible Application Markup Language. *see* XAML (eXtensible Application Markup Language)

F

fetchMenuItemsSucceeded function, 211–212
FindName function
finding XAML object, 104–105, 269
handling events in JavaScript, 267–268
folders, Blend, 68
FontFamily object, 42, 227
fonts, downloading, 133–134
formats
bitmap, 85
CLR for Silverlight 1.1, 192
supported audio and video, 46–47
full screen mode display, 22–24

G

garbage collection, 192
GeometryCollection object, 228
GeometryGroup object, 228
Get Microsoft Silverlight image, 5
GET request, Downloader object, 128
get_element method, 179
GetControlDescriptor method, 177–178
GetDeclarationScript method, 155–157
getElementById method, 4
getElementId method, 182
GetHost function, 104, 269
getItem method, 270
GetResponseText function, Downloader, 131, 132
GetScriptDescriptors ( ) method, 164–165, 177
GetScriptReferences ( ) method, 165–166, 176
getValue method, 270–271
GetVideo function, 211
glyphs, 228
GoFullScreen function, 23–24
Gradient Brushes, 71–73
GradientStop object, 71–73, 229
GradientStopCollection object, 229
Grand Piano Player example, 11–12

H

handleLoad function, 209–211
Hello World, 252
hiding elements, at design time, 65
hierarchy
adding XAML objects to Silverlight player, 260–261
enumerating through objects in element, 111–113
XAML, 258–260
HTML (HyperText Markup Language)
adding multiple Silverlight objects to page, 20–21
creating Silverlight object in, 17–18
from default.html file hosting Silverlight control, 15–16
DOM of, 4
placing Silverlight control on page, 34
hyperlinks, navigational, 43–45

I

icons, Blend, 62, 65
Image control, Blend, 77–78
image objects
downloading, 197
downloading content in packages, 133
layout and design of, 77–78
positioning, 36–37
properties, methods and events of, 229
ImageBrush object, 230
implicit collection syntax, 256–258
initParams parameter, createObject function, 102–103
InkPresenter object, 230
installation, Silverlight, 6–8

Interaction panel, Blend, 63–66
IScriptControl, AJAX, 159
isInstalled function, 103–104
items, adding to project within Blend, 67–68

J

JavaScript, 91–112. *see also* Silverlight.js helper library
accessing Storyboards programmatically, 125–128
adding Silverlight JavaScript library to control, 146–150
adding XAML file to Silverlight player, 260–261
creating default client type for Xaml control, 161–163
creating Silverlight player, 92–95
default files in, 14
event handlers, 267–268
events, Silverlight player, 113–115
events, XAML. *see* XAML (eXtensible Application Markup Language) element events
for full screen mode display, 23–24
getting/setting XAML properties, 106–108
instantiating/inserting XAML elements, 108–113
locating XAML content elements, 105–106
Mouse Capture, 123–125
overview of, 92
setting hyperlink properties, 43–45
Silverlight 1.0 support for, 5
using Silverlight Downloader object, 128–134
using with MediaElement, 49, 134–138
JavaScript Object Notation (JSON) dictionary, 95
JIT (Just-In-Time) compiler, 192
JSON (JavaScript Object Notation) dictionary, 95

K

key frames
applying easing to, 83
defined, 79
snapping, 82–83
keyboard events
in full screen mode, 119
for full screen mode display, 24
implementing, 119–120
input, 118–120
keyboard shortcuts, 118
KeyboardEventArgs object, 230
KeyEventArgs.Key property, 118
KeyEventArgs.PlatformKeyCode property, 119
KeySpline object, 231
KeyTime object, 231

L

layout, of Silverlight content, 31–40
within Canvas object, 31–34
Silverlight 1.1 limitations, 189
Silverlight vs. ASP.NET, 140
using transforms, 38–40
using ZIndex property, 34–38
layout and design, in Blend, 74–79
adding images, 77–78
Design surface, 74–75
overview of, 74
Pen tool, 76
Pencil tool, 76–77
shape tools, 75–76
Layout panels, Blend Toolbox, 64
Line object, 231
LinearColorKeyFrame object, 232
LinearDoubleKeyFrame object, 232
LinearGradientBrush
Brush editor for, 70–71
properties, methods and events of, 232
for reflecting video, 54–56
LinearPointKeyFrame object, 232
LineBreak object, TextBlock, 41, 233
LineGeometry object, 233
LineSegment object, 233
LINQ
dynamically generating XAML using, 170
Silverlight 1.1 Communication APIs, 195
Silverlight 1.1 Data APIs, 194

loadComboBox function, 215
localization, 189
locking elements, at design time, 66
Lumos video player example, 201–220
creating Data layer, 206–207
creating host web page, 207–208
designing application architecture, 202
designing user interface, 202–204
getting started, 202
managing developer/designer workflow, 204–205
preparing media, 205
summary of, 220
Lumos video player example, coding
Button class, 216–219
combo box functions, 213–215
createSilverlight function, 208–209
inserting VideoArea user interface, 211
instantiating video navigation, 211–213
onLoad event handler, 209–211
Scene class, 209
VideoArea class, 217–219

M

markerEventArgs object, 138
MarkerReached event, 50–52, 137–138
markers
adding to video files, 49–52
Blend Properties panel, 69–70
preparing media for application using, 205
working with, 137–138
markup order, Z-Index order vs., 66
MatrixTransforms, 38, 233
Media control, 142
MediaAttributeCollection object, 234
MediaElement object
adding audio or video to web pages, 46, 78–79
adding play, pause, and stop to, 48–49
example application, 217–219
interacting with, 47–49
positioning using ZIndex and Opacity, 36–37
properties, methods and events of, 234
properties exposed on, 47–48
supported formats for audio and video, 46–47
using JavaScript, 49, 134–138
using markers in video, 50–52
MenuItem.cs class, 173–174
Microsoft Expression Blend 2.0. *see* Blend (Microsoft Expression Blend 2.0)
Microsoft Expression Design, 87
Microsoft Intermediate Language (MSIL), 192
Mouse Capture, 123–125
mouse events
controlling Storyboards with, 127–128
creating client-side ButtonBar class, 181–182
example application, 214, 216–219
input, 118, 120–122
MouseEventArgs object, 234
MouseMove event, 122–123, 264–266
MP3 format, 47
MSIL (Microsoft Intermediate Language), 192

N

nameScope parameter, FindName method, 111
naming conventions
ASP.NET custom control project, 143–144
elements, 65
Storyboards, 80
navigation
creating and inserting buttons, 211–213
creating hyperlinks, 43–45
Silverlight vs. ASP.NET, 139
.NET Framework, 2, 5
New Folder, Blend, 68
New Project dialog, 13–14

O

object (content) element syntax, in XAML, 256

object reference, 221–249
ArcSegment object, 221
BeginStoryboard object, 221
BezierSegment object, 222
Canvas object, 222
ColorAnimation object, 222
ColorAnimationUsingKeyFrames object, 223
ColorKeyFrame object, 223
ColorKeyFrameCollection object, 223
DiscreteColorKeyFrame object, 224
DiscreteDoubleKeyFrame object, 224
DiscretePointKeyFrame object, 224
DoubleAnimation object, 224
DoubleAnimationUsingKeyFrames object, 225
DoubleCollection object, 225
DoubleKeyFrame object, 225
DoubleKeyFrameCollection object, 225
Downloader object, 226
DrawingAttributes object, 226
Duration object, 226
Ellipse object, 227
EllipseGeometry object, 227
FontFamily object, 227
GeometryCollection object, 228
GeometryGroup object, 228
glyphs, 228
GradientStop object, 229
GradientStopCollection object, 229
Image object, 229
ImageBrush object, 230
InkPresenter object, 230
KeyboardEventArgs object, 230
KeySpline object, 231
KeyTime object, 231
Line object, 231
LinearColorKeyFrame object, 232
LinearDoubleKeyFrame object, 232
LinearGradientBrush object, 232
LinearPointKeyFrame object, 232
LineBreak object, 233
LineGeometry object, 233
LineSegment object, 233
MatrixTransforms, 233
MediaAttributeCollection object, 234
MediaElement object, 234
MouseEventArgs object, 234
ParserErrorEventArgs, 235
Path object, 235
PathFigure object, 235
PathFigureCollection object, 236
PathSegmentCollection object, 236
PointAnimation object, 236
PointAnimationUsingKeyFrames object, 236–237
PointCollection object, 237
PointKeyFrame object, 237
PointKeyFrameCollection object, 237
PolyBezierSegment object, 238
Polygon object, 238
Polyline object, 238
PolylineSegment object, 239
PolyQuadraticBezierSegment object, 239
QuadraticBezierSegment object, 239
RadialGradientBrush object, 239
Rectangle object, 240
RectangleGeometry object, 240
RepeatBehavior object, 240
ResourceCollection, 241
RotateTransform object, 241
Run object, 241
RuntimeErrorEventArgs object, 241
ScaleTransform object, 242
Silverlight control object, 242
SkewTransform object, 242
SolidColorBrush object, 242
SplineColorKeyFrame object, 243
SplineDoubleKeyFrame object, 243
SplinePointKeyFrame object, 243
Storyboard object, 243
Stroke object, 244
StylusInfo object, 244
StylusPoint object, 244
StylusPointCollection object, 244
TextBlock object, 245
Timeline object, 245

TimelineCollection object, 245
TimelineGroup object, 246
TimelineMarker object, 246
TimelineMarkerCollection object, 246
TimelineMarkerEventArgs object, 246
TimeSpan object, 247
TransformCollection object, 247
TransformGroup object, 247
TranslateTransform object, 247
TriggerAction object, 248
TriggerActionCollection object, 248
TriggerCollection object, 248
UIElementCollectionobjects, 248
VideoBrush object, 249
object tag, HTML, 17–18
Object tools, Blend Toolbox, 64
objects
declaring in XAML, 255–258
referencing properties of, 270–271
Objects and Timeline area, Interaction panel, 63–64, 81–83
onError event, 101–102, 113–115
onFullScreenChange event, 113, 115
online resources
author blogs, 273
keyboard shortcuts, 118
latest Blend 2 Preview, 60
portable key codes, 119
resource Web sites, 274
Silverlight 1.1 Alpha Refresh Release, 191
Silverlight 1.1 example, 199–200
Silverlight influential blogs, 273–274
Silverlight object attributes, 18
Silverlight SDK, 9
Silverlight Streaming Services free account, 46
XAML exporters, 87
onLoad event
example application, 209–211
overview of, 113–114
player initialization, 101–102
onMarkerReached function, 51–52
OnPreRender override, 156
onResize event
defined, 113
resizing Silverlight control, 21–22
working with, 115
Opacity property, positioning objects, 36–37
OpacityMask, 54–56
Open function, Downloader, 128
OpenFileDialog, 197
operating system, Silverlight architecture, 3–4

P

packages, downloading, 131–133
Page Methods, ButtonBar control, 185–186
Page Turner example, 11
painting
with brushes, 41–45
video onto objects, 52–53
panels, Blend, 62–63
parameters
createSilverlight function, 21
event handler, 266–268
optional tags for Silverlight control, 19–20
parameters, createObject function, 95–103
parent and element IDs, 99
player initialization events, 101–102
player initialization properties, 100–101
player initParams, 102–103
XAML source parameter, 97–99
parent IDs, createObject function, 99
ParentElementID property, rendering Xaml control, 154–155, 157
ParserErrorEventArgs, 235
Path object, 235
Path Tools, Blend Toolbox
Combine tools, 77
location of, 64
Pen tool, 76
Pencil tool, 76–77
PathFigure object, 235
PathFigureCollection object, 236
PathSegmentCollection object, 236
Pen tool, 76
Pencil tool, 76–77

PointAnimation object, 236
PointAnimationUsingKeyFrames object, 236–237
PointCollection object, 237
PointKeyFrame object, 237
PointKeyFrameCollection object, 237
PolyBezierSegment object, 238
Polygon object, 238
Polyline object, 238
PolylineSegment object, 239
PolyQuadraticBezierSegment object, 239
portable key codes, 118–119
Presentation APIs, Silverlight 1.1, 196–199
***Professional ASP.NET 2.0 AJAX* (Gibbs/Wahlin), 163**
***Professional JavaScript for Web Developers* (Zakas), 163**
Project panel, Blend, 66–68
Project tab, starter template, 61
properties
  assigning in XAML, 256–258
  getting and setting XAML, 106–108
  marker, 50–51
  MediaElement, 47–48
  player initialization, 100–101
  referencing object, 270–271
  server-side ButtonBar class, 171–176
  UIElement class objects, 30
  Xaml client-side control, 162–163
  Xaml control, 150–154, 160–161
Properties panel, Blend, 68–74
  common property editors in, 69
  layout and design in, 75
  marker system in, 69–70
  overview of, 68–69
  setting image Source property in, 78
  using Brush editor, 70–73
  using transform editors, 73–74
property editors, Blend
  custom, 70
  overview of, 69
  using Brush editors, 70–73
property element syntax, 256, 258
prototype property, client-side ButtonBar class, 183

Q

QuadraticBezierSegment object, 239

R

RAD (Rapid Application Development) tools, 26, 253–254
RadialGradientBrush, 70–71, 239
Rectangle object, 240
Rectangle tool, Blend Toolbox, 75
RectangleGeometry object, 240
referencing
  adding ASP.NET AJAX to your control using, 158–159
  Silverlight player, 104, 269–271
reflections, creating video, 53–56
#region...#endregion, 149
RegisterClientScriptResource method, 166
registering, new client-side type, 164
removeEventListener method, XAML elements, 268
rendering
  Silverlight content, 29–31
  Xaml control, 154–158
RenderTransform property
  creating timeline, 81–82
  defined, 38
  working with, 73–74
RepeatBehavior, 57, 240
resizing, Silverlight control, 21–22
resource, creating Storyboard as, 80–81
ResourceCollection, 241
ResponseText property, Downloader, 130–131
RIAs (Rich Internet Applications), 1–2
Rich Internet Applications (RIAs), 1–2
rich media, Silverlight vs. ASP.NET, 140
root element, of XAML files, 258–259
RotateTransform
  adding to TextBlock using XAML, 252–253
  defined, 38
  properties, methods and events of, 241
  working with, 38–40
Run object, 41, 241

runtime
hiding elements at, 65
installing SDK page for, 9–10
referencing object properties at, 270–271
updating artwork dynamically at, 85
RuntimeErrorEventArgs object, 241

S

ScaleTransform
adding to TextBlock using XAML, 252–253
defined, 38
properties, methods and events of, 242
reflecting video using, 54–56
working with, 38–40
scaling, and bitmaps, 85–87
Scene class, example application
combo box functions, 213–215
defined, 209
inserting VideoArea user interface, 211
instantiating video navigation, 211–213
onLoad event handler, 209–211
Scene.xaml file, 14, 61
Scene.xaml.js file, 14, 61
<script> tag, XAML, 98–99, 262
ScriptControl, AJAX, 158–159
ScriptControlDescriptor, 177
ScriptManager control, creating host page, 207–208
ScriptMethod attribute, 207
Scripts collection property, Xaml control, 160–161
ScriptService attribute, 207
SDK (Software Development Kit), Silverlight
building applications with project templates from, 13–18
examples of, 11–13
installing, 9–11
security, and full screen mode, 24
Selection tools, Blend Toolbox, 64
sender parameter, event handlers, 266–268
server-side code, creating ButtonBar, 170–178
ServiceModel (WCF) support, Silverlight 1.1, 195
setFontResource method, 42
SetSource function, 133
setValue method, referencing object properties, 270–271
shape tools, Blend Toolbox, 64, 75–76
Silverlight, 1.0 case example. *see* Lumos video player example
Silverlight, introduction to, 1–28
adding multiple objects to page, 20–21
creating control in HTML, 17–18
displaying in full screen mode, 22–24
and DOM, 4
getting SDK, 9–13
installing plug-in, 6–8
naming, 2
object attributes, 18–20
resizing control, 21–22
understanding, 1–4
using Visual Studio 2005, 13–17
versions of, 5–6, 103–104, 190–191
and XAML, 25–26
Silverlight 1.1 Alpha Refresh Release, 189–200
base APIs, 193–194
CLR and, 191–192
communication APIs, 195
data APIs, 194
debugging, 199
defined, 5
dynamic language support, 199
example of, 199–200
framework, 192–193
limitations of Silverlight 1.0, 189
presentation APIs, 196–199
versions 1.0 vs. 1.1, 5, 190–191
Silverlight control object, 242
Silverlight JavaScript library, 146–150
Silverlight player
basic XAML to display Hello World in, 252
events, 264–266
referencing, 269–271

Silverlight Streaming Services, 46
Silverlight.js helper library, 96–104
accessing Silverlight player object, 104
adding player to web page using, 92–95
adding Silverlight JavaScript library to control, 146
createObject and createObjectEx functions, 96–103
creating Silverlight player using, 18
defined, 17
element and parent IDs, 99
isInstalled function, 103–104
overview of, 96
player initialization events, 101–102
player initialization properties, 100–101
player initparams, 102–103
XAML source parameter, 97–99
SilverPad example, 11–12
SkewTransform
adding to TextBlock using XAML, 252–253
defined, 38
properties, methods and events of, 242
working with, 38–40
snapping, keyframe, 82–83
SolidColorBrush, 70–71, 242
Solution Explorer, building Silverlight applications, 14
Source property
adding audio or video to web pages, 46
assigning XAML file to Silverlight player with, 260–261
creating inline XAML using script tag, 98–99
setting for images, 78
setting MediaElement, 78–79
specifying Silverlight XAML content in, 97–98
SplineColorKeyFrame object, 243
SplineDoubleKeyFrame object, 243
SplinePointKeyFrame object, 243
starter templates, Silverlight project, 60–62
Status property, Downloader, 130
StatusText property, Downloader, 130
Storyboard Picker, 80–83
Storyboards
accessing programmatically, 125–128
adding animations to button template, 169–170
creating client-side ButtonBar class, 183
creating timeline, 81–83
overview of, 80
properties, methods and events of, 243
timeline support for, 79
Stretch property
positioning objects using ZIndex with, 37–38
setting image size, 78
Stroke object, 244
styles, Silverlight 1.1 lacking, 189
StylusInfo object, 244
StylusPoint object, 244
StylusPointCollection object, 244
SWF2XAML: A Flash to XAML Conversion Tool, 87
System.Web.Extensions library, AJAX, 158–159

T

templates
building Silverlight applications with Visual Studio project, 13–18
creating XAML button, 166–170
Silverlight 1.1 lacking data binding, 189
text
downloading content in packages, 132
drawing with, 41–45
Silverlight 1.1 lacking support for, 189
Text controls, Blend Toolbox, 64
TextBlock object
adding VideoBrush to, 52–53
creating hyperlinks, 43–45
custom transforms using XAML on, 252–253
properties, methods and events of, 245
Silverlight vs. ASP.NET, 140
using markers in video, 50–52
working with, 41–43

textDecoration property, hyperlinks, 44–45
textual data input, Silverlight vs. ASP.NET, 140
TextWrapping property, TextBlock objects, 42
theConverted - SWF to XAML Edition converter, 87
Timeline object, 245
TimelineCollection object, 245
TimelineGroup object, 246
TimelineMarker object, 138, 246
TimelineMarkerCollection object, 246
TimelineMarkerEventArgs object, 246
timelines
creating in Blend, 80–83
creating in video files, 49–52
using keyframe snapping, 82–83
TimeSpan object, 247
toggleFullScreen method, 162
Toolbox, Blend, 63–64, 75–76
TransformCollection object, 247
TransformGroup
defined, 38
properties, methods and events of, 247
working with, 38–40
transforms
adding to TextBlock using XAML, 252–253
positioning objects using, 38–40
reflecting video using, 54–56
using editors, 73–74
TranslateTransform
adding to TextBlock using XAML, 252–253
creating timeline, 82
defined, 38
properties, methods and events of, 247
TriggerAction object, 248
TriggerActionCollection object, 248
TriggerCollection object, 248
Triggers section, Interaction panel, 63

U

UIElement class objects, 29, 30
UIElementCollection, 248
updates, 8
URI parameter, Downloader, 129
UrlProperty attribute, 150
user interface, Silverlight, 166–187
bitmaps and, 86
building with XAML, 2
creating button template, 166–170
creating ButtonBar client-side code, 178–183
creating ButtonBar server-side code, 170–178
example of designing, 202–204
using ButtonBar control, 184–187
UsingKeyFrames animation types, 170

V

versions, Silverlight. *see also* Silverlight 1.1 Alpha Refresh Release
comparing, 190–191
detecting with isInstalled function, 103–104
overview of, 5–6
video, 46–56
creating reflections, 53–56
interacting with MediaElement object, 47–49
overview of, 45
painting onto objects, 52–53
supported formats for audio and, 46–47
using JavaScript and MediaElement, 134–138
using markers and timelines in, 49–52
using MediaElements to add, 46, 78–79
video, example application
coding. *see* Lumos video player example, coding
creating Data layer, 206–207
creating host web page, 207–208
preparing, 205
VideoArea class, 211, 217–219
VideoBrush, 52–53, 249
View tools, Blend Toolbox, 64
Visual Studio 2005
building Silverlight applications in, 13–18
creating new project, 30–31

W

Web Custom Control template, 144–145
Web Services component, 202, 206–207
web-based gaming, Silverlight vs. ASP.NET, 141
WebResource attribute, 147–148
WMA (Windows Media Audio) format, 47
WMV (Windows Media Video) format, 47
workflow, managing developer/designer, 204–205
workspace, Blend. *see* Design Workspace
WPF (Windows Presentation Foundation), 2, 253
WPF/e technology, 1, 2

X

XAML (eXtensible Application Markup Language), 29–58, 251–272
- accessing Storyboards programmatically, 125–128
- adding objects to object hierarchy with, 260–261
- adding video with. *see* video
- animations with, 56–58
- building Silverlight user interface with, 2
- code behind and x:Name, 262–264
- creating sharp gradients with, 72–73
- defining events in JavaScript with, 268
- downloading content in packages with, 132
- drawing with text and brushes with, 41–45
- exporters, 86–88
- getting/setting properties, 106–108
- hierarchy, 258–260
- interacting with MediaElement object, 47–49
- layout and design in Blend with, 74–75
- layout of content using transforms, 38–40
- layout of content using ZIndex property, 34–38
- layout of content within Canvas object, 31–34
- locating content elements, 105–106
- object declaration, 255–258
- referencing Silverlight control in, 269–271
- rendering Silverlight content in, 29–31
- Silverlight player events in, 264–266
- source parameter in, 97–99
- typical file in, 254
- understanding, 25–26, 251–253

XAML (eXtensible Application Markup Language) element events, 115–125
- event handler declaration in, 115–118, 266–268
- handling mouse input, 120–123
- implementing keyboard events, 119–120
- keyboard and mouse input, 118–119
- using Mouse Capture, 123–125

.xaml extension, defined, 254
Xaml.debug.js file, 161
XamlUrl property, 150
XamlXporter for Illustrator, 87
XLINQ, defined, 194
XML, Silverlight 1.1 and, 194
XML comments, 148, 150–151
XMLHTTPRequest browser objects, 195
x:Name attribute, XAML, 110–111, 262–264

Y

YAGNI (You Ain't Gonna Need It) architectural principle, 149

Z

ZIndex property, 34–38, 66
ZIP files
- downloading packages using Downloader object, 131–133
- retrieving content compiled in packages, 131
- SDK, 10